Katherine Austen's *Book M*
British Library, Additional Manuscript 4454

Medieval and Renaissance Texts and Studies

Volume 409

Katherine Austen's *Book M*
British Library, Additional Manuscript 4454

Edited by
Sarah C. E. Ross

ACMRS
(Arizona Center for Medieval and Renaissance Studies)
Tempe, Arizona
2011

Published by ACMRS (Arizona Center for Medieval and Renaissance Studies)
Tempe, Arizona
© 2011 Arizona Board of Regents for Arizona State University
All Rights Reserved

Library of Congress Cataloging-in-Publication Data

Austen, Katherine, 1628-1683.
 Katherine Austen's Book M : British Library, Additional Manuscript 4454 / edited by Sarah C. E. Ross.
   p. cm. -- (Medieval and Renaissance texts and studies ; v. 409)
 Includes bibliographical references and index.
 ISBN 978-0-86698-457-7 (alk. paper)
 1. Austen, Katherine, 1628-1683. Book M. I. Ross, Sarah C. E. II. British Library. Manuscript. Additional 4454. III. Title.
 PR3316.A685B66 2011
 828'.403--dc23
                                                          2011045760

Cover Art:
Austen Memorial in St. Leonard's Church, Shoreditch.
Photograph reproduced by permission of the London Metropolitan Archives.

Appendix:
Extracts from Daniel Featley's *Clavis Mystica* (1636) and Jeremy Taylor's *The Rule and Exercises of Holy Living* (1650) are reproduced © The British Library Board, shelfmark 475.c.3 and shelfmark E. 1257.
Extracts from Jeremy Taylor's *Eniautos* (1653), and from John Donne's *LXXX Sermons* (1640) are reproduced by permission of *The Huntington Library, San Marino, California.*

∞
This book is made to last. It is set in Adobe Caslon Pro,
smyth-sewn and printed on acid-free paper to library specifications.
Printed in the United States of America

*For my mother, Susan,
and my daughter, Amelia,
with love*

Contents

Acknowledgments	ix
Abbreviations	xi
Introduction	1
Textual Introduction	41
Book M	51
Appendix	173
Bibliography	205
Topical Guide	215
Concordance to Biblical References	217
General Index	219

Acknowledgments

I first encountered *Book M* in my first week as a doctoral student in Oxford, and Katherine Austen's trials and tribulations, her determined and at times fractious voice, and her modest brown book became my first encounter with the "real" early modern woman of the manuscript archive. I have worked on Austen, on and off, over a long period of time.

I have accumulated in this time a large number of intellectual and personal debts—with enormous pleasure on my part. Nigel Smith, who supervised my doctoral thesis, has been a formative influence in this work, as has Elizabeth Clarke, who has been a generous mentor, discussant, and friend. Thanks must also go to Jane Stevenson and Peter Davidson, who directed me to *Book M*, and to numerous scholars and friends with whom I have talked of Austen over the years: Victoria Burke, Marie-Louise Coolahan, Jonathan Gibson, Erica Longfellow, Peter McCullough, Paul Salzman, and Helen Wilcox. Those who have assisted me with particular references include Elizabeth Clarke, Elizabeth Gray, Patricia Crawford, Glynnis Cropp, France Grenaudier-Klijn, Alison Holcroft, and Jamie Reid-Baxter. Anonymous readers for ACMRS provided thoughtful and engaged comments on the draft edition. Averil Coxhead, Elizabeth Gray, Nikki Hessell, Ingrid Horrocks, and Karen Jillings have provided invaluable conversation and friendship in the Massey University community.

This edition was completed with the assistance of a St Hilda's College, Oxford, Association of Senior Members Studentship, which allowed me to pursue sources in London archives in 2004. Massey University has also provided research funding that has made the completion of this work possible.

I am enormously grateful for the insight and wisdom of the team at ACMRS: Bob Bjork, Roy Rukkila, Todd Halvorsen, Leslie MacCoull, and Bill Gentrup. Leslie's meticulous copyediting and vast knowledge enabled me to trace several of Austen's sources that had previously eluded me. Bill, most particularly, has seen this project through to its conclusion with care, patience, and an admirable unflappability; it has been a pleasure to work with you, Bill. Anne Austin provided efficient and cheerful copyediting expertise at the Palmerston North end.

I would like, last but not least, to thank the two families whose lives have run along in the background to the production of this book: Sue and Campbell Ross, who first sent me off on this particular journey; and Andru, Milly and Henry Isac, who have watched the cross-referencing process from afar, and with a remarkable capacity to remain interested. Here, you see, it is.

Abbreviations

BCP *Book of Common Prayer (1636)*

CSPD *Calendar of State Papers, Domestic Series, Elizabeth, James I, Charles I, Charles II*

IGI *International Genealogical Index*

KJV Bible, King James Version (1611)

ODNB *Oxford Dictionary of National Biography*, ed. H.C.G. Matthew and Brian Harrison (Oxford: Oxford University Press, 2004)

OEDO *Oxford English Dictionary Online*

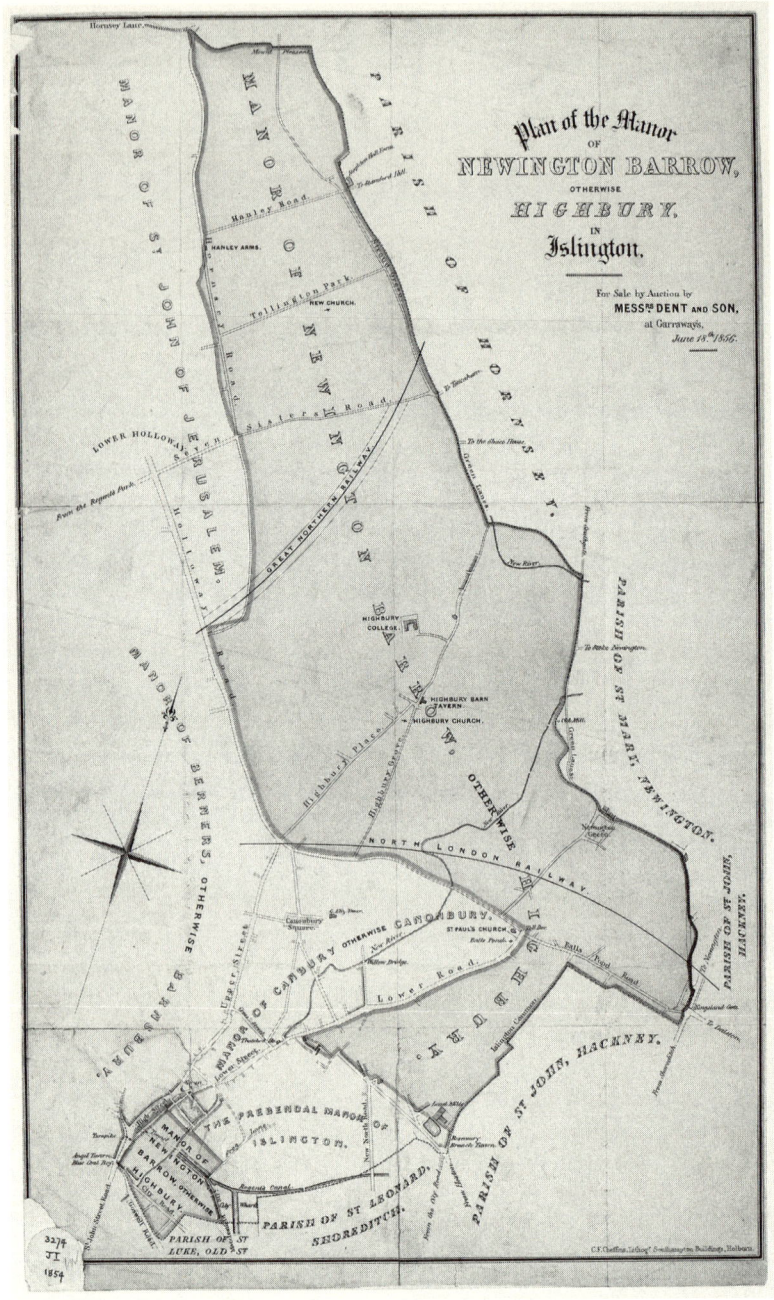

Figure 1. "Plan of the Manor of Highbury" (1856),
London Metropolitan Archives. Reprinted by permission.

Introduction

Katherine Austen's life-writing

> When I view over the assurances and hopes I have had in this book of my meditations As sometimes I am puting on wreathes of victory, I have overcome my enemies and my feares But such is the vnsurenes of every ground in this world to Anchor on. as I soone come to wade in deep places againe. (fol. 112ᵛ)

So writes the young widow Katherine Austen (1628–1683) towards the end of her *Book M*, a manuscript volume which she describes as "this book of my meditations." Katherine Austen's life, as it is documented in *Book M* over two years between 1664 and 1666, was indeed full of enemies and fears, tribulations and uncertainties: a gentlewoman widow aged between thirty-five and thirty-eight, living in London and Middlesex, Austen was the guardian of three underage children, and was occupied (and spiritually preoccupied) with defending her own and her children's interests. Her topics for meditation and prayer include everyday misfortunes of illness, accidents, and death, the temptation of a second marriage, the Great Plague outbreak of 1665–66, and the ill-will of relatives and associates; running throughout *Book M* are reflections on her ultimately successful campaign to safeguard her eldest son Thomas's inheritances of the manor of Highbury in Islington and the estate of the Red Lion in Fleet Street, both the subject of numerous legal challenges. *Book M* may be a "book of my meditations," but much of its liveliness for a twenty-first-century reader resides in its author's preoccupation with matters secular, social, and financial, even as those matters are conceptualized and written through a deeply providential world view.

Austen's preoccupation with secular and social, as well as godly, affairs has seen *Book M* widely cited by social historians, particularly as a rich source of insight into seventeenth-century women's experience of widowhood.[1] Austen

---

[1] Barbara Todd, "The Remarrying Widow: A Stereotype Reconsidered," in *Women in English Society, 1500–1800*, ed. Mary Prior (London: Methuen, 1985), 54–92; eadem, "'I do no injury by not loving': Katherine Austen, a Young Widow of London," in *Women and History: Voices of Early Modern England*, ed. Valerie Frith (Toronto: Coach House

articulates throughout *Book M* her determination to avoid remarriage in order to protect her children's financial interests, and she refers repeatedly to challenges to these interests. Little has been known until this point about the specific nature of these tribulations, but it is now possible to situate *Book M* in the context of extensive legal and parliamentary documents concerning her son's inheritance of Highbury and the Red Lion, and so to sharpen our understanding of her worldly affairs. Austen's meditations have also been cited in recent explorations of dreams in early modern culture, although her extended meditations on dreams and visions, angels and portents, demand more extended attention,[2] and *Book M* contains thirty-four poetic meditations in rhyming couplets, which have attracted the interest of scholars working in early modern women's poetry.[3] Austen's poems add significantly to our understanding of women's engagement with the lyric in the early modern period, and of the lyric's devotional, social, and literary functions.

Book M's appeal to social and literary historians alike is indicative of its elusiveness to generic classification, occupying a space between the historical artefact and the text of literary interest. It is perhaps most useful to begin a

---

Press, 1995), 207–37; eadem, "The Virtuous Widow in Protestant England," in *Widowhood in Medieval and Early Modern Europe*, ed. Sandra Cavallo and Lyndon Warner (Harlow, Essex: Pearson Education, 1999), 66–83; Ralph Houlbrooke, ed., *English Family Life, 1576–1716: An Anthology from Diaries* (Oxford: Basil Blackwell, 1988); Sara Heller Mendelson and Patricia Crawford, *Women in Early Modern England, 1550-1720* (Oxford: Clarendon Press, 1998), 174–84; *Women's Worlds in Seventeenth-Century England: A Source Book*, ed. Patricia Crawford and Laura Gowing (London and New York: Routledge, 2000); Raymond Anselment, "Katherine Austen and the Widow's Might," *Journal for Early Modern Cultural Studies* 5 (2005): 5–25.

[2] Patricia Crawford, "Women's Dreams in Early Modern England," in *Dreams and History: The Interpretation of Dreams from Ancient Greece to Modern Psychoanalysis*, ed. Daniel Pick and Lyndal Roper (London and New York: Brunner-Routledge, 2004), 91–103; Mary Baine Campbell, "Dreaming, Motion, Meaning: Oneiric Transport in Seventeenth-Century Europe," in *Reading the Early Modern Dream: The Terrors of the Night*, ed. Katharine Hodgkin, Michelle O'Callaghan, and S. J. Wiseman (New York: Routledge, 2008), 15–30, esp. 27 (and 148 n.).

[3] Pamela Hammons, "Despised Creatures: The Illusion of Maternal Self-Effacement in Seventeenth-Century Child Loss Poetry," *English Literary History* 66 (1999): 25–49; eadem, "Katherine Austen's Country-House Innovations," *Studies in English Literature* 40 (2000): 123–37; eadem, "Widow, Prophet, and Poet: Lyrical Self-Figuration in Katherine Austen's 'Book M' (1664)," in *Write or Be Written: Early Modern Women Poets and Cultural Constraints*, ed. Barbara Smith and Ursula Appelt (Aldershot: Ashgate, 2001), 3–27; eadem, *Poetic Resistance: English Women Writers and the Early Modern Lyric* (Aldershot: Ashgate, 2002), 100–63; Sarah Ross, "'And trophes of his praises make': Providence and Poetry in Katherine Austen's *Book M*, 1664–1668," in *Early Modern Women's Writing: Selected Papers from the Trinity/Trent Colloquium*, ed. Victoria E. Burke and Jonathan Gibson (Aldershot: Ashgate, 2004), 181–204.

consideration of genre with Austen's own self-styling as a godly writer who must "endeauour to trace the loue and fauour of God. to me in his many kind dispensations to me" (fol. 111ʳ). Her articulated sense of a godly duty to pay attention to the operations of providence in her life, common in seventeenth-century women's autobiographical texts,[4] is matched by a less conventional insistence on the value of "Ingenuity" (fol. 44ᵛ), and her ingenuity manifests itself in one of *Book M*'s most striking aspects. Austen collates snippets and anecdotes from a wide range of sources, drawing widely, freely, and often without acknowledgement, on the Bible, on sermons of prominent English divines such as Jeremy Taylor, John Donne, John Gauden, and Daniel Featley, and on poetry and drama. She creates long passages of related anecdotes gathered from diverse sources, arranging them according to her own preoccupations and weaving into them her own associated reflections. *Book M* verifies and extends recent insights into women's reading practices[5] and into the relationship between reading and writing as it is revealed in the comparable autobiographical manuscripts of Lady Anne Halkett and Lady Sarah Cowper.[6] Austen moves freely between compilation of others' texts and consideration of the operations of divine providence in her own life, without any of Lady Sarah Cowper's sense of this as "errant plagiary."[7] *Book M* thus develops our understanding of compilation as an activity richly constitutive of a textual self,[8] revealing reading, contemplation, compilation, and original writing as interrelated means by which one early modern woman negotiates her self in relation to the world around her.

Austen's practice of extended paraphrase and personalized compilation is a mode of life-writing which coexists with her use in *Book M* of occasional meditation and psalm meditation, both popular devotional practices for seventeenth-century women. Occasional meditation was advocated and practiced by Joseph Hall, Robert Boyle, and numerous other seventeenth-century divines, whose influential manuals and examples of the practice advocated the meditation on ran-

---

[4] See p. 28, below.

[5] See Sasha Roberts, "Reading in Early Modern England: Contexts and Problems," *Critical Survey* 12 (2000): 1–16, and the articles in that special issue, esp. Mary Ellen Lamb, "The Sociality of Margaret Hoby's Reading Practices and the Representation of Reformation Interiority," 17–32; and Edith Snook, *Women, Reading, and the Cultural Politics of Early Modern England* (Aldershot: Ashgate, 2005).

[6] See Suzanne Trill, *Lady Anne Halkett: Selected Self-Writings* (Aldershot: Ashgate, 2007), esp. xxvii–xxviii; Anne Kugler, *Errant Plagiary: The Life and Writing of Lady Sarah Cowper, 1644–1720* (Stanford: Stanford University Press, 2002).

[7] See Kugler, *Errant Plagiary*.

[8] For compilation as a form of authorship see, e.g., Victoria Burke, "Women and Early Seventeenth-Century Manuscript Culture: Four Miscellanies," *The Seventeenth Century* 12 (1997): 135–50; eadem and Sarah C. E. Ross, "Elizabeth Middleton, John Bourchier, and the Compilation of Seventeenth-Century Religious Manuscripts," *The Library*, 7ᵗʰ ser., 2 (2001): 131–60.

dom occurrences as an opportunity for contemplating the spiritual self or, as in Austen's case, the operation of divine providence in everyday life.[9] The titles of many of Austen's meditations—"On *the* Birds Singing in my Garden" (fol. 4ᵛ), "Vpon paying for the fal of Mr Riches house" (fol. 39ʳ), "Vpon Sis*ter* Austens vnkindnes to me vpon all occasiones" (fol. 45ʳ)—indicate their emergence out of this tradition, although her pieces at times approximate the modern diary entry rather than the spiritualized reflection that is the occasional meditation.[10] If the occasional meditation was one mode of focusing on God's providence on a daily basis, the reading of the Psalms was another, and the extent to which the Psalms became a discourse for self-expression in early modern women's writing has been explored fruitfully in recent criticism.[11] Lady Margaret Hoby, Alice Thornton, Lady Mary Rich,[12] and Lady Anne Halkett all draw extensively on the Psalms in their life-writings and provide close comparisons to Austen. Austen's identification with David and the Psalms, however, is particularly strong, as she draws on Psalm 118:17 in her repeated declaration that "I shal not dye but live. and declare the workes of the Lord" (fols. 21ʳ, 75ʳ).

Austen's description of *Book M* as "this book of my meditations" notwithstanding, the volume is only in part a book of occasional meditations; it is also in part a book of Psalm meditations and paraphrases, part diary, part mother's advice book, part family record, part literary miscellany, and part manuscript of original poetry. *Book M* is cohesive as a piece of self-writing or life-writing[13]

---

[9] Marie-Louise Coolahan, "Redeeming Parcels of Time: Aesthetics and Practice of Occasional Meditation," *The Seventeenth Century* 22 (2007): 124–43, esp. 124. Three recent discussions of the occasional meditation in relation to women's writing are Coolahan, "Redeeming Parcels of Time"; Trill, *Lady Anne Halkett*, esp. xxxiv–xxxvii; and Raymond Anselment, ed., *The Occasional Meditations of Mary Rich, Countess of Warwick*, MRTS 363 (Tempe: ACMRS, 2009).

[10] See, e.g., her dated entry on the death of her servant William Chandeler, fol. 38ᵛ. For a similar evolution, see Trill, *Lady Anne Halkett*, xxxvi.

[11] See, in particular, Margaret P. Hannay, "'So May I with the Psalmist Truly Say': Early Modern Englishwomen's Psalm Discourse," in *Write or Be Written*, ed. Smith and Appelt, 105–34; Suzanne Trill, "'Speaking to God in His Phrase and Word': Women's Use of the Psalms in Early Modern England," in *The Nature of Religious Language: A Colloquium*, ed. Stanley E. Porter (Sheffield: Sheffield Academic Press, 1996), 269–83; and eadem, *Lady Anne Halkett*; Anselment, "Katherine Austen"; idem, "Seventeenth-Century Manuscript Sources of Alice Thornton's Life," *Studies in English Literature* 45 (2005): 131–55; idem, *Occasional Meditations of Mary Rich*.

[12] See Anselment, *Occasional Meditations of Mary Rich*.

[13] I use "self-writing" and "life-writing" relatively interchangeably. For useful discussions, see Elspeth Graham, "Women's Writing and the Self," in *Women and Literature in Britain, 1500–1700*, ed. Helen Wilcox (Cambridge: Cambridge University Press, 1996), 209–33; eadem, Hilary Hinds, Elaine Hobby, and Helen Wilcox, eds., *Her Own Life: Autobiographical Writings by Seventeenth-Century Englishwomen* (London:

which exemplifies the generic fluidity of women's personal writings in the period, individual women's use of multiple and various genres,[14] and also the coexistence of generically diverse modes of personal writing within a single document. *Book M* not only reminds us in its individual passages that "textual form and the subjectivity it produces are mutually constitutive,"[15] but that the discourses and textual forms available to seventeenth-century women were multiple, complex, and at times conflicting. It is only in reading *Book M* as a complete text that it can be understood, not as a series of discrete fragments, but as a complete piece of life-writing in which Austen writes herself in and through numerous modes of discourse that are available to her, including the biblical, devotional, maternal, legal, social, and literary; the textual forms she employs include meditation, prayer, advice piece, letter, and poem. Austen describes herself to her suitor as "like pennelope, always employed," (fol. 96^r) and *Book M* is the physical manifestation of her industrious time, spent "with method, vsefully, and comfortably" (fol. 56^r). Like Penelope, Austen defines her time according to her husband's absence, and *Book M*'s generic complexity may reflect the ill-defined nature of widowhood as a social role, as well as the challenges for women "discovering [. . .] the voices of authorship."[16] Austen creates in *Book M* a thick textual tapestry, in which a wide range of sources, discourses, and genres are incorporated into a weave and weft governed by her own idiosyncratic preoccupations.

Book M also demands investigation as a material object, a purpose which a printed edition can only partially serve. Austen's main meditational chronology in *Book M* runs from 1664 to 1666; however, added onto spare folios and into spaces after entries, and inserted between some lines, are additions, modifications, and further compilations which run as late as 1682. Austen clearly reviewed her own writing over the years, reflecting further on her written meditations, and adding depth and texture to her original thoughts (see, for example, fols. 55^v, 78^r, 112^v); in doing so, she follows the instructions and practices common to occasional meditation.[17] Margaret Ezell has recently argued for the need to investigate

---

Routledge, 1989), 16–21; Michelle M. Dowd and Julie A. Eckerle, eds., *Genre and Women's Life Writing in Early Modern England* (Aldershot: Ashgate, 2007), 1–13; Trill, *Lady Anne Halkett*, xxxvii.

[14] See Sara Heller Mendelson, "Stuart Women's Diaries and Occasional Memoirs," in *Women in English Society, 1500–1800*, ed. Prior, 181–210, esp. 181–82; Elspeth Graham, Hilary Hinds, Elaine Hobby, and Helen Wilcox, "'Pondering All These Things in Her Heart': Aspects of Secrecy in the Autobiographical Writings of Seventeenth-Century Englishwomen," in *Women's Lives/Women's Times: New Essays on Auto/Biography*, ed. Trev Lynn Broughton and Linda Anderson (Albany: State University of New York Press, 1997), 51–71, here 51; Dowd and Eckerle, *Genre and Women's Life Writing*, 1–13.

[15] Dowd and Eckerle, *Genre and Women's Life Writing*, 1.

[16] Nigel Smith, *Literature and Revolution in England, 1640–1660* (New Haven and London: Yale University Press, 1994), 5.

[17] See Coolahan, "Redeeming Parcels of Time," 131.

the manuscript context and physical characteristics of early modern women's life writing; Victoria Burke similarly insists on the need to "get physical" in interpreting manuscript writing, a major mode of women's writing in the early modern period.[18] Physical characteristics, alongside *Book M*'s content, not only reveal Austen's life-writing process, but also provide indicators that Austen envisaged an audience for her manuscript, perhaps the "perticular relatives and General" to whom she refers in one meditation (fol. 77ᵛ). Certainly, as she writes elsewhere, the "vnfained desier of [her] soule" to "glorify [God's] name in all the pathes of thy providences" rings clear in the content and form of *Book M*, a densely-woven textual artifact of Austen's worldly activities and "the manifestations of [God's] Love to me" (fols. 71ʳ, 21ʳ).

Katherine Austen's life

Katherine Austen,[19] née Wilson, was born in the parish of St Mary Colechurch, London, on 30 April 1628, the daughter of Robert Wilson and his wife Katherine, née Rudd.[20] Robert was a well-to-do member of the Drapers' Company and a citizen of the City of London, operating from premises attached to the front of the Wilsons' dwelling quarters in Cheapside, but he died in 1639, leaving a widow and several young children: Robert (who followed his father into the Drapers' Company), Richard, Thomas, Anne (who seems to have died between 1639 and 1648), Katherine (the author of *Book M*), Mary, and Martha.[21] Robert Wilson provided well for his widow and young family: his widow and sons acquired properties in Middlesex, Essex, and London, and Orphans' Ledgers and Finding Books for the City of London detail the administration of payments to them. Katherine's husband, Thomas Austen, received a payment of £2478 upon her marriage to him in 1645, and comparable payments were made on her sisters'

---

[18] Margaret Ezell, "Domestic Papers: Manuscript Culture and Early Modern Women's Life Writing," in *Genre and Women's Life Writing*, ed. Dowd and Eckerle, 33–48, here 34; Victoria Burke, "Let's Get Physical: Bibliography, Codicology, and Seventeenth-Century Women's Manuscripts," *Literature Compass* 4/6 (2007): 1667–82, here 1667.

[19] Austen is variantly spelt Austin and Austinn in some records.

[20] See *Book M*, fols. 40ʳ and 77ʳ; Katherine Austen's will, National Archives, PROB 11/375; Joseph Jackson Howard and Joseph Lemuel Chester, eds., *The Visitation of London, Anno Domini 1633, 1634, and 1635*, 2 vols. (London: The Harleian Society, 1880), 2: 355. Katherine Rudd / Wilson / Highlord's will names "my deare mother Mrs Anne Rudd" (National Archives, PROB 11/205).

[21] Howard and Chester record the Wilson children as Robert, Richard, Anne, Katherine, and Mary. See also Robert Wilson's will, National Archives, PROB 11/182 (proved 18 January 1640); Katherine Rudd / Wilson / Highlord's will, National Archives, PROB 11/205; A.H. Johnson, *The History of the Worshipful Company of Drapers of London*, 5 vols. (Oxford: Clarendon Press, 1914–1922) 3: 468, 342 n.

marriages and to her brothers on their comings-of-age.[22] These were not inconsiderable sums. Austen describes her inheritance from her father as "the happy instrument to raise me to my Marriage without other assistance" (fol. 79ᵛ), and the dowry of her youngest sister, Martha, was sufficient to enable her to marry a baronet, Sir Edward Cropley.[23]

Katherine's mother, Katherine Rudd / Wilson, rapidly married a second husband, John Highlord, a member of the Skinners' Company, a committee member of the East India Company, and an alderman of the City of London.[24] Highlord's standing among London citizens was higher than Wilson's: there was a property qualification of £10,000 for the office of alderman, and he resided from at least 1638 in the parish of St Olave's, Hart Street, a fashionable and expensive area near the Customs House in East London.[25] Katherine Rudd / Wilson / Highlord's second marriage was short-lived—John Highlord died in 1641—but it clearly boosted further the financial and social status of herself and her young children, both during and after Highlord's lifetime. John Highlord bequeathed the income from lands in Essex and Oxfordshire to his widow for the duration of her natural life,[26] and while Highlord's will makes no provision for his stepchildren, this income seems likely to have contributed to the legacies Katherine Rudd / Wilson / Highlord eventually left for her children. Katherine Austen states in *Book M* that her son Robert's estate "came perticularly from my portion from my Good father *your* Grandfather Robert Wilson: And my vnparraleled Father in Law. Ald*erman* Highlord" (fol. 93ʳ),[27] and she writes "Blesed Alderman

---

[22] Corporation of London Record Office, *Orphans Finding Book, 1643–1661*, fols. 49ʳ, 123ʳ, 199ʳ; *Orphans Ledger, 1627–1648*, fol. 303 (opening); *Orphans Recognizances, 1639–1644*, fols. 108ᵛ–110ʳ.

[23] Fol. 72ʳ; John Burke, *A Genealogical and Heraldic History of the Commoners of Great Britain and Ireland*, 4 vols. (London: Henry Colburn, 1838), 4: 142. By way of comparison, Sarah Holled, the future Lady Sarah Cowper, took around £500, plus an £800 pin money provision, into her marriage in 1664 (Kugler, *Errant Plagiary*, 1). For KA's pin money, see p. 8 below.

[24] A.B. Beavan, *The Aldermen of the City of London*, 2 vols. (London: The Corporation of the City of London, 1908), 2: 63; Valerie Pearl, *London and the Outbreak of the Puritan Revolution: City Government and National Politics, 1625–43* (Oxford: Oxford University Press, 1964), 303; Robert Brenner, *Merchants and Revolution: Commercial Change, Political Conflict, and London's Overseas Traders, 1550–1653* (Cambridge: Cambridge University Press, 1993), 90.

[25] T.C. Dale, *The Inhabitants of London in 1638*, 2 vols. (London: The Society of Genealogists, 1931), 1: iv, 166; Tai Liu, *Puritan London: A Study of Religion and Society in the City Parishes* (London: Associated University Press, 1986), 35.

[26] John Highlord's will is National Archives, PROB 11/187 (proved 18 December 1641).

[27] "Father-in-law" was used interchangeably in the seventeenth century to refer to a spouse's parent, or to a step-parent (*OEDO*).

(Highlord) How doe I revere thy memory, who wast the Foundation in a great part: of my second and later Fortune" (fol. 79ᵛ); in a later related meditation she refers to "the Legacy my D*eare* mother left me (at her Decease.)" (fol. 105ʳ). This evocation of Highlord as a financial benefactor alongside her own father is a striking aspect of Austen's identity in *Book M*—all the more so given that she would have been twelve or thirteen years old at the time of Highlord's death in 1641, that her mother cannot have been married to him for more than two years, and that *Book M* is composed more than twenty years after his death.

Katherine married Thomas Austen on 10 July 1645, at the parish church of St Stephen's, Coleman Street, in London,[28] and her mother died three years later, in 1648. Katherine Rudd / Wilson / Highlord left her daughter with money of her own: she received £2000 "for her owne vse & by her to be disposed of at her pleasure," to be paid to Katherine at the rate of £100 per annum for the duration of her marriage. Katherine Rudd / Wilson / Highlord evidently saw the importance of independent female wealth: she made similar provisions for Austen's surviving sisters, Mary and Martha, and her bequests appear to be deliberately tailored to circumvent her daughters' loss of independent property under marital coverture.[29] Austen not only refers in *Book M* to "the Legacy my D*eare* mother left me (at her Decease.)" but states that "the succes of two thousand poundes. hath been the growth of most of my Fortune" (fols. 105ʳ, 49ʳ). It is clear that she regards her mother's legacy and the projects in which she has invested it as her own distinct contribution to her marital family's financial success.[30]

Austen's new husband, Thomas, was from an upwardly-mobile gentry family with significant landholdings across the county of Middlesex. The Austen family had owned land in and around Hoxton (where they lived) and Shoreditch, adjacent Middlesex parishes, since at least 1550.[31] *The Victoria County History of Middlesex* describes Katherine Austen's father-in-law, also Thomas, as a cheesemonger,[32]

---

[28] *IGI*, microfiche for London, 5, 295.

[29] The will of Katherine Rudd / Wilson / Highlord (National Archives, PROB 11/205). Amy Louise Erickson discusses "separate estate" and pin money for married women, *Women and Property in Early Modern England* (London: Routledge, 1993), 103. She also suggests that female testators in early modern England tended to prioritize giving to female relatives in their wills, as a corrective to women's susceptibility to loss of economic agency (19, 209–17, 228; summarized in Pamela Hammons, "Rethinking Women and Property in Sixteenth- and Seventeenth-Century England," *Literature Compass* 3/6 [2006]: 1386–1407, here 1392).

[30] See also p. 13, below.

[31] *The Victoria County History of Middlesex*, ed. T. F. T. Baker, vol. 11: *Early Stepney with Bethnal Green* (Oxford: Oxford University Press for the Institute of Historical Research, 1998), 167. Hoxton and Shoreditch are now part of metropolitan London, but in the seventeenth century they were parishes in the rural county of Middlesex.

[32] *The Victoria County History of Middlesex*, ed. T. F. T. Baker, vol. 8: *Islington and Stoke Newington Parishes* (Oxford: Oxford University Press for the Institute of Historical

but he had by 1632 acquired the manor of Newington Barrow or Highbury in Islington, an extensive manor in two parts, located in the north and east of the parish with a small, separate area to the south (see Fig. 1, p. ix). (St. John's Wood and Highbury Wood had at one time been part of the manor, but were no longer so during the Austens' tenure.[33]) There was in the seventeenth century no manor house—it had been destroyed in the late fourteenth century and not rebuilt—but the manor comprised some 987 acres, and would have generated significant income.[34] Katherine Austen's husband Thomas received an education befitting the emergent status of his family: he matriculated at Lincoln College, Oxford, in 1640, and in June 1646 he was admitted to Lincoln's Inn, as was his younger brother John.[35] The two sons' status was evidently a source of pride in the family: they are buried in the church of St Leonard's, Shoreditch, on either side of their "worthy Father," memorialized by a stone tablet describing "two most dearly affectionate Brothers [. . .] who were both of the Hon*ourable* house of Lincolns Inn."[36]

Their father, Thomas Austen the elder, had, however, acquired Highbury under circumstances which gave rise to legal contestation for several decades, including the years of *Book M*'s composition. Highbury and several other manors and Crown lands had been conveyed in 1629 from the Crown to Sir Allen Apsley, Lieutenant of the Tower of London (and father to Lucy Hutchinson). Apsley was victualler to the Navy, and the lands were intended to offset costs that he had incurred in this activity;[37] however, Apsley died very shortly afterwards in 1630, and Highbury ended up in Thomas Austen the elder's hands. Sir Allen Apsley's creditors complained in 1634/5 and 1639 that Thomas Austen should have conveyed the manor to them. The creditors' petition also concerns the forest or park of Galtres (or Gaultres) in Yorkshire, another former Apsley estate that was in the hands of Austen and Stephen Alcock.[38] Alcock was the deputy victualler and accountant of the Navy, and is accused of "not deliver[ing] a just state of the accounts between his Majesty and Sir Allen," and Austen and Alcock are described

---

Research, 1985), 56. No source is given. He is described as a clothworker and brewer in National Archives, E214/215.

[33] Like Hoxton and Shoreditch, Islington was in the seventeenth century part of rural Middlesex rather than of metropolitan London.

[34] John Nelson, *The History and Antiquities of the Parish of Islington, in the County of Middlesex*, 2nd ed. (London: for the author, 1823), 131–38.

[35] Joseph Foster, *Alumni Oxonienses*, 4 vols. (Oxford: Parker, 1891), 1: 45; *The Records of the Honourable Society of Lincoln's Inn*, 2 vols. (London: Lincoln's Inn, 1896), 1: 253.

[36] London Metropolitan Archives, SC/PHL/02/1190–143.

[37] *CSPD 1625–1649*. Apsley petitions the king, claiming £100,000 is "due to him and his creditors for victuals delivered for the provision of your Majesty's ships and fleets," and arranging for £20,000 to be raised by the conveyance of lands to Apsley for sale at fixed-term purchases (246–47).

[38] *CSPD 1639*, 101, 148; see also National Archives, E214/225.

in the 1639 petition as "both patentees and trustees."[39] Austen is accused in 1639 of having failed to meet an order of 1635, "whereby he and the other trustees were to make a declaration of the execution of the trust, what manors and lands were conveyed to them, what they have sold, for how much, and how the moneys have been employed."[40] Apsley's trustees are accused, in petitions throughout the seventeenth century, of misappropriating lands intended for the satisfaction of the creditors. The nature of Thomas Austen's connections to Apsley, which warranted him acting as a trustee, are unclear, and it is also unclear whether Highbury had been purchased or appropriated by him.[41] But his family's possession of Highbury certainly gave rise to extensive legal contestation, a dominant concern for Katherine Austen throughout *Book M*.

Katherine Austen's husband, Thomas Austen the younger, had inherited Highbury from his father in or before 1653,[42] before himself dying prematurely at the age of thirty-six on 31 October 1658.[43] Katherine became a thirty-year-old widow with three surviving children, Thomas, Robert, and Anne, all of whom were significantly underage: Thomas, her eldest son and heir, was twelve years old upon his father's death in 1658.[44] Thomas Austen's will names her as executrix and guardian "during her Widdowhood," and, as the head of her family, Austen engaged in the complex management of her children's estates. Sir Allen Apsley's son, also Sir Allen, tried to recover Highbury and Galtres from Austen's son, Thomas, in 1662: in the second folio of Chancery proceedings is Thomas Austen's response to Apsley's Bill of Complaint, and it is entitled "The severall Answeares of Thomas Austen vnder the age of one and Twentie yeares that is to say of the age of Sixteene Yeares [. . .] Completed by Katherin Austen widdow his Mother and Guardian."[45] Apsley's creditors also petitioned the House of Commons in February 1664/5,[46] and Austen refers in *Book M* to being "appointed" on the ninth of that month "to be that day at the Com*mittee* of Parlia*ment*" (fol. 60ᵛ). She entitles a poem "Vpon Courtiers at *th*e Com*mittee* of parlia*ment* striving for Highbury: *th*e 14th Feb*ruary*: that I was there. 1664" (fol. 59ᵛ), and her discussion of this period indicates that she went to Westminster "about 6 times," despite her

---

[39] *CSPD 1634–1635*, 459–60; *CSPD 1639*, 101.

[40] *CSPD 1639*, 101.

[41] Nelson, *History and Antiquities of the Parish of Islington*, 137, describes Highbury as being sold to Thomas Austen.

[42] See London Metropolitan Archives, Courts Leet and Baron ACC/2844/012; Thomas Austen the younger's first Court Leet and Baron is dated 19 May 1653.

[43] *Book M*, fol. 1ʳ.

[44] The memorial tablet for Thomas Austen in St Leonard's, Shoreditch, indicates the birth of another daughter, but KA does not mention her in *Book M*.

[45] National Archives, C5/41/3, fol. 2. This wording is echoed in the proceedings relating to the Red Lion (see pp. 11–13, below).

[46] *Journals of the House of Commons*, vol. 3 (25 April 1660–29 July 1667), 594, 612.

own and her eldest son's illnesses (fol. 61ʳ). The committee to which the creditors' petition had been referred reported to parliament on 2 March 1664/5, but the verdict on Highbury was inconclusive. Austen meditates on a further challenge to the ownership of Highbury, feared or actual, at a sitting of parliament in June 1665 (fols. 79ᵛ, 84ᵛ).

Katherine Austen's guardianship saw her concerned not only about the outright ownership of Highbury but about the expiry of a lease period that the Crown had imposed upon the lands in question. Sir Allen Apsley had petitioned the king in 1627, when the conveyance of lands including Highbury was being arranged, to clarify precisely how many years' purchase was being granted.[47] The period agreed upon appears to have been thirty-six years, for *Book M* contains Austen's "Discourse to: L: vpon the New*ington* Barrow," in which she dwells on the significance of this period (fols. 48ʳ–49ʳ).[48] She celebrates the expiry of the lease period at Michaelmas 1665 (fol. 103ᵛ). State records, however, continue to focus on the estate's original misappropriation. A petition to Whitehall on 10 April 1666 calls for the lands to be recovered by the Crown,[49] and it is most likely in response to this that Austen writes in September 1666, under the title "S*ir* Ieffery Pamers teling me. our busines was ordered to be brought before the privy Counsel" (fols. 112ᵛ–113ʳ).[50] Austen's extended campaign for Highbury was ultimately successful: her son Thomas (under his own auspices) successfully opposed a 1670 bill to the House of Lords to recover the estate for the Crown,[51] and Highbury passed to Thomas's son John after 1683.[52]

Highbury was not the only one of her children's legacies to prove troublesome for Katherine Austen. She was also engaged during the period of *Book M*'s composition in extended wrangling with "Sister Austen," who can be identified as her sister-in-law Susanna, née Winstanley, the wife of Thomas Austen's younger brother John.[53] John Austen died not long after his brother, in 1659, and the terms of his will generated considerable tension between the two young widows. John Austen left his numerous properties to his wife Susanna until 25 June 1669, and then to his daughter; however, these properties were to pass to his

---

[47] *CSPD 1625–1649*, 246. Apsley complains that the Lord Treasurer has caused the order for Apsley's repayment in land "to be made 'so conditional with ifs and ands' as no man will deal with petitioner."

[48] Further meditations on the lease's expiry occur on fols. 48ᵛ–49ʳ and 103ᵛ.

[49] *CSPD 1665–1666*, 344–45.

[50] The precise occasion for a poem entitled "Iune 16: 1665: on L: Barks shuite with me for: H*ighbury*" is unclear (fol. 84ᵛ).

[51] *Historical Manuscripts Commission 8ᵗʰ Report*, part 1, section 1 (Darlington: HMSO, 1881), 148b; and *Journals of the House of Lords*, vol. 12 (1666–75), 362, 369.

[52] Thomas's son John sold Highbury to James Colebrooke in 1725 (*The Victoria County History of Middlesex*, 8: 56).

[53] Thomas Austen's will, National Archives, PROB 11/285.

nephew, our author's son Thomas, in the event of his daughter's death.[54] John and Susanna Austen's daughter died very young—Katherine Austen discusses the death of her infant niece in *Book M*—and expectations of inheritance for Katherine Austen's son therefore arose.[55] *Book M* documents most closely Katherine Austen's wrangling with Susanna and her father James Winstanley over the Red Lion (fols. 45[r], 64[v], 81[r]-83[v]), an estate in Fleet Street in the parish of St. Dunstan's in the West, London, "the greatest part whereof is now vsed as an Inne and comonlie called or knowne by the name of the red Lyon."[56] Susanna petitioned in 1662 for Katherine Austen to hand over documents of title and other "writings" relating to the Red Lion that were in Katherine's possession, complaining that without them she is unable to collect rents from the Red Lion's tenants and is therefore unable to pay legacies to which her husband's will had committed her. Katherine Austen (acting for her son) responds that she is keeping the documents "for the preservacon & maintennance of her [. . .] sonnes interest therein," and in order to prevent Susanna Austen from "cancelling surrendring or other distroying of the originall Lease if the same should come into her hands."[57] It is clear that there was no love lost between these two young widows, the wives of the "two most dearly affectionate Brothers" memorialized on the stone tablet in the church of St. Leonard's, Shoreditch.[58]

Book M and legal records document continued enmity and division over the Red Lion and over John Austen's main estate of Durhams, in the parish of South Mimms, Middlesex.[59] Katherine Austen was permitted to retain the Red Lion's title and lease in her possession,[60] but she refers in *Book M* to Susanna Austen renewing her petition for the estate in May 1665 and in February 1665/6 (fols.

---

[54] John Austen's will is National Archives, PROB 11/296.

[55] *Book M*, fol. 83[v]. John and Susanna Austen's daughter, another Katherine Austen, is named in her father's will and in Chancery court records regarding the Red Lion. John Burke incorrectly describes John and Susanna Austen as having "no issue" (*Genealogical and Heraldic History of the Commoners*, 1: 363).

[56] London Metropolitan Archives, HB/C/027. Thomas Austen the elder had acquired a 40-year lease over this estate in 1638 (National Archives, C10/109/4).

[57] National Archives, C10/78/1 (1662). KA discusses this dispute in *Book M*, fol. 83[v].

[58] KA also writes bitterly of Susanna Austen's father, James Winstanley, even though he had served as the steward for her husband Thomas Austen in administering the estate of Highbury (fol. 82[r]; London Metropolitan Archives, Courts Leet and Baron ACC/2844/012).

[59] Durhams is alternatively spelt Derhams. South Mimms is near modern-day Barnet, north London. See National Archives, PROB 11/296; and also John Burke and John Bernard Burke, *A Genealogical and Heraldic History of the Extinct and Dormant Baronetcies of England, Ireland, and Scotland*, 2nd ed. (London: John Russell Smith, 1844), 30. KA discusses the earlier line of inheritance of Durhams on fol. 51[v].

[60] *Book M*, fol. 83[v]; National Archives, C10/96/1 and C10/98/1.

81ʳ, 108ʳ). Chancery court records include a Bill of Complaint by Katherine Austen and her son Thomas against Susanna Austen in May 1666, with replies from Susanna Austen in October 1666 and February 1666/7,[61] Susanna denying acting in "any way to defeat or defraud the [. . .] Compl*ainan*t of any matter or thing whatsoever that is given him by the last Will of the said John Austen."[62] Katherine Austen reflects despondently late in *Book M* "If we loose Fleetstreet Estate [i.e., the Red Lion]. And tho we neuer shal posses that Gift of Durhams" (fol. 111ᵛ); however, it is clear that John Austen's properties did revert to her son Thomas. Thomas eventually resided at Durhams, and his son John sold the manor in 1733.[63]

Quite apart from defending her eldest son's interests so actively, Katherine Austen appears to have acquired further property in her own right in the period of her widowhood. She meditates twice in *Book M* on a "second addition" to her family's fortune, with a clear sense of pride that she has "added to our estate by Gods great blesing. vpon me these seaven yeares of my widdowhood. such another estate as was left to me and my children" (fols. 79ᵛ, 105ʳ). This second estate is discussed elsewhere as "the Swan my buildings," and it is the source of further tribulation, as Austen meditates repeatedly on an extensive and delayed building project and on losses associated with the project (fols. 90ʳ, 100ʳ, 109ᵛ, 112ᵛ). It seems likely that Austen's buildings were located around "the house called the Sign of the Swanne in Islington" at which her late husband Thomas had held his Courts Baron and Leet for the manor of Highbury,[64] but it is clear that the finances for them did not derive from her husband's estate (see fol. 105ʳ). Austen addresses the first of her meditations on this "second" estate to her stepfather John Highlord, describing him as "the Foundation in a great part: of my second and later Fortune" (fol. 79ᵛ); she is probably referring to her mother's legacy of £2000, enhanced by her mother's second marriage to Highlord, which she describes in her meditation "Of Ho*nour*: Contraries" as "the growth of most of my Fortune" (fol. 49ʳ).[65] Elsewhere in *Book M*, Austen also refers to rents for a property or properties in Essex (fols. 100ʳ, 109ᵛ), indicating that her property ownership stretched further afield.

Book M thus documents, very extensively, the preoccupations of a widow engaged in extensive legal action over several familial legacies. *Book M* can, like Alice Thornton's roughly contemporaneous diaries, be described as a "record of

---

[61] National Archives, C10/96/1 and C10/98/1.

[62] National Archives, C10/96/1, fol. 2.

[63] *The Victoria County History of Middlesex*, ed. Baker, (1985), 5: 284. Sir John Austen, M.P., is incorrectly identified here as the grandson of John Austen, the owner in 1653; he was in fact his great-nephew.

[64] London Metropolitan Archives, Courts Leet and Baron ACC/2844/012, 1653–1657.

[65] John Highlord's will documents no direct legacy to KA. See p. 7, above.

mid-seventeenth-century gentry squabbling over their estates-pie."[66] Austen's legal engagements are vitally coupled with a determination to maintain her status as *feme sole*,[67] as *Book M* reveals her making a highly conscious decision not to remarry because of her desire to preserve her independent responsibility for her children's estates and fortunes. She rejects a suitor's advances out of fear that acceptance would "doe real Injuries. where I am already engaidged. To my Deceased Friends posterity" (fols. 95ʳ⁻ᵛ), and she defines a "dishonourable Marriage" as one that "impair[s] the prosperity God hath given use [i.e. us]" (fol. 94ᵛ).[68] Austen is determined to maintain her marital independence for the sake of her children's estates, and Barbara Todd and Ralph Houlbrooke see her as exemplifying a broad social trend among seventeenth-century widows toward eschewing remarriage to protect their children's financial interests.[69] Austen's determination notwithstanding, it is clear that she finds her role as an independent widow a trying and exhausting one, and our new insight into the extent of her legal engagements makes it clear why this should be so. She reflects in *Book M* on her own mother, whose "strong nature [was] worne out by [. . .] the many cares and busneses w*hi*ch a great Family gave occasions to her [. . .] D*ear*e Mother thou hadst a great estate. and a great burden too" (fol. 51ʳ). She also wishes that such burdens may not be the lot of her own daughter, Anne. Observing that "My Nansy is busie and inquisitive in to all things of Husfry," she wishes "if it be the Will of God may she neuer come to such a taske as I haue" (fol. 107ᵛ).

Austen remained a widow, resident at the Austen family's home in Hoxton, Middlesex, until her death in 1683, by which time she had thoroughly succeeded in securing her children's legacies and advancing their financial and social position. Thomas and Robert, her two sons, inherited "all my Lands houses and Tenements Together with all my Stock in the Indy Company" and her "Estate in Blackfriers which I leased out to the Scotch Company."[70] Thomas continued

---

[66] Margaret George, *Women in the First Capitalist Society: Experiences in Seventeenth-Century England* (Brighton: Harvester Press, 1988), 173. For further comparison of KA's and Alice Thornton's journals, see pp. 28–29 and 37–38, below.

[67] Legally, the *feme sole* held rights to property and to make business contracts which were denied the wife, who under English common law was *feme coverte*, her legal identity subsumed into that of her husband. For explanations of these legal concepts, see Hammons, "Rethinking Women and Property"; and Mendelson and Crawford, *Women in Early Modern England*, 37–38. Tim Stretton discusses early modern English widows' engagement in litigation, emphasising that widows frequently "had *cause* to go to court" for reasons comparable to KA's: *Women Waging Law in Elizabethan England* (New York: Cambridge University Press, 1998), 108–19, esp. 109.

[68] KA writes elsewhere that "A Rich woman must not marry with a p*er*son of meane Fortune" (fol. 50ʳ).

[69] See fols. 68ᵛ, 69ᵛ, 76ʳ, 91ʳ; Todd, "The Remarrying Widow," 54–92; Houlbrooke, *English Family Life*, 54, 79, 242; and Anselment, "Katherine Austen."

[70] KA's will is National Archives, PROB 11/375.

to own Highbury and Durhams, and his son John (d. 1742) became an M.P. for Middlesex and a baronet.[71] It is somewhat surprising, given Austen's mother's care to provide independent incomes for her daughters, that she left in her own will only her "best Cabinet" for her daughter Anne. Numerous relatives, friends, and neighbours received small cash sums for mourning and, in the liberal tradition of her father and stepfather, Austen left donations to parish poor (Shoreditch and St Mary Colechurch, "where I was borne"), and to Christ's hospital. Katherine Austen's life spanned fifty-four years and perhaps, as she says of her own widowed mother, she was "worne out by too much stirring and walking" (fol. 51^r). Even if this were the case, her advice piece to her daughter Anne is her own best testament to a widowhood of prodigious activity in her own and her family's advancement:

> have y*our* Granmother (Anne) Austen's virtue and goodnes. Yet may you be defended from the passion of her Mallancholy. and bare with more Courage the encounters of endeard separations which must neccesarily attend us. [. . .] And Remember my D*eare* Mother. Y*our* Grandmother. (Katherine Wilson, Highlord,[)] Take industry from her and me. And as I have practised virtue and imployment. (I hope to be vseful in my life) From my Deare Mother be you an cxsample and patterne to y*our* children. (fol. 93^v)

Katherine Austen's providential world view

It is clear in *Book M* that her state of independence since her husband's death held imaginative as well as legal significance for Katherine Austen. She meditates repeatedly on the passing of seven years since Thomas's death, a period which she sees as one of unstinting tribulation.[72] "I may say for these 6 yeares that are past," she writes, "I have never been off from the waters of peril. from one danger, one violence, one opresion, one desertment. one Crose or another" (fol. 38^r).[73] Barbara Todd claims that provisions in Austen's husband's will "made it financially prohibitive for her to marry during the first seven years of her widowhood," but Thomas Austen's will contains no such proviso.[74] *Book M*,

---

[71] *The Victoria County History of Middlesex*, ed. Baker, 11: 167; Burke and Burke, *Extinct and Dormant Baronetcies*, 30.

[72] Lady Anne Halkett also meditates repeatedly on the period of her widowhood, and provides an illuminating comparison for KA; see Trill, *Lady Anne Halkett*.

[73] KA also refers to this time period on fols. 40^r, 56^v, 60^r, 62^r, 65^v, 68^r–69^r, 86^r, 99^v–100^r, 101^r, 102^v.

[74] Todd, "The Remarrying Widow," 76. The claim is repeated in Virginia Blain, Patricia Clements, and Isobel Grundy, *The Feminist Companion to Literature in English* (London: B.T. Batsford, 1990), 40–41; and Hammons, "Country-House Innovations," 123.

rather, reveals two other reasons that Austen set such store on this time period. She refers to a "demonstration" to her, predating *Book M*, that she would live to the same age as her husband (fol. 75ᵛ)—that is, thirty-six years, two months, and twenty-one days, as she delineates carefully on her first title page (fol. 1ʳ). This milestone age will occur towards the end of her sixth year of widowhood, in mid-1664,[75] and its passing is the subject of several meditations (see, for example, fols. 62ʳ, 63ᵛ, 65ᵛ). Prior to its passing, she has received a "Counterintimation" in the form of her "dream of monition," which indicates to her "a contradiction: that I shal not dye but live. and declare the workes of the Lord" (fol. 21ʳ; and see fols. 74ᵛ–75ᵛ). Austen regards her dream of monition as indicating to her a preservation akin to that of Hezekiah (see fols. 21ʳ and 75ʳ⁻ᵛ), but she also comes to associate herself in her preservation beyond a sixth year with the biblical sufferer Job, who experienced six years of trials (Job 5.19, "He shall deliver thee in six troubles: yea, in seven there shall no evil touch thee"):

> Has Conduct carried me through seaven great yeares
> Great in perplexities, and great in feares.
> Great Griefes with Iob: could hardly be exprest
> Neither by sighings, or by teares redrest
> Six folded trials. and a seaventh as great. (fol. 102ᵛ)

The emotional importance to Austen of her "resolution to continue seaven yeares" (fol. 68ᵛ) is clearly related also to this identification with Job. She reiterates on several occasions her hope for a deliverance parallel to his. She reflects at one point, "I thought my troubles grew to an end, now my 6 years is near at conclusion, But low I find them rather augmented" (fol. 56ᵛ); at another, she prefaces a list of expenses, "Through six afflictions God has promised to cary his children. and in the seaventh they shal be delievered. Six I have pased. six yeares of Divers mixtures full of accidents and encounters extrordinary for a single woman to pas" (fols. 99ᵛ–100ʳ).

Austen's interpretative logic in imputing significance to the seven-year period illustrates a simultaneous engagement with Hezekiah, Job, and the Psalmist David.[76] Her identification with these male biblical figures notwithstanding, she also repeatedly genders her sufferings in a trope of widows' and orphans' paradoxical weakness and privilege in relation to God. God is he who "relieveth the Fatherles and widowes" (fol. 57ʳ); she reflects that "all widdowes and orphanes. all Fatherles and Friendles may put their trust in God" (fol. 62ᵛ); and she quotes from Isaiah 10:1–2, "Woe unto them that decree unrighteous decrees [. . .] to take away the right from the poor of my people, that widows may be their prey, and

---

[75] KA reflects on the coincidences of these dates on fols. 40ʳ and 78ʳ; for her birth date, see fol. 77ʳ.

[76] For David, see pp. 26–32, below.

that they may rob the fatherless!" (fol. 82ᵛ). Through the biblical trope of afflicted widows and orphans, Austen is able to construct herself and her children as the meek who shall inherit the earth—either in death, or in vindicated glory in their estate battles. She reflects, "Surely my God is preparing for me Halcione daies for daies of trouble and Molestation I have found from men. Who considers not afflicted widowes"; and she continues, "My God if it be thy will to consigne me quiet and repose, if not in this life, I am sure in another" (fol. 35ᵛ).

Austen's imaginative reliance on her own and her family's deliverance as God's children typifies a providential world view of the kind that permeated seventeenth-century English society.[77] She regards her tribulations as the design of God, "the great governour of the world [who] orderes it by the variety of changes, and accidents" (fol. 37ʳ), and her confidence in the providential ordering of the world enables her to endure adversity through a belief in what Keith Thomas has termed "sanctified affliction."[78] Austen explicitly reflects that "sanctified aduersity is better then Fortunes. where heaven denyes it" (fol. 61ᵛ), and while she notes that David "pray[s] to be delievered. from men which are thy hand o Lord," she is also able to reassure herself "That when I find troubles from men. That it hath pleased thee to make them the instruments of rebukes to me" (fol. 57ᵛ). Austen draws extensively on the popular Church of English divine Jeremy Taylor's reflections on providence, paraphrasing his advice to "Consider afflictions. are the excercises of wisdome. the nursery of virtue, the venturing for a crowne and the gate of Glory" (fols. 36ʳ⁻ᵛ).[79] Austen's providential world-view underpins her identification with Job (a favored model of innocent suffering for the providential thinker) and with widows and orphans, as she derives what Keith Thomas would describe as "stoical consolation" from "the tempests and inquietudes of this life" (fol. 70ᵛ),[80] and shores herself up against the fear of defeat in her estate wrangling.

In a typical, if somewhat paradoxical, element of seventeenth-century providentialism, Austen's adoption of a stance of afflicted sanctity does not prevent her from equating godliness and virtue with industry and prosperity in the world. Citing John Donne's funeral sermon for Sir William Cockayne, Alderman and Lord Mayor of London, she reflects:

> The most remarkable points I have observed out of all the workes of Doc*ter* Dun. I doe refer to two points. Which are prosperity. and Aduarsity.

---

[77] See Alexandra Walsham, *Providence in Early Modern England* (Oxford: Oxford University Press, 1999) for an excellent and comprehensive discussion.

[78] Keith Thomas, *Religion and the Decline of Magic* (London: Weidenfeld and Nicolson, 1971), 81; see Walsham, *Providence*, 15–17.

[79] KA is paraphrasing Taylor, *The Rule and Exercises of Holy Living* (1650), 153.

[80] Thomas, *Religion and the Decline of Magic*, 81.

> & Not withstanding ^that^ great aduersity and Crosses attend us in this world. we are not to slaken our duty of industry and vsefulnes in the course of our race. (fol. 91ᵛ)

Cockayne's appeal as a role model for Austen is clear. Donne describes, "though he were of Parents of a good, of a great Estate, yet his possibility and his expectation from them, did not slacken his own industry." Cockayne, indeed, "multiplied his estate so, as was fit to endow many and great Children."[81] Austen's extrapolation on Donne's sermon for Cockayne accords with Keith Thomas's somewhat wry description of the providential mindset as, to a large extent, "self-confirming": "if a godly man was smitten then he was being tested and tried," but at the same time, "the overwhelming majority of clerical writers and pious laymen sincerely believed that there was a link between man's moral behaviour and his fortune in this world."[82] Austen reflects that constant industry is required of the godly in the face of whatever adversities; her meditation prescribes industry as godly duty, a "strict command," and prosperity is industry's worldly result and manifestation.[83]

Austen's belief in godly industry also underpins a highly materialistic set of criteria for individual and familial honor. She defines her family's honor according to wealth—the sign of godly industry—and "Liberality," a definition that is deeply anti-aristocratic. Folios 49ᵛ–50ʳ contain a prose contemplation "Of Honour," and here she writes:

> I esteeme Honour not any thing worth, vnles it be well guarded with wealth, that it ravil not out to a degree, farre meaner then Yeomandry is. So that the Fortune I Iudge to be the real Honour. And the Title is the ornament, the embellishing of that Fortune, w*h*ich makes it look a litle brighter to dazle common eyes. (fol. 49ᵛ)

Austen has drawn a horizontal line in the left hand margin just over halfway down folio 49ᵛ, and has returned to recast her definition of honor in a different pen, perhaps at a later date: "True Honour consists not so much in those preferments and titles of the world, [. . .] But in holy wisdome, grauity and constancy" (Fig. 6, p. 93). She implicitly acknowledges the worldliness of

---

[81] John Donne, Sermon LXXX, "Preached at the funeral of Sir William Cokayne, Knight, Alderman of London, December 12. 1626," *LXXX Sermons* (1640), 816–26, here 824–26.

[82] Thomas, *Religion and the Decline of Magic*, 82, 88–89.

[83] Max Weber's assertion that Calvinism elevated "intense worldly activity" to the significance of a "calling," and that it became "indispensable as a sign of election" (*The Protestant Ethic and the Spirit of Capitalism* [London: Allen & Unwin, 1976], 112, 115), is particularly apt in the case of Austen and her colleague in the multiplication of estates, Cockayne.

her previous distinction between fortune and titles, and it is possible to read her as articulating some unease with acquisitiveness as an end in itself. "Surely Mediocrity is the happiest condition we can obtaine,"[84] she writes, but she muses that "the Active man stayes not at it but climbes far beyond it: Til he paces all the degrees, from competency, to superfluites. And from thence Ambition tempts him with Titles, and emenency" (fol. 50^r). Austen's professed abnegation of worldly and fiscal concerns is belied by her work ethic and the preponderance of meditations in *Book M* that focus on her estate tribulations. This attempt to celebrate "Mediocrity" notwithstanding, Austen's individualistic identification of godliness with industry and economic achievement defines her constructions of social virtue and honour. The absoluteness with which industry equals honor for Austen would seem to be inflected by, and to reinforce, the upwardly-aspirant status of her families (by birth, marriage, and childrearing).

Austen's emphasis on industry and activity in godliness and honor is also evident in her attitude towards and participation in her eldest son Thomas's Oxford education. Thomas, like his father, was a university and Inns-of-Court man: he matriculated at Balliol College in 1664 and he was admitted to Lincoln's Inn in 1669.[85] Austen sees her son's education as his father's legacy, and includes a description of it as such in an advice piece that she writes for him before making a journey to Essex at the height of the Great Plague in August 1665: "You must know an honour and duty is to be performed to the Ashes of y*our* most worthy Father from whence your being sprung. and who did surpase confering nature to you while he was with you by an ardent affection for your Education" (fol. 92^v). *Book M* is contemporary with Thomas's Oxford years, and Austen returns to his education several times. She is not wholly commendatory. Folios 43^r–44^r are addressed "To my S*on* T*homas* A*usten*," and comprise a tirade against a "very rude Fashione" of leaving one's hat on, which "creates abundance of pride in Colledges"; however, on folio 44^v she relents, describing her son's education as preferable to "Court breeding" on its own. Later, she is delighted to hear from Thomas's tutor of "his sobriety and temperance," qualities that will "fit him to a Heavenly inheritance" (fol. 82^v). For Austen, the virtues of her son's university education are religion and "sollid Learning."

The value that Austen places on industry and activity in the acquisition of a godly education is also manifest in her own contemplative activities, as represented in *Book M*. Katherine Austen did not have her son or husband's educational opportunities—as a woman, she would not have attended grammar school, let alone university, and her education in secular matters would necessarily have

---

[84] KA is implicitly evoking Ecclesiastes 4:6, to which she refers directly in relation to "mediocrity" on fol. 112^r.

[85] Foster, *Alumni Oxonienses*, 1: 46; *The Records of the Honourable Society of Lincoln's Inn*, 1: 305.

been piecemeal.[86] But she connects her son's education to her own, following the advice to her son Thomas with an exploration of ingenuity that insists on the importance of her own contemplation and thoughtful reflection. She writes "There is nothing I adoar more in this world then Ingennuity," and she explores her own definition of the term:

> What is Ingennuity.
> I take it to be dexterity and aptenes to vndertake all things readily, with life and apprehention, with Iudgement and sollidity, as suites with the vndertaking. And for the proper deriviation of the word I am not a schollar to know from whence it comes./ (fol. 44ᵛ).

"To spend time," a later meditation, reinforces the value that she places on contemplative activity:

> Consider how to spend my time, Not trifling away, but with method, vsefully, and comfortably, And to waigh the howeres of the day, to divide them in several studies. imployments. In Devotion, in Sobernes. In educating my children. In History, in a portion for retirement: In seecking knowledg: Tis observed. the ignorant man is compared to a Beast: But he is far worse then a Beast. their nature is to be ignorant: Tis mans fault if he be so./. (fol. 56ʳ)

Austen implicitly includes women in this statement, and elsewhere in *Book M*, she refers to her own diligence and knowledge with pride: she reports that her suitor said "he never taulket with me but learned Something of me" (fol. 96ʳ). Austen may disclaim pretensions to scholarship on account of her gender; however, ingenuity and studious activity, "Iudgement and sollidity," are manifest throughout *Book M* as she uses her meditations to make sense of the world around her.

Katherine Austen's compilations: portents, visions, and the theology of dreams

Katherine Austen's ingenuity takes, first and foremost, the form one might expect from one who equates "sollid Learning" and religion: she reads and reflects extensively upon the scriptures and on the exempla they provide. She describes and reflects on men and women in the scriptures who, like herself, have received God's "succours and assistances": "Abram and Isack: As well as David: and St Peter and St Paul. As well as Ester and Iudeth and Deborah" (fol. 85ᵛ). It is not always clear whether Austen has collated lists of exempla such as this herself, or

---

[86] See Kenneth Charlton, *Women, Religion, and Education in Early Modern England* (London and New York: Routledge, 1999). Thomas Austen's 1658 will, notably, leaves his books to be divided between his two sons; the legacy excludes his daughter Anne (National Archives, PROB 11/285).

whether she has lifted them from a secondary source. But she certainly draws freely and flexibly on diverse sources at other points in *Book M*. She relates, for example, a tale about Lady Margaret Beaufort (whom Austen describes as "a most pious woman (as that age went)") which is to be found in Camden's *Remaines*, and she follows it immediately with a snippet from Francis Bacon's *Historie of the Reigne of King Henry the Seventh* (fol. 33ʳ). Two folios later, she borrows from Thomas Fuller's *The Holy State* when she describes Hildegard von Bingen as "a gracious virgin" and a pious prophet (fol. 34ʳ). Austen borrows widely from scripture and beyond as she slips freely in and out of differently gendered models of forbearance; she subscribes to the general wisdoms offered by the male, yet freely assumes the particular statuses offered to the female godly.

Austen's preoccupations, as well as her religious, political, and social allegiances, are clear in her extensive practice of collation and compilation. Jeremy Taylor and John Donne, in particular, are paraphrased extensively, frequently in relation to dreams and visions, or on providence and its operation in everyday life; for example, Austen borrows from Donne's sermons to assert her belief "That every man hath a particular Angel to assist him" (fol. 6ʳ and following). The paraphrase is, characteristically, unattributed, and she concludes it with an indication of her own association of texts, "See: D*oc* Feat*ly*," a reference to Daniel Featley, the Church of England controversialist from whose sermons Austen paraphrases elsewhere (fols. 17ʳ–20ʳ). Austen also excerpts Bishop John Fell's *Life of Henry Hammond*, and she paraphrases extensively from Bishop John Gauden's funeral sermon for Bishop Ralph Brownrig. I have not been able to locate the source of every borrowing or paraphrase in *Book M*, but enough sources have been located to give a sense of Austen's practice. Many of her borrowings derive from common printed sources; for example, John Donne's *LXXX Sermons* and Jeremy Taylor's *Eniautos*, as well as his *Rules for Holy Living*. But it is also clear that Austen recorded material in oral circulation: she refers to "the Dreame of Lady Burtons Cosen" (fol. 10ᵛ), Lady Frances Burton being the aunt of her husband, Thomas,[87] and when retelling a story about the deaths of Sir Edward Thurland and Sir Thomas Twisden, she remarks "this Thurland told one that told us" (fol. 10ᵛ). Factual errors are present in Austen's version of this anecdote (see note to fol. 10ᵛ), and similar errors occur in her retelling of dream anecdotes printed in Izaak Walton's *Lives* (see fols. 11ʳ–12ʳ). It is possible that she had personal acquaintance with Walton and his circle, as her father's will refers to an Izaak Walton living in one of his houses in Chancery Lane in the late 1630s.[88]

Austen's traceable sources are, without exception, impeccably Church of England and royalist, but her deeply orthodox religious allegiances do not preclude a fascination with portents and omens, visions and dreams—a fascination of

---

[87] She is named in the wills of Thomas Austen and his brother, John Austen, National Archives, PROB 11/285 and National Archives, PROB 11/296.

[88] Robert Wilson's will, National Archives, PROB 11/182.

the kind that scholarship has, inaccurately, associated with either uneducated superstition or a "hotter" kind of Protestantism in early modern England.[89] Austen records tales such as that of a drop of blood falling from the ceiling at Greenwich, a murderer condemned "some 10 or 20 yeares" after the act by the victim's severed hand (fol. 10ᵛ), and a man thrown from his horse and killed when riding past the bones of a horse he had unjustly slain one year previously (fol. 33ᵛ). A boy who falls from a churchyard monument and "dashet his braines out" has been warned by a voice saying "Goe away" (fol. 31ᵛ), and Austen herself has been fortunate not to be killed in a fall from a tree that is haunted by spirits (fol. 98ʳ). Austen's eagerness to commit tales of portents and fortunate escapes to the pages of *Book M* may seem unorthodox, but her compilation of such anecdotes is mirrored in the print culture of the time. "Strange and wonderful newes" of providential disasters and comeuppances proliferated in the cheap pamphlet press between 1560 and 1640, and providential anecdotes were compiled into encyclopedic anthologies, such as Thomas Beard's *The Theatre of God's Judgements* (1597). Alexandra Walsham regards these printed compilations as representing "moments of coalition" between unlearned and elite modes of thinking, and those of Protestants across the religious and political spectrum. "Strange newes" may have been a staple of the cheap and popular press, but our knowledge of providential ephemera is due largely to its preservation in the collections of "gentlemen bibliophiles like John Selden, Anthony Wood, Samuel Pepys, and Robert Harley." Equally, the compilation of such anecdotes became a staple in the personal papers and spiritual diaries of providential thinkers, from the Puritan diarist John Beadle, to the moderate Parliamentarian Ralph Josselin,[90] to a Church of England royalist such as Katherine Austen.[91]

Alongside her records of portents and omens, Austen affords considerable space in *Book M* to compiling anecdotes of dreams and visions, and she gives careful and explicit consideration to the theological implications of her belief in these as forms of God's immediate intervention in everyday life. She considers the role "Of Angeles" early in *Book M*, reflecting that "sometimes God delievers

---

[89] See Walsham, *Providence*, 2.

[90] Ralph Josselin, the vicar of Earls Colne, Essex, from 1641 to 1683, also recorded thirty-three dreams in his diary, reflecting "why should not I when I see many of the thoughts of my head fulfilled trust in god for the accomplishment of the rest, apprehending there is something of god in those thoughts and visions, agreeing with the scripture": Alan MacFarlane, ed., *The Diary of Ralph Josselin, 1616–1683* (London: Oxford University Press for The British Academy, 1976), 304, 335. While Josselin was a parliamentarian, he pursued a course moderate enough to ensure his survival as vicar at Earls Colne from 1641 to 1683, and he is notably troubled by the separatist sects of the 1650s, particularly the Quakers.

[91] I am indebted to Walsham for this contextual description; see *Providence*, esp. 2, 33, 37, 51, 66, and 69.

his Will by the Voyce of an Angel . . . Sometimes without voyce as by Dreames . . . And sometimes by Visiones . . . These visiones are revealed onely to the elect of God" (fol. 7ʳ).[92] She is careful to qualify her assertion here, referring to Daniel Featley to remind herself that "we must bles God for [angels] but not pray to them" (fol. 6ʳ).[93] Her primary concern in her consideration of angels is to insist that "God dus give signes" to his children in times of trouble (fol. 7ʳ); in this way, angels "were an integral part of the [early modern] providential world-view which Protestantism powerfully reinforced."[94] Austen is elsewhere categorical that God may work via miracle or revelation, paraphrasing Donne's assertion that:

> We are genneraly to receive our instructions from Gods word: and where those meanes are duely exhibited. in his Church. we are to rest. as being sufficient to instruct us without revelation. Yet we are not to conclude God in his Law. as that he should have noe prerogative, nor so to bind him up in his ordinances, as that he never can, or never does work by an extrordinary way of Revelation. (fol. 15ʳ)

Austen paraphrases excerpts from Bishop John Gauden's funeral sermon for Ralph Brownrig, Bishop of Exeter, which focus on divine visitations, and her selections give such visitations ongoing status as one form of God's providential intervention in the lives of his chosen people: "God is not prodigal of these special favours. but for some great designes are they indulged" (fol. 13ʳ).[95]

Immediately following the consideration of angels (fols. 6ʳ–9ʳ) is an extended compilation of dream anecdotes (fols. 10ʳ–17ʳ); this dream compilation confirms Austen's interest in the prophetic qualities of dreams and visions, as well as reinforces the orthodox nature of the authorities on which she draws. She paraphrases from John Fell's *Life* of the royalist Henry Hammond a description of a dream that visited Hammond in 1643, "About the beginning of the troubles";[96] she retells the story of Donne's vision of his wife with a dead child in her arms; and she recounts equally well-known dreams recorded by members of the Wotton

---

[92] I have not been able to trace KA's source for this passage. KA's free association of voices, dreams, and visions is commonplace. Crawford has commented that "Contemporaries were often hard pressed to determine the differences between dreams, waking dreams, visions and prophecies. Visionary insights might be perceived as dreams, and the nature of prophecies was complex" ("Women's Dreams," 94–95). See also KA's own reference to "*Book* I: pag 260 of Dreames & of prophesies" (fol. 33ʳ).

[93] It is not clear to which Featley text KA is referring.

[94] Peter Marshall and Alexandra Walsham, eds., *Angels in the Early Modern World* (Cambridge: Cambridge University Press, 2006), 14–15.

[95] John Gauden, *A sermon preached in the Temple-chappel, at the funeral of the Right Reverend . . . Dr. Brounrig* (1660), 8 and 116–17. See footnote to fol. 13ʳ.

[96] John Fell, *The Life of The most Learned, Reverend and Pious Dr. H. Hammond* (1661), 27–28.

family (see fols. 11ʳ–12ʳ). The exclusively orthodox nature of Austen's sources and authorities illustrate that she was participating in a culture of recording and interpreting dreams that was common across the religious spectrum, not only among radical sects. Sir Thomas Browne regarded the "phantasmes of sleepe" as more likely to be generated by the ingestion of certain foods than supernatural visitations, but he insists that "divine impressions" are possible.[97] Joseph Hall, whom Austen cites, is among those "known to have taken at least some dreams seriously,"[98] and even Archbishop Laud, to whom Austen may refer (fol. 12ʳ), recorded dreams in his diary (although he rarely entered into interpretation).[99]

Folios 10ʳ–17ʳ conclude with a consideration of the doctrinal concerns raised by a belief in dreams' significance, in which Austen echoes the terms of contemporary debate. Thomas Hill's *The moste pleasunte Arte of the Interpretacion of Dreames* (c. 1576) had been countered by Reginald Scot's *The Discoverie of Witchcraft* (1584), and educated divines who recorded dreams frequently demonstrate an anxiety to dissociate themselves from the "vulgar enthusiasms" of opponents such as George Fox.[100] Archbishop Laud, for example, observes of a dream with an obvious premonitory meaning, "I am not moved with dreams; yet I thought fit to remember this";[101] Austen (paraphrasing John Fell) echoes this disclaimer in commenting that Henry Hammond "was no valuer of trifles," but "had so extraordinary a Dream he could not then despice, nor ever after forget it" (fol. 10ʳ). Austen paraphrases Jeremy Taylor's version of the standard check on overenthusiasm when she comments "Now w*h*at a man pretends he hath herd we

---

[97] Thomas Browne, "On Dreams," in Geoffrey Keynes, ed., *The Works of Sir Thomas Browne*, 6 vols. (London: Faber and Faber, 1931), 5: 183-85. Nigel Smith explains the proximity of visions and dreams in seventeenth-century thought and cites Browne, who concludes that "Most of the 'visions' and 'revelations' which were so common during the Interregnum were probably what we should call dreams" (Nigel Smith, *Perfection Proclaimed: Language and Literature in English Radical Religion, 1640-1660* [Oxford: Clarendon Press, 1989], 74). Izaak Walton, like Thomas Browne, believes it possible for dreams to be divine revelations. Relating the stories of Nicholas Wotton's dreams, he states that "Almighty God (though the causes of Dreams be often unknown) hath even in these latter times, by a certain illumination of the soul in sleep, discovered many things that humane wisdom could not forsee" (*The Life of Sir Henry Wotton*, unpaginated preface to Sir Henry Wotton, *Reliquiæ Wottonianæ* [1651]).

[98] Thomas, *Religion and the Decline of Magic*, 129.

[99] Kathleen McLuskie, "The 'Candy-Coloured Clown': Reading Early Modern Dreams," in *Reading Dreams: The Interpretation of Dreams from Chaucer to Shakespeare*, ed. Peter Brown (Oxford: Oxford University Press, 1999), 147–67, here 160. See also Charles Carlton, "The Dream Life of Archbishop Laud," *History Today* 36 (1986): 9–15; and *Reading the Early Modern Dream*, ed. Hodgkin, et al.

[100] Peter Holland, "The Interpretation of Dreams in the Renaissance," in *Reading Dreams*, ed. Brown, 125–46, here 130; McLuskie, "The 'Candy-Coloured Clown'," 160.

[101] McLuskie, "The 'Candy-Coloured Clown'," 160.

can enquier if it agree to Gods word" (fol. 14ʳ).[102] She goes on to paraphrase an unidentified sermon on Paul's epistle to the Hebrews, "God, who at sundry times and in divers manners spake in time past unto the fathers by the prophets, Hath in these last days spoken unto us by his Son" ([Hebrews 1:1]; fols. 16ʳ–17ʳ), and she determines that contemporary saints must "keep to the word of God. and that will keep you from delusiones" (fol. 16ʳ). She dwells extensively on the perils of being too eager to accord divine origins to all dreams, reflecting that "when persons by an over curiosity have anticipated their desier to know their Fortune. it seldome hath been a good succes to them," and she again illustrates her point by compiling illustrative anecdotes—this time from literary sources (fols. 32ʳ⁻ᵛ). Misleading prophecies, she describes, are "begotten by *th*e Devil," and she then paraphrases from Thomas Fuller's life of Andronicus to warn that "men had need take heed of curiosity to know things to come. which is one of the Kernals of the forbiden fruit" (fols. 32ʳ⁻ᵛ).[103] Nonetheless, Austen begins her next folio with an undinted conviction that "Some Dreames are not to be slited" (fol. 33ʳ).

Austen's compilation of anecdotes and theology relating to dreams and revelation culminates, thematically, in her elaborate interpretation of several dreams of her own. She records "My Dreame on 2d: of I*an*uary 1664," in which she attends a wedding, climbing "a high paire of Staires" and coming to a room in which her husband was conversing with a gentleman in a gown. Leaving by a set of back stairs, Austen returns for her muff, descending by only eight or nine steps for the second time when she awakes. Austen states that the dream "ran in my minde divers dayes afterwards," and she seeks what John Fell describes as a dream's "correspondent event" (*Book M*, fol. 10ʳ). She decides that "the First paire of staires signified to me to the end of I*an*uary and the second was so many dayes in Feb*ru*ary and then something wud fall out to me." Austen's feeling about the dream's significance is borne out in the events of her lawsuits: she is summoned to attend the Committee of Parliament in the Highbury business on 9 February 1664/5, and she asserts that when she does so, the room "was the same as I saw in my Dreame," and the presiding judge, Sir John Birkenhead, is the man with whom her husband was conversing (fol. 60ᵛ). She reports another dream of her father-in-law and brother-in-law engaged in a game of cribbage with herself and her husband, and she reflects, similarly, that the "troublesome busines [of Highbury] might wel be compared to a game at Cards. wherein my Father Aus[ten] and all of us have been concerned in *th*e takeing care of and defending" (fol.

---

[102] Nigel Smith has noted of Philip Goodwin, in his *The Mystery of Dreames, Historically Discoursed* (1658), that "What separates the more orthodox Protestant from the radical sects is his Scripturalism" (Smith, *Perfection Proclaimed*, 78).

[103] Thomas Fuller, *The Holy State and the Profane State*, 4th ed. (1663), 492.

64ʳ).[104] Austen does not hesitate to impute real-life significance to the precise details of these dreams: in each case, her oneirocriticism takes the form of deliberate reflection, and retrospective ascription of the dream's referents. She also records in verse a dream "Vpon [. . .] the 20th Oct*ober* 1664: when I Dreamet I saw 4 Moones in a clear Sky," and she regards this dream as a prompt to speculate upon what form her deliverance from tribulation will take. The meaning of this dream is unclear, but Austen resolves in the poem to "willingly agree" to whichever "state is fittest Lord for thee," and she supplicates that she be filled with God's purposes (fol. 63ᵛ).

Austen's analysis of one further dream defines a key aspect of the relationship she perceives between her godly self, her text, and the world around her. She follows her exploration of dreams and visions at the opening of *Book M* (fols. 10ʳ–17ʳ) with an "Observation on my Dream. of Monition" (fol. 21ʳ)—that is, of instruction, warning, or intimation. Austen claims not only the ability rightly to construe and interpret her own dreams, but also that the particular dream recorded here contains a monition—an instruction or omen—more plain and certain than most intimations of which she has heard, of a public godly role for herself: "I shal not dye but live. and declare the workes of the Lord. As if that was the meaning, After the being excercised with divers trials and afflictions: that I should continue to declare the workes and manifestations of his goodnes." Quoting directly from Psalm 118:17, Austen here claims a monition which overturns that received in an earlier dream (see p. 16, above); her discussion of both reveals a willingness to base a personal *raison d'être* on dreams and the interpretation of them, a mode of thinking which is sanctioned in the passages of scripture to which she refers. Supported by the authorities and anecdotes which feature in her paraphrases and compilations, she claims the ability to interpret her own dream as a monition, and identifies herself directly with the Psalmist David. Austen's belief in omens and portents, dreams and visions, not only informs her view of her life as a catalogue of providences "shewed to me a private. to me a particular person" (fol. 21ʳ), but underpins her monition that she ought to declare these providences to others—an activity in which *Book M* appears to play a part.

Occasional meditation, the Psalms, and Katherine Austen's poetic voice

Katherine Austen's identification of herself with the Psalmist David, in her monition that "I shal not dye but live. and declare the workes of the Lord," underscores two further vital generic strands in the text of *Book M*: occasional meditation and—its close relative—Psalm paraphrase and meditation. Austen's meditations very frequently fall into the category of the occasional meditation,

---

[104] KA's rejected suitor, who died in 1665, was also "one that much observed Dreames"; see fols. 96ᵛ–97ᵛ.

the brief, apparently spontaneous, meditation on a random event, in order to focus on that event as evidence of the relationship between the self and God.[105] Joseph Hall, Jeremy Taylor, John Donne, and Thomas Fuller, all of whom Austen read, were advocates and practitioners of the occasional meditation,[106] with Hall's *Occasional Meditations* (1630; enlarged in 1631 and 1633) becoming a particularly popular and exemplary collection.[107] Austen follows his model (in spirit, rather than through imitation of specific pieces) in meditations such as "Vpon Lending Mr C: money." This meditation seems at first to be an opportunity for Austen to vent about "His abominable rudenes for my kindnes to him," but she is able within a few lines to construe such losses as "instructions to teach me piety and hollines to cast my dependenc on the God of comfort" (fol. 52^r). Her meditation "On my Fall off the Tree," with its reference to "Revoulted spirits [which] that place did haunt" (fols. 98^v–99^r) comes close to being "too farre-fetcht, or fauouring of Superstition," a risk warned against by Hall,[108] but for the most part, Austen models the seventeenth-century occasional meditation as it was practiced widely by women as well as men. Her occasions for meditation often coincide with familial events worthy of memorialization. She meditates, for example, on 5 December 1664 on her son "Robin Austins recovery of the smal pox. and Coronal Popons son Iohn diing of them" (fols. 46^{r-v}); this poetic consideration prompts her into a further poetic "Meditation on my death" (fols. 46^v–47^r). She also meditates in poetry "On the Death of my Neece Grace Ashe. 4 years old" (fol. 53^v), and a meditation "On the Death: of Mr Franceis Duffeild my Husbands Cosen Germaine" becomes an opportunity to reflect in prose on the passing of numerous friends and relatives, and to reflect that "These may be preparations to me. I may make my self ready" (fol. 54^r).

Occasional meditation occupies a vital space in seventeenth-century spiritual diaries which, like *Book M*, are concerned to trace more broadly the presence of God and his providences in the writer's life. It is clear that for Austen, isolated or individual events such as her fall from the tree and her preservation from injury represent God's immediate intervention in her life:

It might have bin a fatal Tree,
And my last acts catastrophe.
Yet all wayes from that remote part,
My Genius ever did divert. (fol. 98^v)

---

[105] See Coolahan, "Redeeming Parcels of Time," 124; and pp. 3–4, above.
[106] See Coolahan, "Redeeming Parcels of Time."
[107] See F. L. Huntley, *Bishop Joseph Hall and Protestant Meditation in Seventeenth-Century England*, MRTS 1 (Binghamton, NY: Medieval & Renaissance Texts & Studies, 1981).
[108] Coolahan, "Redeeming Parcels of Time," 133.

These preservations are the "special" or "particular" acts of providence by which God meted out the care of his chosen people,[109] and to a very large extent, it is her duty to record these "particular" providences to her and hers that drives Austen's meditations in *Book M*. She expostulates at one point, "O that I may live to tell the singular providences of God to me" (fol. 62ᵛ), and references to providences "shewed to me a private. to me a particular person" (fol. 21ʳ) are numerous. John Beadle's *Journal of a Thankful Christian* (1656) describes the Christian duty to keep a journal "of all Gods gracious dealings with us," and such "account keeping" of particular providences motivates a large number of women's spiritual journals in the period. Alice Thornton styles her *A booke of remembrances* in providential terms, as a notice of "all the remarkable deliuerances of my selfe, Husband & Children";[110] like Austen, she alludes repeatedly to Job and David, and her "predication of selfhood on suffering and deliverance"[111] is directly comparable to Austen's. Elizabeth Walker, similarly, entitles one third of the manuscript that she left "Some Memorials of God's Providences to my Husband, self, and Children."[112] Such spiritual account-keeping merges in *Book M* with literal account-keeping, as already intimated in Austen's meditation "Vpon Lending Mr C: money." That Austen viewed the success or otherwise of her worldly estate tribulations as indicative of God's providences to her is indicated most clearly when she prefaces a two-page opening of household accounts as a spiritual ledger, of "the divers emergincies I have bin put to for the supplying great vndertakeings. and how I have pased through not withstanding my preventions" (fol. 99ᵛ).[113]

The most influential scriptural model of the occasional meditator was David, whose Psalms constituted an ur-text for the daily meditations of many seventeenth-century women, including Katherine Austen. The Psalms' role in daily devotional life was underpinned by the *Book of Common Prayer*'s prescription of the daily Psalm readings, which guided the reader through the whole Book of Psalms each month;[114] and the close proximity of occasional meditation and Psalm reading, paraphrasing, and meditation is indicated by Joseph Hall's publication of Psalm paraphrases along with his occasional meditations in *Holy Obseruations* (1607). Calvin famously described the Psalms as "the Anatomy of all the partes of the Soule," in which is "lyvely set out before our eyes, all the greefes, sorowes, feares, doutes, hopes, cares, anguishes, and finally all the trubblesome

---

[109] See Walsham, *Providence*, 12.

[110] Yale University Library, Microfilm MISC 326, [p. 1].

[111] Graham, et al., "Pondering All These Things," 53.

[112] Effie Botonaki, "Seventeenth-Century Englishwomen's Spiritual Diaries: Self-Examination, Covenanting, and Account Keeping," *Sixteenth Century Journal* 30 (1999): 3-21, here 12.

[113] For spiritual and secular accounting, see Botonaki, "Spiritual Diaries," esp. 14, 17.

[114] Trill, "Speaking to God," 271.

motions wherewith mennes mindes are woont to be turmoyled."[115] The words of the Psalms could thus be used to express and define almost any emotional state, and this is likely to have been particularly so for early modern women for at least two reasons. Women's education beyond religious precepts, principles, and texts was more restricted than that of men, and the Psalms may have provided "an acceptable form for self-expression in a culture that exalted silence as a feminine virtue."[116] Certainly, Margaret Hannay has argued that "The words of the Psalms so permeated early modern consciousness that quoting Psalms often became the deepest personal expression of the inner life for both men and women," and "Psalms could thus become life-writing."[117] Interaction with and meditation through the Psalms permeate the life-writings of Lady Margaret Hoby, Alice Thornton, Lady Mary Rich, and Lady Anne Halkett, although none identifies herself as closely and explicitly with the Psalmist as does Katherine Austen.

Austen's interpretation of her dream of monition, "that I shal not dye but live. and declare the workes of the Lord," is a direct quotation of Psalm 118:17. Her dream interpretation thus involves an audacious identification of herself as a second David, and she continues her reflection on her dream of monition, "thou hast shewed thy wonders to me as well as to David: as well as to Kings." She describes the significance of David's model to her own writing on folio 107^r: "King David was the great example of trouble and confidence in that trouble to his meditations I resort to, and he that was his retreate shal be mine," and her response to Psalm 147 describes David's speaking voice as a model for her own:

> [David] incites to give praise for our birth. Let Israel rejoyce in him that made him. Let the children of Zion be Ioyful in their King. Nay and let my soule and my body too, Every Faculty of soule. every member of my body, sing vnto my God that hath made me. (fol. 77^r)

Austen thus centers her interpretation of her dream of monition on the figure of David, and she reiterates throughout *Book M* the exemplarity of his speaking voice and his Psalms to her own mode of meditational writing.

Austen meditates throughout *Book M* on David's afflictions and his responses to these, often noting the numbers of the Psalms to which she is responding. For example, in a meditation reacting to Susanna Austen's lawsuit over the Red Lion, she meditates on Psalm 121, the Psalm guiding her response to the particular affliction in her own life:

---

[115] Quoted in Barbara Lewalski, *Protestant Poetics and the Seventeenth-Century Religious Lyric* (Princeton: Princeton University Press, 1979), 43. Lewalski outlines the history of the Psalms' devotional significance, 39–53, 231–37.

[116] Hannay, "So May I," 118.

[117] Hannay, "So May I," 107.

The CXXI: Salme: tels me w*ha*t I shal find if I lift up my eyes to the hills: whence cometh all my help: a help that will not suffer my feet to be moved if I stand in his wayes. (fol. 82ʳ)

She moves fluidly here within the language of the Psalm (she moves in the lines quoted from verse 1 to 3), altering the pronouns to the first person and thus applying the Psalm directly to her particular, personal circumstance. The Lord's protection is also rendered more directly personal than it is in the Psalm itself: "In all those perils and evils w*hi*ch is for his glory. w*hi*ch is for my benefit. he wil preserve my soule. out of them." (Psalm 121:7 is simply "The Lord shall preserve thee from all evil: he shall preserve thy soul.") Austen moves, as is typical in her Psalm meditations, from an exposition of free Psalm paraphrase into a direct discussion of her particular, immediate circumstance—in this case, her sister-in-law's challenge to the Red Lion—before concluding with a prayer in which she apostrophizes God. Such meditations on secular events that draw heavily on Psalm discourse run throughout *Book M*; indeed, they are too numerous to discuss individually here. Austen seems, most frequently, to be working with the King James Version of the Psalms, although there is at least one adherence to a variant *Book of Common Prayer* (i.e. Coverdale) version (of Psalm 68; see fol. 55ʳ).

Austen's response to Psalm 147 ("and let my soule and my body too, Every Faculty of soule. every member of my body, sing vnto my God that hath made me") not only describes the process of her reading and meditational activities, but may also say something about her inspiration to poetic authorship. David was regarded as the epitome of the godly poet, evoked by female and male religious poets alike: Philip Sidney regarded the Psalms as a "divine poem"; Anne Southwell describes David as "that sweet singer of Israell"; and Robert Southwell, S. J., declares "With David verse to vertue I apply, / Whose measure best with measured wordes doth sit."[118] Joseph Hall describes his aim in his Psalm paraphrases to "be a Poet with David," and to create "holy measures rightly composed."[119] To "be a Poet with David" is to fit holy prayer to measure, and into the sharply-crafted poetic form. "Every Faculty" of Katherine Austen's soul thus sings to God in *Book M*, not merely through reading and stepping into the Psalms' poetic voice, but also through casting "the words of my mouth and the meditation of my heart" (Psalm 119:14) into verse lines of her own. Her prose deliberations transform into verse on several occasions. For instance, she writes at the top of folio 57ᵛ, "I here David pray to be delievered. from men

---

[118] Katherine Duncan-Jones and Jan van Dorsten, eds., *Miscellaneous Prose of Sir Philip Sidney* (Oxford: Clarendon Press, 1973), 77; Jean Klene, ed., *The Southwell-Sibthorpe Commonplace Book*, Renaissance English Text Society, 7th ser., 20 (Tempe: Medieval & Renaissance Texts & Studies, 1997), 5; James H. McDonald and Nancy Pollard Brown, eds., *The Poems of Robert Southwell, S. J.* (Oxford: Clarendon Press, 1967), 1–2.

[119] Hall, *Holy Obseruations*, sig. Gʳ.

which are thy hand o Lord"; beneath it, after half a page of prose meditation, she begins a poem which is entitled simply "Read Salme 27: of Supportation" (Fig. 7, p. 102). A poem on folios 106ᵛ–107ʳ is similarly contextualized, preceded and followed by prose references to David, and Austen's versification also interacts directly with the Psalms during her concern with the 1665 plague outbreak. She terminates a prose meditation with the note that "Da*vid* composed this 91 Sal*me* when 70000 died in 3: daies," and follows this note with a poem that apostrophizes "My God," and asks that "thy peculiar hand" and "providence divenely sent" protect her and hers from "Fierce Contagion" (fol. 89ʳ).

The relationship between occasional meditation, the divine poem that is the Psalms, and lyric poetry more broadly is an intriguing and complex one, and one which *Book M* can help us better to understand. Barbara Lewalski is among those who outline the extent to which the Psalms were seen not only as an "anatomy of the soul" in the seventeenth century, but also as "the compendium *par excellence* of lyric poetry,"[120] and sixteenth- and seventeenth-century English Psalm paraphrase and lyric poetry developed in conjunction with each other.[121] Katherine Austen, however, does not achieve, and does not seem to aim for, the technical variety, diversity, or accomplishment for which the Sidney Psalms are acclaimed.[122] Her versification is for the most part "rhetorically modest,"[123] in simple rhyming couplets. The only exception in formal terms is her brief but effective poem on the death of her four-year-old niece, Grace Ashe (fol. 53ᵛ); her most rhetorically ambitious lyric is "Come all my thoughts, awake, awake," an exploration of the impossibility of expressing God's perfection in human language which echoes the tone of Donne's Holy Sonnets (fol. 67ʳ). Austen's inspiration to poetic authorship clearly lies in the occasional and lyric model of King David, and the simplicity and

---

[120] Lewalski, *Protestant Poetics*, 39.

[121] See Hannibal Hamlin, *Psalm Culture and Early Modern English Literature* (Cambridge: Cambridge University Press, 2004); Margaret P. Hannay, "Joining the Conversation: David, Astrophil, and the Countess of Pembroke," in *Textual Conversations in the Renaissance: Ethics, Authors, Technologies*, ed. Zachary Lesser and Benedict S. Robinson (Aldershot: Ashgate, 2006), 113–27; Roland Greene, "Sir Philip Sidney's Psalms, the Sixteenth-Century Psalter, and the Nature of the Lyric," *Studies in English Literature* 30 (1990): 19–40.

[122] See Beth Wynne Fisken, "Mary Sidney's Psalmes: Education and Wisdom," in *Silent But for the Word: Tudor Women as Patrons, Translators, and Writers of Religious Works*, ed. Margaret P. Hannay (Kent, OH: Kent State University Press, 1985), 166–83, on the "dazzling variety of stanzaic forms and metrical patterns" employed by Mary Sidney in her Psalm translations (167). See also J.C.A. Rathmell, ed., *The Psalms of Sir Philip Sidney and the Countess of Pembroke* (New York: New York University Press, 1963), xii; and Margaret P. Hannay, Noel J. Kinnamon, and Michael G. Brennan, eds., *The Collected Works of Mary Sidney Herbert, Countess of Pembroke*, 2 vols. (Oxford: Clarendon Press, 1998), 2: 469–84.

[123] Coolahan, "Redeeming Parcels of Time," 130.

modesty of her verse reinforces its primary affinity with devotional thought and the godly ejaculation, in which the "holy measure" and the poetic measure serve a mutual purpose, disciplining the mind and the pen in godly reflection and exercise.[124] Devotional aims and aesthetic ones did not have to be mutually exclusive, as the poetry of the Sidneys and George Herbert exemplifies, but Austen's poetry adheres to devotional impulses and conventions rather than highly literary ones.[125] It reminds us of the wide range of generic choices, aesthetic ambitions, and rhetorical fluencies in seventeenth-century women's texts, and of the variant poetic identities constructed through these generic choices and fluencies.

The rhetorical modesty of Austen's verse notwithstanding, her interest in literary texts of a certain order is indicated by the numerous literary fragments scattered throughout *Book M*. Austen's compilation of dreams and prophecies includes the prophecy of Henry IV's death in Shakespeare's *Henry IV, Part 2*, in which Henry is falsely confident that he will not die until he has heard Mass in Jerusalem; he dies in Jerusalem Chamber in Westminster (4.4.363–68). She follows this immediately with an anecdote told in the opening lines of Richard Brome's play, *A Jovial Crew; or, The Merry Beggars*, and the proximity of her wording to Brome's suggests that she is working directly from a printed copy (fol. 32^r; Fig. 5, p. 75).[126] These anecdotes are not attributed to their sources in *Book M*; neither are two couplets from Samuel Daniel's *The Complaint of Rosamond*, which Austen writes onto the final folio of her manuscript (fol. 114^v). Austen's only attribution of a literary fragment is, in fact, incorrect: six lines describing Venus's grief on the death of Adonis, which Austen describes as being "Out of a poeme of Doc*ter* Corbets: to his Friend: when she might be a widow" (fol. 71^v), are in fact from Henry King's "The Legacy." The presence of these fragments clearly illustrates a degree of literary interest on Austen's part, but it is also clear that she has chosen them all because they appeal to her personal preoccupations: the Shakespeare and Brome extracts are integrated into her compilation of omens and portents, while the direct application of King's lines to her own life is indicated by a cross-reference to an earlier meditation in *Book M*, focusing on her deceased husband's ongoing "influence" in her life (fol. 23^r).

Austen's misattribution of Henry King's lines to Richard Corbett, the Oxford coterie poet and Arminian bishop, is itself of interest, as it may be suggestive of not only of her sources but of poetry's social associations for Katherine Austen.

---

[124] See Elizabeth Clarke, "Herbert's House of Pleasure? Ejaculations Sacred and Profane," *George Herbert Journal* 19 (1996): 55–71. Ramie Targoff, *Common Prayer: The Language of Public Devotion in Early Modern England* (Chicago: University of Chicago Press, 2001) also provides a useful discussion of rhymed prayer.

[125] Coolahan, "Redeeming Parcels of Time," explores the tension between "simplicity and eloquence, utility and aesthetics" in poetic occasional meditation (135).

[126] Brome's play, the last to be performed before the closing of the theatres in 1641, was published in 1652 and 1661.

Introduction 33

Corbett and King's poetry circulated widely in manuscript;[127] misattribution is frequent in these manuscripts,[128] and Austen's belief that the lines she quotes are Richard Corbett's probably indicates that she had access to a manuscript source. There are two identifiable avenues by which Austen may have accessed such manuscript poetry. One is through her husband, educated at Oxford and in the Inns of Court, where commonplace books of poetry such as Richard Corbett's were enormously popular. The other is through her father, the draper in the City of London, who may well have known the linen-draper-turned-biographer Izaak Walton (see p. 21 above, and fols. 11^r–12^r); Walton's associates included Donne and Henry King. For Robert Wilson and Thomas Austen, coterie poetry and poetic literacy no doubt carried the kind of social connotations described by Marotti of the university classes:

> Since students at the universities [. . .] came from different levels of the social hierarchy, it is fair to say that in this environment the practices of manuscript transmission cut across social classes most dramatically. In fact, one of the obvious reasons for the persistence of the manuscript system of literary transmission through the seventeenth century was that it stood opposed to the more democratizing force of print culture and allowed those who participated in it to feel that they were part of a social as well as an intellectual elite.[129]

Is it possible that Austen's versification in *Book M* is inflected by the social aspirations and cultural identifications that Marotti describes? Pamela Hammons has also considered the social and cultural functions of Austen's versification in her literary treatment of Austen's verse, particularly of the one non-devotional verse in *Book M*, and her discussion is useful in this regard. "On the Situation of Highbury" (fol. 104^r) is a country-house poem, its references to Parnassus and Helicon isolated and anomalous in the context of Austen's predominantly devotional mode. Austen openly declares the inadequacy of her poetic skills to the task of country-house poet, but she nonetheless evokes the secular and courtly verse tradition in relation to the estate which is the focus of her social ambitions. Hammons discusses Austen's innovative use of the country-house genre (most country-house poets are, after all, outsiders or loyal retainers), and argues that

---

[127] Corbett's poems were published only posthumously, in *Certain Elegant Poems* (1647) and *Poëtica Stromata, or A Collection* (1648). King's poetry was first published in 1657 (with a second edition in 1664) but had previously circulated very widely in manuscript (see Mary Hobbs, ed., *The Stoughton Manuscript* [Aldershot: Scolar Press, 1990]).

[128] Beal, for example, lists numerous spurious ascriptions of poems to Corbett in seventeenth-century miscellanies (Peter Beal, *Index of English Literary Manuscripts*, vol. 2.1, *1625–1700* [London: Mansell, 1993], 159).

[129] Arthur F. Marotti, *Manuscript, Print, and the English Renaissance Lyric* (Ithaca: Cornell University Press, 1995), 34.

Austen utilizes the genre to "ascribe value to the estate" and, simultaneously, to legitimate "the authority and propriety of her verse." "On the Situation of Highbury" enacts a multifaceted legitimation: of Highbury as an estate worthy of monumentalization, and of Austen as its literal and poetic owner.[130] Austen's use of the country-house genre, thoroughly explored by Hammons, therefore articulates her ownership of the estate that is the focus of her social ambitions. "On the Situation of Highbury" claims for her a lived and verbal affiliation with the social and cultural elite.[131]

"On the Situation of Highbury" is indeed isolated and anomalous in *Book M*, but its meaning is modified if its physical location in the manuscript is taken into account. "On the Situation of Highbury" is given a page to itself (fol. 104ʳ), and the verso of the leaf is also left blank (fol. 104ᵛ); such profligate use of textual space is rare at this point in *Book M*, and indicates that Austen is affording the poem a kind of special presentation status. The poem is, however, immediately preceded by another poem about the embattled family estate, "On that day Highbury came out of Lease. Mic*h*aelmas 1665" (fol. 103ᵛ); the two poems occur on the same opening of *Book M* and thus contextualize each other (as Fig. 9, p. 157 illustrates). Austen reflects in prose at the top of folio 103ᵛ, "Am I the person am to reap the first fruites of that long expectation, and enter into those pleasant feeldes of a faire inheritance. [. . .] Tis a blesing I know not how to receive." She is then moved to versification, and she writes because it is her Christian duty to meditate on and be thankful for the "many Blesings" that "richly shine" upon her on this occasion. "On that day Highbury came out of Lease" contemplates her own and her family's "accessiones" as a providential favor: "Tis more then can. be vnderstood," and it "Beyond my apprehension comes." "On that day Highbury came out of Lease" concludes with a circumspect reflection that the receipt of blessings requires an increase in godly duties, and it is only then that Austen moves to her country-house poem, "On the Situation of Highbury." Secular poetics are just one small element of Austen's discourse(s) in *Book M*, and to read "On the Situation of Highbury" in isolation is to risk distorting its function. Even Austen's one secular poem is framed, physically and conceptually, by her providentialism, with its coexistent strains of stoical submission to worldly trials and the prioritization of worldly industry and its badge, prosperity.

---

[130] Hammons, "Country-House Innovations," 123–24. Hammons usefully compares "On the Situation of Highbury" to Ben Jonson's "To Penshurst" and Aemilia Lanyer's "The Description of Cooke-ham." See also eadem, "Widow, Prophet, and Poet," esp. 4, 12.

[131] See also Ross, "Trophes of his praises make."

Book M and the question of audience: "to my perticular relatives and General"

On one of her prefatory pages, Austen gives prominent place to the following statement:

> Whoso euer shal look in these papers and shal take notice of these personal occurrences: wil easily discerne it concerned none but my self: and was a private excercise directed to my self. The singularity of these conceptions doth not aduantaige any. (fol. 4ᵛ)

Austen's disclaimer is of course paradoxical, assuming as it does a readership even as it protests the manuscript's privacy. Her disclaimer, furthermore, contradicts her expostulation on her dream of monition: "I shal not dye but live. and declare the workes of the Lord [. . .] that I should continue to declare the workes and manifestations of his goodnes." Her expressed desire to "declare" the works of God's goodness to her would seem to be, itself, a declaration of an intended audience for *Book M*. Coyness about claiming public authorship is typical of female-authored devotional texts in the period, and statements such as Austen's opening disclaimer frequently need to be read against the grain. Margaret Ezell is just one critic to challenge the assumption that "a manuscript text written by a seventeenth-century woman, unpublished, its contents described as religious devotions is ipso facto a 'closet' text."[132] Ezell has argued in the case of Elizabeth Delaval's (prose) spiritual journal that literary qualities (Delaval employs dramatic and romance narrative techniques) and the volume's physical characteristics indicate that the manuscript is first and foremost a presentation piece. Austen's opening disclaimer thus needs to be read alongside other statements and declarations in *Book M*. What evidence is there of an intended audience for *Book M*, and how is this audience characterized?

Sara Heller Mendelson claims that many seventeenth-century women destroyed manuscript volumes such as *Book M* "when the dangers of childbirth or a serious illness made them apprehensive of a posthumous discovery."[133] Mothers' advice or legacy books, however, constitute a tradition of deliberate creation of family records for the event of a mother's death, and Austen clearly intended *Book M*, at least in part, to fulfil this function.[134] On travelling to Essex at the height of the plague outbreak in August 1665, Austen wrote into *Book M* a piece

---

[132] Margaret Ezell, "Elizabeth Delaval's Spiritual Heroine: Thoughts on Redefining Manuscript Texts by Early Women Writers," *English Manuscript Studies* 3 (1992): 216–37, here 236.

[133] Mendelson, "Stuart Women's Diaries," 184.

[134] For mothers' advice books, see Sylvia Brown, *Women's Writing in Stuart England: The Mothers' Legacies of Dorothy Leigh, Elizabeth Joscelin, and Elizabeth Richardson* (Thrupp,

to her son Thomas, bequeathing him her providential jewel; a series of three advice pieces, one to each of her children; and a concluding piece to "all my three Deare children," entitled "my wishes." She follows the pieces with a florid signature and date, suggesting that she intended the pieces to carry some posthumous authority (see fols. 92ʳ–94ʳ; and see Fig. 8, p. 145). Folio 51ᵛ is another direct address "To my Children," in which she advises, "Let the example following divert your wishes and your aimes at the estate of Friendes," and she also addresses her children directly on fol. 42ʳ. There is no question that Austen utilizes *Book M*'s potential to provide posthumous evidence of her desires and intentions.

Book M's final folio, moreover, suggests that Austen may have intended an audience for the volume within her lifetime, and beyond her immediate family. Folio 114ʳ bears in large letters the inscription "My strength will I ascribe vnto my God" (an echo of Psalm 68:34), and the publicness of this declaration, suggested by its size, is reinforced by an address below: "D*eare* Sis*ter*: I hope now this Callamity [the plague] is allmost gone. to haue an oppertunity to see you. The absence of Friendes in a time of so many feares was with more impatience then when safety and health gave more confidence of the well fair one of another." The suggestion is perhaps that Austen's sister will see *Book M* before she sees Austen herself, although a further address on folio 114ᵛ complicates any real-life chronology. Under the title "To Willy Wilson. when Nansy was with him. 1665," Austen writes "Deare nephew y*our* pretty letter was very acceptable, and am well pleased your Cosen Nancy and you are loueing Comerades"; the message is signed "Y*our* Lo*ve*i*n*g Aunt: K*atherine*" (see Fig. 10, p. 170). The familial addresses could be drafts of letters completed elsewhere, rather than indicators that *Book M* itself was circulated; however, these addresses coexist with extended familial details or "remembrances" which would seem to render the sense of audience specific to *Book M*. Austen's final page records familial details such as "22 Feb*ruary* Robin went to Schoole" and "Tom went to Ox*ford*." While the evidence of *Book M*'s final two pages is not straightforward, it seems to suggest that Austen expected the manuscript to circulate at least to members of her extended family.

Austen's bold claims in *Book M* to a particular godliness certainly merge at several points in the volume into a declaration of a public audience for the pages of *Book M*. As a record of God's providences to her, *Book M* is potentially beneficial not only to herself, and she concludes a poem with the hope that:

> to all I may display
> The Love of Iesu, and his soveraigne stay.
> And by an outward, and an inward Story,
> Render my praises to that immense glory. (fol. 101ᵛ)

Glos: Sutton, 1999); and Kirsten Poole, "'The Fittest Closet for All Goodness': Authorial Strategies of Jacobean Mothers' Manuals," *Studies in English Literature* 1 (1995): 69–88.

These lines, juxtaposing the "outward" and "inward Story," perhaps reveal an ongoing ambivalence about claiming a public role in declaring God's love to her; elsewhere, too, she expostulates, "O that Heaven wud direct me what I should doe whether I shal glorify his name by a contemplative private life. or by an active publike life" (fol. 105ᵛ). But any uncertainty suggested here occurs within the context of the self-construction that arises out of her reflections on her dream of monition, and her likening of herself to Hezekiah, Job, and David. She has drawn on the Psalms of David in interpreting her dream of monition, aligning herself with him in the belief that "I shal not dye but live. and declare the workes of the Lord"; she also asks "if it be the Will of Heaven to enlarge my daies as once to Hezekiah was knowne. I beg of his Maj*estie* a thankful heart. to declare and tel the manifestations of his Love to me" (fol. 21ʳ). She later returns to the idea of herself as Hezekiah, the God-fearing king of Judah whose life was extended by fifteen years (2 Kings 20): "And it may be God hath a further end to serve of me, A̶n̶d̶ that I should live to praise his name as Iob and Hezekiah did" (fol. 75ʳ). In both her initial interpretation of her dream of monition and this later reflection upon it, she aligns herself to crucial biblical models not only of providential suffering but also of public godliness and, in the case of David, the composition of godly texts for the sustenance of others. Borrowing David's words again at the same time as she likens herself to Hezekiah, Austen asks in this later reflection, "Has my God lengthend out my threed of life; and am I to tel his wonderful workes. *that others may see them as well as I*: Open my lipes o God. and my mouth shal shew forth thy praise" (fol. 75ᵛ; emphasis added; she is quoting the Mattins/Evensong antiphon, Psalm 51:15). She then describes herself, not long afterwards, as "an obliedged person. to perform those duties commanded from my Creator, To my soule my body. to my perticular relatives and General" (fol. 77ᵛ). Here, most explicitly, she appears to claim for *Book M* at least the possibility of an audience beyond her extended family.

Alice Thornton's life-writing in manuscript provides an illuminating parallel to *Book M* in its performance of a godly function that is not only both personal and public, but also distinctly social. Thornton (née Wandesford) began *A booke of remembrances* in or soon after 1668; in that year she was widowed and left in a woeful financial position, a result of the indebtedness of her father's estates (income of which was reserved for Alice and other children) and her husband's financial incompetence. She soon expanded *A booke of remembrances* into a three-volume series of autobiographies, in which piety is clearly not her only motivation for writing.[135] Katherine Austen's estate wranglings are paralleled by Thornton's

---

[135] *A booke of remembrances* is Yale University Library, Microfilm MISC 326, excerpted in Graham, et al., *Her Own Life*, 147–64. Charles Jackson's edition, *The Autobiography of Mrs. Alice Thornton, of East Newton, Co. York*, [London: The Surtees Society, 1875], is a heavily edited conflation of the three later autobiographical manuscripts. See also Graham, et al., "Pondering All These Things."

thwarted attempts to prevent her mother's estate of Laistrop being regarded, under marital coverture, as liable for her late husband's bad debts, and Thornton's three-volume series of autobiographies gives a detailed account of her financial standing and transactions.[136] She deals, in addition, with an accusation levied by a kinswoman's maidservant that she, Thornton, was having an affair with the local clergyman. Thornton prefaces her autobiographical manuscripts with a version of her manifesto statement in *A booke of remembrances*, that "it is the dutie of every true Christian to remember and take notice of Almighty God our Heavenly Father's gracious acts of Providence over them," but she also describes her manuscript being put to use in the service of her worldly honour, in a passage "Of Dafeny's shewing my freinds the First Book of my Life. Anno Domini 1668":

> I sent her my owne Book of my Life, the collections of God's dealings and mercys to me and all mine till my widowed condittion. That she might be able to sattisfy all my freinds of my life and conversation,—that it was not such as my deadly enymyes sugested [. . .] this poore woman did shew the said bookes to my aunt Norton and severall other freinds, as my lady Wivell, which sent to her to lett her know how much I was wronged, and to speak to her about me, with great greife and many teares did expresse her concerne, and pittied my case, saing that I had ever bin a most vertuous woman all my life.[137]

Thornton's and Austen's writings echo each other in the combination of providential piety and convictions of their mistreatments by society in general, and Thornton's passage, quoted above, illustrates that devotional writings could stand as testimony to a woman's godliness and honour. Elspeth Graham *et al.* note that "it becomes evident that she writes to vindicate herself," and Raymond Anselment comments on the extent to which "spiritual journal and rhetorical apology are integrally related."[138] Graham *et al.* write that Thornton's manuscripts were probably intended "for manuscript circulation amongst members of her family and immediate circle, and to serve as a record to be handed down to her children and descendants, explaining her financial actions and defending herself against accusations of improvidence, of having lowered the family name and estate, and of dishonest transactions."[139] *Book M* contains no concrete evidence that it was circulated beyond Austen's extended family, but there are suggestions enough that it took on a public aspect in at least an extended familial, and quite possibly a wider communal, sense.

---

[136] George outlines the background to Thornton's estate: *Women in the First Capitalist Society*, 173–76.

[137] Jackson, *Autobiography*, 258–59.

[138] Graham et al., *Her Own Life*, 148; Anselment, "Seventeenth-Century Manuscript Sources," 142.

[139] Graham et al., *Her Own Life*, 148.

There remains one other factor to consider in evaluating the intended audience of *Book M*—and, in particular, the audience of the verse contained therein. Austen has sequentially numbered certain of her poems in the margin: beside the third poem is written "First," beside the fourth is written "2d," and the fifth poem in the volume has "3d" beside it (fols. 41ʳ, 46ʳ, 53ᵛ; and see the numbering of poems thereafter). Austen has not numbered every poem in *Book M*, and so the numbers seem to indicate some kind of selection process. I have discussed Austen's apparent sensitivity to the social and coterie value of "literary" writing, above; in this context, it is notable that her poetry alone is numbered. It is possible that she extracted and collected the verses in another lettered volume, or a manuscript of a different, more formal kind, or that she intended to do so; if so, her numbers would suggest an extraction of "literary" pieces mirrored in the modern anthologization of Austen's verse.[140] We have no evidence of *Book M*'s reception, and the manuscript itself does not contain any clear indicators of the giving or receiving of manuscript poetry on Austen's part.[141] One can only speculate that the poem "On the Death of my Neece Grace Ashe. 4 years old" may have been suitable to circulate among relatives and friends; and it is possible that "On *th*e Birds Singing in my Garden," unnumbered and written into previously vacant space at the end of Austen's table of contents, is not her own. Austen also describes in one verse the creation of devotional poems as "Trophes of his praises" (fol. 67ʳ), a phrase which may suggest not only careful crafting, but also the possibility of extraction and display. Ezell's insistence on the importance of literariness as an indicator of publicness may assist us in reading *Book M* and its poetry in particular. Austen's selection numbers may well indicate that she regarded her verses, in their "singularity," as godly and literary "Trophes" to be extracted for presentation to a wider public audience.

---

[140] Two of Austen's verses appear in Jane Stevenson and Peter Davidson, eds., *Early Modern Women Poets (1520-1700): An Anthology* (Oxford: Oxford University Press, 2001).

[141] Anna Cromwell Williams' 1650s manuscript, in contrast, includes verse by Williams' aunt and mother-in-law, indicating and perpetuating the existence of a tradition of female versification in the family: "The sisters newyearsgift ^from Mrs^ Elizabeth ^Cromwell^ to ^Mrs^ Mary ^Price^ a happie mother of good children" and "Verces made by Mrs Battina Cromwell, wife to Henry Cromwell esqr Sir Oliver Cromwells sonne" (British Library, Harleian MS. 2311, fols. 20ʳ, 21ʳ).

Textual Introduction

Book M is now preserved in the British Library as Additional MS. 4454, having been bequeathed to the British Museum by Thomas Birch (1705–1766) as part of his miscellaneous collection of manuscripts (British Library, Additional MSS. 4101-4478). It is a small quarto volume of 116 leaves that has been rebound in a modern brown cloth and leather binding, the covers measuring 210 × 205 mm. The original leaves each measure 200 × 155 mm, and have been tipped onto 30 mm stubs throughout; three modern front flyleaves and three end leaves have been added. The modern British Library binding bears on its cover the stamp of Thomas Birch's collection ("E Bibliotheca Birchiana") and on its spine the title "Katherine Austen's Miscellanies."

The manuscript is in a single hand throughout, a legible italic that I presume to be Austen's own. On folios 1^r and 2^r, Austen writes her name and family details in a large and florid italic script; she uses an equally elaborate style to subscribe her name after the advice pieces on folios 92^r-94^r, and for the inscription, "My strength will I ascribe vnto my God," on folio 114^r. Her hand is otherwise an unprepossessing but legible italic, and additions and corrections are liberally added. The florid signatures at the beginning of the volume and after specific entries aside, there is little sense of the manuscript being prepared for presentation. Pages have had margins ruled on left and right in simple pencil. On folio 6^r, the first page of Austen's main text, pencil lines have been ruled for the title "Of Angeles," but the only other occasion on which title lines are ruled are for the more elaborate of two title pages on folio 2^r. Catchwords are common, and are usually (but not exclusively) run into the text rather than set apart. They are not consistently used, but are frequently useful indicators of whether meditations continue from one page or folio to another.

The manuscript was foliated in pencil in June 1874, with the folio numbers running at the top right-hand corner of each recto (not including the front flyleaves or the end leaves). There are two omissions: one leaf between folios 24 and 25 and one leaf between folios 31 and 32 have not been foliated. Each of these unfoliated leaves is blank except for Austen's page number at the top right-hand corner of each recto; these are Austen's p. 20 and p. 28. Austen's own paginations begin with page 1 on folio 6^r, and both her pagination and her use of the manuscript's available leaves alters notably as the volume progresses. Until folio 45, the rectos only are included in the sequence of her pagination; up until this point, she frequently leaves versos blank, or uses them to backfill with new entries. For example, her description of Hammond's dream runs mid-sentence from folio 10^r to folio 11^r, pages 5 and 6 in Austen's numbering. Folio 10^v is headed with the dream of Lady Burton's cousin; the verso is unnumbered and the anecdotes on this page do not feature in the table of contents, indicating that they were added to the blank verso at a later date. Austen's use of recto space, however, increases as *Book M* progresses. Initially, she leaves versos which she has used unpaginated (these are indicated as [*unp*] in this edition). She then begins to give the same page number to both leaves on a single opening; thus, folios 35^v and 36^r are both numbered page 33, folios 38^v and 39^r are both numbered page 36, and folios 39^v and 40^r are both numbered 37. From folio 45, Austen includes both rectos and versos in her sequential numbering, although this does not become entirely systematic until folio 56. Both Austen's page numbers and the nineteenth-century foliations are given in this edition. Folio numbers are given in the left-hand margin, and Austen's page numbers in the right-hand margins.

The second of the two "title pages" is inscribed "Katherine Austen 1664," apparently dating the commencement of the manuscript, and a list of familial birth and death dates below this title ends with 11 November 1668 (fol. 2^r). *Book M*'s contents seem to fall predominantly between 1664 and 1666: the earliest date in the manuscript is April 1664 (fol. 2^r), and one of the last references to a date in the principal text is on folio 113^r, "Now tis in Sep*tember* 66." It is clear, though, that Austen added material to the volume subsequent to her initial use and initial chronology, backfilling in adding to her catalogues of dreams and omens.[1] No indication of date is usually given when material is added; most frequently, a slight variation in handwriting or ink quality, or a distinction in spacing (as she strives to make an addition fit available space) is the only indicator that an addition has been made. The latest dated anecdote makes it clear that Austen added to *Book M* until late in her life: the deaths of Sir Edward Thurland and Sir Thomas Twisden in 1683 are recorded under a horizontal line at the bottom of folio 10^v. Austen's own "Table" of contents on folios 3^r–5^v lists meditations on key topics which follow in the volume. She evidently left folios 3^r–5^v blank in the first instance, filling them as she filled the volume: the "Table" peters out on folio 4^r, and folios 4^v–5^r are filled with her authorial disclaimer and a poem, apparently added at a later date.

Austen's aspiration to organized reflection and scholarship is manifest in her use of cross-references throughout *Book M*. She frequently cross-references related material within *Book M* itself; for example, during a discussion of prosperity in relation to godliness, she adds a cross in ink and the number "107" (fol. 80^r); on her page 107, there is a corresponding cross and a continuation that appears to arise from later contemplation (fol. 82^v). She also makes frequent notes

---

[1] See also p. 5, above.

referring to other volumes, indicating that *Book M* is one of a series of interrelated notebooks in which she wrote during her lifetime. For example, at the end of a discussion of honor, she writes, "Book I: pag: 12: of Mediocrity: and of Honour" (fol. 49^v); she finishes her paraphrase of Jeremy Taylor's sermon "Of the Feare of God" with a reference, "see B*ook* C: what the fear of the Lord is: p*ag* 121: I wil teach you the fear of the Lord" (fol. 30^r); and at the end folio 33^r, having paraphrased from William Camden, Francis Bacon, and other unidentified sources in quick succession, she writes, "See B*ook* I: pag 260 of Dreames & of prophesies." Most if not all of Austen's references of this kind seem to be to volumes like *Book M*, rather than to volumes by other authors. The dream of Lady Burton's cousin is "in book of Browne paper" (fol. 10^v); a dream about her suitor is recorded in "B*ook*: K: pag. 213" (fol. 97^v); and she writes on folio 77^r, "See Medit*ation* in Parchment book. P*ag* 73: on my 36t yeare: This on my 37th April 30th 1665: being Sabbath day." References to books lettered from "A" to "M" suggest that her network of manuscript volumes was very extensive.[2]

Austen's use of textual space in *Book M* emphasizes an immediate material connection between her lived experience and *Book M*. Sara Jayne Steen has written of editing Renaissance women's letters, "I feel a responsibility to a woman . . . who once existed in bodily form, walked on rush mats, laughed, and put her pen to paper."[3] This kind of response to a woman's early modern manuscript text has at times drawn scorn, as if responding to the material text is to fetishize the physical object, and therein fail to evaluate its literary qualities with due rigour. David Colclough, among others, has criticized the tendency to see manuscript texts as offering more direct access to the lived past than print texts, asserting the need to see print and manuscripts in a continuum with each other.[4] Texts such as Austen's, however, foreground the need to differentiate between kinds of manuscripts — in particular, between presentation documents and those which are, for want of a better term, cumulative. Volumes of meditations such as Katherine Austen's do give a very vivid sense of writing as a daily — or at least regular — response to lived experience. Changes in handwriting, ink, and spatial layout convey a sense of when and where ideas were added — rather as a printed volume with handwritten marginalia gives us a different sense of living, reading, and thinking in the past than a uniform printed volume does. It is, indeed, impossible to reproduce in a modern edition all of the manuscript's material indicators of addition and cumulative writing: changes in pen ink, changes in the neatness or

---

[2] No other manuscripts of KA's authorship are known to be extant.

[3] Sara Jayne Steen, "Behind the Arras: Editing Renaissance Women's Letters," in *New Ways of Looking at Old Texts: Papers of the Renaissance English Text Society, 1985–1991*, ed. W. Speed Hill (Binghamton, NY: Medieval & Renaissance Text & Studies, 1993), 229–38, here 231.

[4] David Colclough, review of Burke and Gibson, eds., *Early Modern Women's Manuscript Writing, Early Modern Literary Studies*, 11 (2005): 8.1–3.

size of the handwriting, the squashing of additional entries into small available spaces. This edition aims to be as faithful as possible to Austen's original manuscript, attempting to do justice to Austen's varied and fluid methods of constructing her manuscript text while recognizing that there are constraints to what can be viably or valuably reproduced in print.

Editorial Principles

I have worked with Michael Hunter's useful article on "How to Edit a Seventeenth-Century Manuscript,"[5] although I deviate from some of his principles, as I do not regard my role as editor as comparable to that of a seventeenth-century printer, regularizing a manuscript text for print publication. I aim to reproduce as far as possible a distinctively manuscript, cumulative text; however, I also recognize that there are points at which the attempt to replicate in print the physical features of a manuscript text can obfuscate the author's clear intention rather than reveal them. I have therefore aimed to retain *Book M*'s characteristics as far as possible while regularizing elements which do not translate well to the print medium, replication of which can make the text seem more fragmentary than it really is.

Lineation, Formatting, and Presentation

Book M's physical layout presents some challenges for the editor. Austen's practice of backfilling, in particular, results in sections of text on versos which effectively interject meditations which run continuously from recto to recto. This is more frequent in the early sections of the manuscript, as discussed in the Textual Introduction, above. I have chosen to place very minor uses of previously blank versos into the footnotes; for example, Austen's reference to Jeremy Taylor on folio 37ᵛ. I have, however, placed larger sections of text from backfilled versos in the main text of the transcription, indented from the left-hand margin. They thus interrupt the main "narrative" as they do in *Book M*, but their slightly different status is indicated. Square-bracketed editorial directions indicate the continuation of a meditation after the indented text.

I have otherwise reproduced Katherine Austen's formatting only in the following ways. Lineation of poetry has been reproduced. Lineation of prose has not been reproduced, except in the following cases: i) where a line ending indicates a new "paragraph" or topic; ii) where a line ending is material to syntax or sense, as there are places where Austen uses a line break in place of terminal punctuation. Hyphenations over line endings have been silently omitted. I have presented prose as running text, indicating page breaks with a vertical line (|)

---

[5] *The Seventeenth Century* 10 (1995): 277–310.

in the text. Folio numbers are indicated in the left-hand margin; Austen's page numbers are indicated in the right-hand margin. Pages that Austen has used but which she has not paginated are recorded as [*unp*] in the right-hand margin, as her increased pagination of the manuscript as it progresses is notable. I have omitted from the running sequence pages that are blank in the manuscript, including Austen's pages 32, 110, and 151 (fols. 35^r, 84^r, 104^v).

I have also chosen, for the sake of clarity, not to reproduce horizontal lines which Austen sometimes draws below or between meditations. There is no discernible distinction in *Book M* between Austen's use of a horizontal line and her separation of two meditations by leaving space between them. Both practices are variable and variably used; inevitably, there are points at which a difficult editorial decision has been made as to whether a meditation continues or is nominally separate from one which is clearly related. I have chosen to indicate separation consistently via a simple line break, as Austen does more commonly in the manuscript. Changes in ink color or the size of Austen's hand have been noted only where they are striking in indicating differentiation between meditations.

One indicator of whether meditations continue from page to page in *Book M* is the presence of catchword, which Austen uses commonly but not consistently. The presence of catchwords is indicated in the textual notes at the foot of the page. Textual notes have been reserved for information which is likely to interest only the most specialist and closely interrogative of readers. All other information is presented in the main footnotes.

Spelling, Punctuation, and Capitalization

I have retained Katherine Austen's original spelling, capitalization, and punctuation throughout this edition. I have retained her use of i/j and u/v graphs, although I have amended a few uses of a "j" as an initial vowel (for example, "jnstrumental"); these instances are noted in the textual notes. Austen's use of capital letters and / or lower case letters is at times difficult to discern, particularly in the cases of "c," "o," "m," "p," and "s"; I have based editorial judgements on size, form, and patterns of use evident throughout the manuscript. Austen's original punctuation is very unlike modern usage: full stops are frequently used to reflect mid-sentence pauses, as are commas, and related ideas and related clauses commonly flow from one to the next in a free way. To modernize Austen's punctuation would be to impose onto the text a large number of substantive judgements about what is and is not a complete sentence; in my view, this would represent too great a level of intervention on the part of myself as an editor. For this reason, her idiosyncratic punctuation is retained in this edition, with one exception: on a few occasions, she follows a phrase with both a comma and a full stop; in these cases I have silently chosen one over the other. Austen also uses a colon in two ways: as mid-sentence or terminal punctuation, or to indicate an abbreviation. Where a colon has been used to indicate an abbreviation, I have expanded the abbreviation and omitted the colon; where no expansion has taken place or where the colon is being used as punctuation, the colon is retained.

Abbreviations, Contractions, and Editorial Corrections

- Abbreviations are expanded, with the added letters indicated in italics. Superscript letters are silently lowered.
- Abbreviations are expanded to the author's favored spelling (for example, "da" is expanded to "da*ies*"; "Cos" is expanded to "Cos*en*"; "Dr" is expanded to "D*eare*"); "p" is expanded to "pag" (not "page")
- where I have not been able to decipher Austen's abbreviations, the abbreviation symbol is retained as a superscript ⁓
- most titles (Mr, Mrs, and St) are not expanded, although superscript letters are silently lowered. There are two exceptions: S^r is expanded to "S*ir*," and "D:" is expanded to "D*oc*" (that is, Dr), to reflect Austen's favored useage. "Doc:" is expanded to "Doc*ter*."
- "Y^e" and "y^t" are expanded as "*th*e" and "*tha*t"
- "ff" is transcribed as "F"
- the ampersand (&) and the use of "&c" for "et cetera" are not expanded
- numbers are not expanded as words
- words ending in "-nig" have been silently regularized to "-ing," as have words containing "-ni" (for example, "benig" has been regularized to "being")
- on some occasions, a missing letter has been added in square brackets (for example, "coah" becomes "coa[c]h")
- Austen's pound symbol has been reproduced as "£"

Emendations, Additions, and Deletions

Words or passages struck through in the manuscript are indicated with the use of strike-through (~~strike-through~~). Insertions appear, as they frequently do in the manuscript, between two carets (^insertion^). Where caret symbols are not used in the manuscript, I have silently inserted them. Editorial insertions are enclosed in [square brackets]. Illegible passages are indicated inside <diamond brackets>, with a full stop for each discernable letter. Austen's use of shorthand has also been indicated in this way.

In several places in the manuscript, particularly in the poems, Austen has added alternative words without striking through her original choice. In these cases, she usually parenthesizes those words which she appears to be replacing; for example, "(O) ^ Lord^ raise my soul, from earth vnto the sky" (fol. 5^r) and "May thy (refreshes) guard) ^revivements shield^ dispaire" (fol. 41^v). I have transcribed both the original and apparent replacement words in this edition, using carets to indicate the insertion but not reproducing Austen's use of interlinear space (above or below the line) to suggest the alternative.

Austen usually uses a simple cross to indicate marginal annotations or cross-references in her manuscript. For clarity, I have represented cross-references uniformly with a dagger symbol (†).

Dates

Austen's discussion of the Committee of Parliament meeting to discuss Highbury indicates that she uses old-style dates in *Book M*. I have retained her old-style dating, adding clarification in footnotes where any confusion may arise from discrepancies between Austen's dating system and those in court records.

Book: M:

All common people have the eutarist of the Suns esifting /

My Husb: was born Sunday ye 11 August 1622
He died 31 oct: 1658 being 36 yeares 2 weeks 2¹ daies

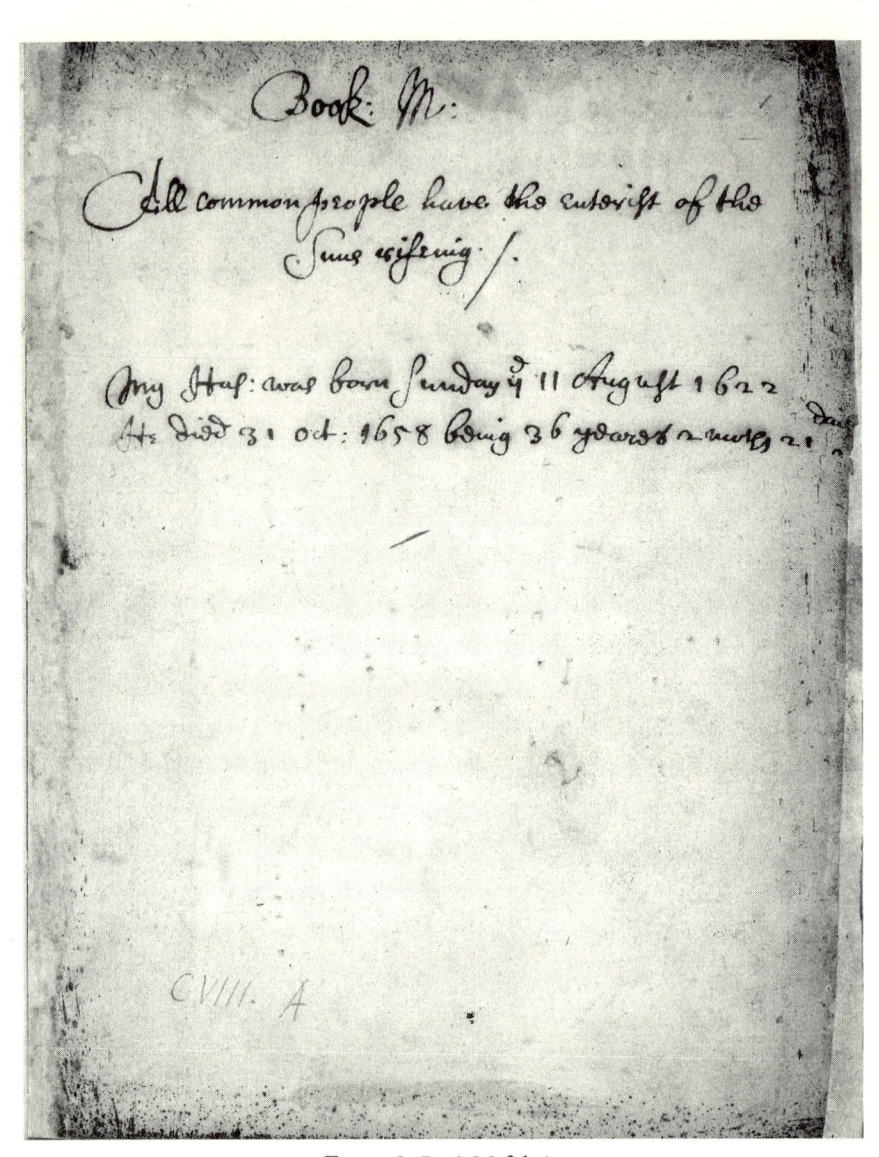

CVIII. A

Figure 2. *Book M*, fol. 1ʳ.
©The British Library Board, Additional Manuscript 4454.

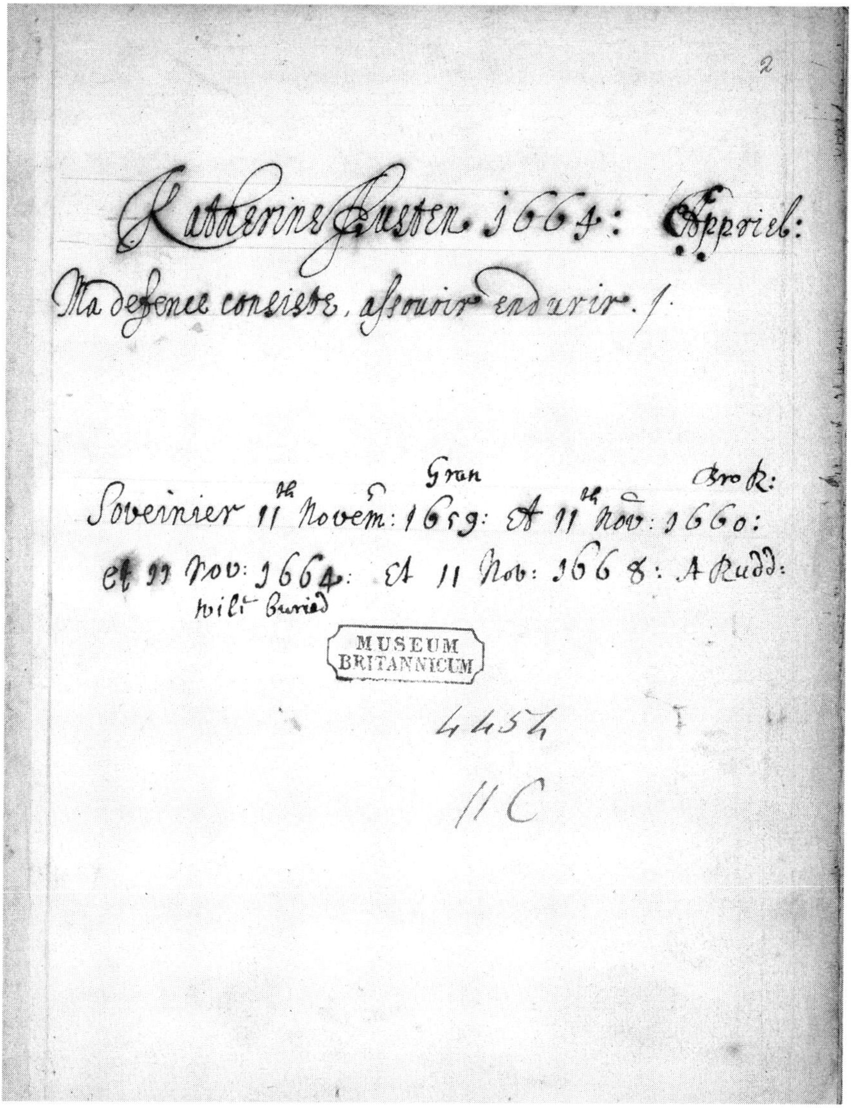

Figure 3. *Book M*, fol. 2ʳ.
©The British Library Board, Additional Manuscript 4454.

[1ʳ] # Book: M: [unp]

All common people have the enterist of the Suns riseing./.

My Hus*band* was born Sunday *th*e 11 August 1622

He died 31 Oct*ober* 1658 being 36 yeares 2 mo[n]ths 21 da*ies*[1]

[2ʳ] # Katherine Austen 1664: /Appriel:[2] [unp]

Ma defence consiste, assouoir endurir./.[3]

Soveinier[4] 11th Novem*ber* 1659: ^Gran^[5] et 11th Nove*mber* 1660: ^Bro[ther] R:^[6] et 11 Nove*mber* 1664: ^wilc buried^[7] et 11 Nove*mber* 1668: A Rudd:[8]

---

[1] KA's husband, Thomas Austen. For the significance to KA of Thomas's age at his death, see fol. 75ᵛ and Introduction, p. 16.

[2] i.e., April

[3] *Ma defence consiste, assouoir endurir*: "My defence consists of/in suffering patiently," or perhaps, with a slightly different emphasis, "I defend myself, that is by suffering patiently."

[4] *Soveinier*: remember

[5] KA's maternal grandmother Anne Rudd? See fol. 54ʳ.

[6] KA's brother Richard Wilson? See fol. 54ʳ.

[7] KA's servant William Chandeler. See fol. 38ᵛ.

[8] A relative on KA's maternal (Rudd) side.

[3ʳ]   Table.   [unp]
Of Angeles.................... 9 1
Of providences by Angeles 2
Gods Comforts in afflic*tions* by Angeles................ 3
Doc Ham*monds* Dreame of *th*e Troubles in 43 5
Doc Duns Apparit[ion] of Wife................... 6
Divers other Dreames: & of Germaine prince D:˜ H<.>:˜ 7
Of the Sybeles their transportations. not heeded 8
Of Common thinges miracles, if with held................. 9:
Ser*mon* Why miracles in the Law. Not in *the* Gosp[el]........... 11
Ser*mon* Doc Featly: whom have I in Heaven................ 12
Observal of my Dreames 16
The feare of God keepes from vaine oberuals................ 21
Ser*mon* of Last Iudgem*ent*: D*oc* Taylor 26
How ill to desier to know our Fortune................... 29
Some Dreames not to be slighted: of S: of Serpent 30
The Virtue of Afflictiones 33
Comfort of God gives in our Trouble 35
Of Williams Death 36
To be satisfied in Losses......................... 36
To beg we may discharge our Duty 37
Meditation to be sustained....................... 38
Of Oxford to T*om* 40
Of Sis*ter* Austen............................ 42
Of Newington Barrow.......................... 47
[3ᵛ] Of Robbins Recovery......................... 44 . [unp]
Of Contraryes 48
Of Honour. Slender without wealth 49
Disturbences shorten life 50
Of Cos*en* Duffelds death......................... 53
Of spending ones time.......................... 55
Of my troubles. 1664.......................... 56
Vpon Courtiers supplanting....................... 61
Meditations of praising God .... ^and Dreames:^............ 65: ^73^
Common things. Miracles........................ 9 – 0⁹
Of opprestion. complaining Meditations................. 77:
Of receiveing assistance from Saints: &c................. 85
Of *th*e English and Duches Quarrel 89
Vpon restoreing me health....................... 90
The providences of my Iewel 91

---

⁹ KA's referent here is not clear.

Book M 53

On my birth day. 96
To Rejoyce 99
Vpon the Benefit to me From my Father in Law. 101
On the Trial of my sister Austen 104
Meditations in poesy 111
On The sickenes. 114
On an emergency a Discourse 123: 131
Of Doc Dun on Aduersity & prosperity 125
Discours to my children. 127
[4ʳ] Vpon my Fall . . . . 138 [unp]
Of Gods help to me in my disaduantagies. 141
Meditations of praise 145
Vpon Highburys its situation. 150
For Gods Assistance in my straightes . . . . .155.

[4ᵛ] Whoso euer shal look in these papers and shal take notice of these personal oc- [unp]
currences: wil easily discerne it concerned none but my self: and was a private
excercise directed to my self. The singularity of these conceptions doth not ad-
uantaige any.

Surely I <. . .> dark <. . . . . .> nearest friends behold me in a cloud: those <.> know
<. .> superficially.[10]

On *the* Birds Singing in my Garden[11]

Nature provides a Harmony for me
This Airy quire, chanting out Mellody
So sweet, so pleasant by zephires pride,[12]
I haue a satisfaction here t'abide,
But, what's this Nature, w*hi*ch such order keepes,
That every plant, in its due season peepes,
Tis from 'theternal order which imprintes
Their Anual vertue, And then gives their Stintes.
When they haue flourisht, then for to decline,
Such is the Nature, God has made to mine,
I haue my flourish too, And I must fade,

---

[10] KA here uses shorthand symbols which I have been unable to decipher.

[11] There is a clear change in the ink used for this poem. KA is likely to have added it at a later date.

[12] i.e., the zephyr (soft, mild, gentle breeze) in its prime; a slightly forced rhyme with "abide."

I must returne to an Etternal shade.
And leaue these harmonies & pleasant thinges,
The end of w*hi*ch, much greater Joyes bringes.
[5ʳ] Yet as an Antepast of those to com: [*unp*]
by Earthly Ioyes, those future are begun
By humaine Ioyes, prepaires us for Divine
The Deity in outward thinges doe shine
The workes of a great Master does appeare
Through out the Current of each day and yeare
Natures a Glas, of his supernal[13] hand
In it we comprehend, and Vnderstand
His power, his loue, w*hi*ch dus all thinges Create
And of his Glory to participate.
(O) ^ Lord^ raise my soul, from earth vnto the sky
My Great Creator I may magnify
And see beyond the glas of finet[14] thinges,
A Future state, Aduance me with those winges
Of Faith, and hope, I may fly up to thee.
Then shal be perfect, their perfection see

[6ʳ]   Of Angeles: 1
That every man hath a particular Angel to assist him. (enjoy your christian Liberty:): Yet know you doe all in the presence of Gods Angels. And tho to consider we doe all in the presence of God, who sees clearely into our hearts. Yet itis a bridle to refraine us from sin that the Angels behold us.[15]
A thankful acknowledgement of the Minestry and protection of Angels. and of the praiers of the Saints in Heauen for us. All these concur to our assistance.[16] and we must bles God for. but not pray to them: See: D*oc* Feat*ly*[17]

---

[13] that is above or on high; existing or dwelling in the heavens (*OEDO*)

[14] i.e., finite

[15] "That every . . . behold us": paraphrases from John Donne, Sermon XLII on Genesis 18:25, *LXXX Sermons* (1640), 412–23, here 422.

[16] "A thankful . . . our assistance": paraphrases from Donne, Sermon LI on Psalm 6:2-3, *LXXX Sermons*, 509–21, here 520.

[17] Daniel Featley (1578–1645), Church of England controversialist. His writings are possibly the source of the two preceding phrases. See fols. 17ʳ–20ʳ for KA's paraphrase of his sermon on Psalm 73:25, in which he criticises papists who pray to saints and angels as mediators (Daniel Featley, *Clavis Mystica: A Key Opening Divers Texts of Scripture* [1636], 546–47).

Assistances by Ang*eles*[18]

Good Angels often give good assistances to men. Invisibly, and sometimes visibly. in such Form as best befits the matter, which is to be delievered: and the capacity of the party.

It hath been presented in the form of a wheele. Beasts. a man with winges,[19] a young man, a shepard. &c.

How did God alwayes refresh his church and Servants with love. And therefore taught them to look beyond *th*e Cloud. and that their stood Glories behind their curtain. to which they could not com but by passing through the waters of affliction.[20] And as the world grew more dark with mourning and Sorrowes. God did therefore send sometimes a light of Fire. and pillar of a Cloud,[21] and the[i] |
[7ʳ] brightnes of an Angel. and the Lustre of a star. and the sacrament of a rainebowe. 2 to guide his people through their portion of sorrowes. and to lead them through troubles to rest.

And sometimes God delievers his Will by the Voyce of an Angel, without any visible sight, as to Hagar, to Abram. to Samuel:[22]

Sometimes without Voyce as by Dreames. For the soules being spirits, and the Angels being spirits also. have noe need of corporal organs to communicate what God hath commanded.

And sometimes by visiones, as to Abraham:[23] And Paul by a vision was assured, that God had called him to *th*e preaching of the Gospel.[24] These visiones are revealed onely to the elect of God. (plal: itis thus).[25] God in a Vision hath spoken to his Saints. And the ministry of the Angels at last shal be to gather them together from all parts.

Sometimes where there is not any thing of Nature to be seene. God puts himself to the cost of a miracle. for the comfort of his children in their troubles.

A special favour God gave to Gideon. gave him a signe. & to Joshua:[26] When God dus give signes, he gives also illustrations of the vnderstanding, that they

---

[18] The following almost certainly paraphrases from a sermon or similar, but I have not been able to trace KA's source.

[19] Imagery drawing on Ezekiel 1 and 10; and Revelation 4.

[20] 1 Kings 22:27; 2 Chronicles 18:26; Isaiah 30:20; and (variant) Psalm 81:7; and related texts.

[21] Exodus 13:21–22; Numbers 14:14

[22] Genesis 21:17–18; Genesis 22:11–12 and 15–18; 1 Samuel 3:4–14

[23] Genesis 15:1

[24] Acts 16:9–10; Acts 26:16–19

[25] I have not been able to trace this source.

[26] Judges 6; Joshua 10:13

---

[i] Catchword: bright

may be discerned to be his signes. and not esteemed natural accidents. God gives signes. to illustrate the case. and to confirme the person. w*h*ich are high demon-
[8ʳ] strations of his mercy, | And this is the Signe of his love to me. That God hath 3 had such a care of all men. is an exspresion and testification to me. he hath likewise a care of me.

Truly[27] Man is encompassed with a Cloud of witnesses of his own infirmities, and the manifold afflictions of this life. in the departure of Friends, of parents. and wife and children. out of this World. Every day makes him learneder then other. in this sad knowledg: And surely Man that has so many dark clouds to pas through, had need of some light to shew him the right way, and some strength to enable him to walke safely in it: One help to him is the assistance of an Angel.

The Angels are Faithful and diligent attendants upon all our steps. They doe attend the Service and good of men.

For evermore itis best for every thing to doe that for which it was ordained, and made. And they were made Angels, for the service, and assistance of man. They are messengers from God to man. Tho they stand in the presence of God, and enjoy the fulnes of that contemplation[28]

Naturally Angels doe not vnderstand thoughts. Curs not the king. for that w*h*ich hath winges shal tel the matter. is vnderstood of Angeles. Yet they may have a perticular power given them. to vnderstand thoughts.[29]

[9ʳ] The slendernes. the delieveranc of the body from the encumbranc of much flesh. 4 gives us some conformity. and likenes to the Angels/

We may enquier of the nature of evil spirits. as we doe of poysons in phisique: of impure and revolted spirits. degenerate spirits –/

The paralatick man which christ had cured. He was overloaded with himself. He had a soule in a sack, noe Limbes to move:[30]

[10ʳ]   Doc: Hammonds Dreame:[31]   5
About the beginning of the troubles: 1643: when minesters was put out of their liveings. Tho he was no valuer of trifles. or any thing, that lookt like such. He had so extraordinary a Dream he could not then despice, nor ever after forget it.

---

[27] KA here begins to paraphrase from Donne; see note below.

[28] "Truly . . . contemplation": paraphrases a paragraph from Donne's Sermon XLV on Apocalypse 7:2, 3; *LXXX Sermons*, 445–56, here 447 (incorrectly paginated as 457).

[29] "Naturally . . . thoughts": paraphrases from Donne's Sermon XLV, 453.

[30] Mark 2:3–12

[31] The following account is lifted almost verbatim from John Fell, *The life of . . . Dr. Hammond* (1661), 27–28. The royalist Henry Hammond was made archdeacon of Chichester in 1643, and helped raise a troop of horses in the king's service in July of that year. He later removed to the king's headquarters in Oxford, and he addressed a letter on the king's behalf to Fairfax and the council of officers before the trial of the king in 1648 (*ODNB*).

Book M   57

He thought himself and a multitude of others, to have been a broad in a bright and chearful day, when on a sudden there seemed a separation to be made. and he with the far les number to be placet at a distance. from the rest: And then clouds gathering, a most tempestuous Storme arose, With Thunder, and Lightnings. with Spouts of impetuous raine, and violent Gusts of Wind, and what elce might ade to a scene of horrour. particular Bals of Fire that shot themselues in among the ranks of those that stood in the lesser party. When a Gentle Whisper seem'd to interrupt those other louder noises saying.
Be stil, and ye shal receive noe harme.[32]
Amidst these terrours the Docter falling to his praiers. Soone after the tempest ceasd. And then he heard began that Cathedral Antheme, Come Lord Jesus.[33] Come away. with which he awaked./. The correspondent evvent of all which. he found verrified in the preseruation of himself and Friends. in the doeing of their duty. The[ii] [continues on fol. 11ʳ]

[10ᵛ]   See the Dreame of Lady Burtons Cosen:[34] that Dreamet she shud   [unp]
         keep a coa[c]h & 4 horses. & she married at the Hage[35] a Lord: &
         did soe: in book of Browne paper[36]

         Tis Certainly declared That their was a drop of blood fel from
         the Sealing at Greenwich upon the Face of the Statue: ^old K^ &
         *w*hich spot or marke of it, could never be got out at this day. This
         was when the old King and *t*he Nobles came to see the Curiousnes
         of *t*he statue worth £1000

         A man was murdered. one cut off his hand & hung it up in the
         Castle of Camberig: some 10 or 20 yeares after he that murdered
         him came in to the Castle & by accident nichet[37] that dry hand &
         it bleed. He confesed and was hanged: twas thought the soul of the
         murdered lay in *t*he hand til the murderer appeared.

---

[32] KA uses a slightly larger font to differentiate this pronouncement (as well as placing it on a line of its own).

[33] KA also uses a slightly larger font to differentiate "Come Lord Jesus" from the text on either side of it.

[34] Lady Frances Burton was an aunt of KA's husband, Thomas (named in the wills of Thomas and his brother John, National Archives, PROB 11/285 and National Archives, PROB 11/296).

[35] i.e., The Hague

[36] Presumably another of KA's manuscript volumes. See Introduction, pp. 42–43.

[37] i.e., nicked

[ii] Catchword: *wh*ich

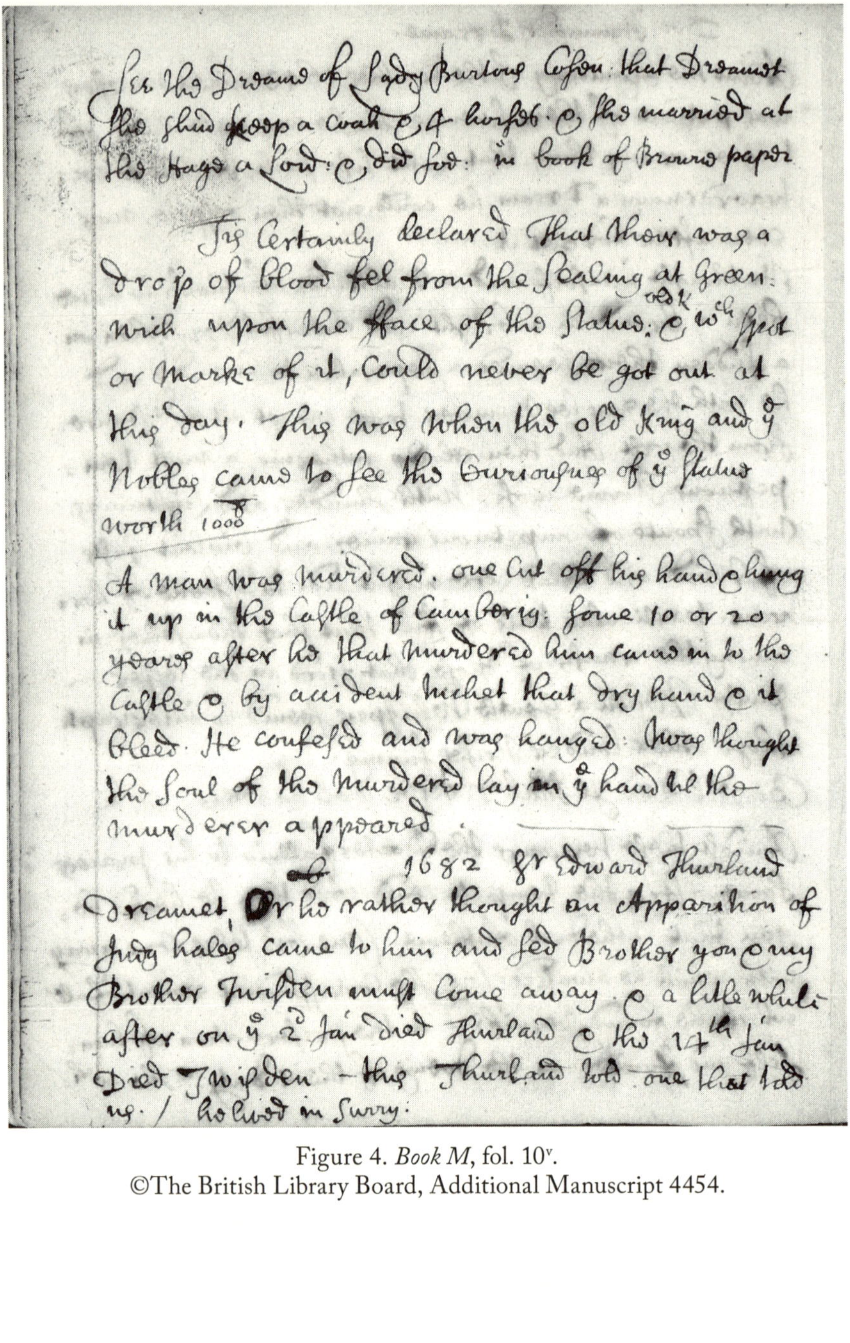

Figure 4. *Book M*, fol. 10ᵛ.
©The British Library Board, Additional Manuscript 4454.

Book M   59

    ab 1682 S*i*r Edward Thurland[38] dreamet, Or he rather thought an Apparition of Judg hales[39] came to him and sed Brother you & my Brother Twisden[40] must Come away. & a litle while after on *th*e 2d Jan died Thurland & the 14th Jan Died Twisden. -this Thurland told one that told us./[41] he lived in Surry:

[11ʳ] | which he was wont often to mention Besides being himself taken to the Quir 6 of Angels, at the close of that Land torrent of ours. And their was too literal a completion of his dream. by his Death. He herd the King proclaimed: and then died a while after./.

When D*oc* Dun was in France, with S*i*r Henery Wotten:[42] He left his wife in Engl*and* big with child. One day the Docter was a siting a reading. in a passage Roome w*hi*ch had two dores. He saw his wife goe by him with a dead child in her Armes, and she lookt as paile as if she had been dead. This apparition did so affright him. that his hair stood up right: S*i*r Henry seeing him thus. did not regard any expence. immediately sent poast to England. And they found that about that very time. his wife was brought to bed of a dead Child. very hardly escaping her life.[43]

---

 [38] Sir Edward Thurland (1607–1683), lawyer and politician. KA had some personal dealings with Thurland, which may have heightened her interest in this anecdote: Thurland and three others were given a warrant in March 1670 to investigate (further) the misappropriation of Highbury and other crown lands (*CSPD 1670*, 101).

 [39] There are three lawyers by the name of Hales, all of whom died in the sixteenth century, listed in the *ODNB*. It is not clear to whom KA is referring.

 [40] Sir Thomas Twisden (1602–1683), judge and politician.

 [41] KA transposes the two men's dates of death: Twisden in fact died on 2 January and Thurland on 14 January 1683 (*ODNB*). See Introduction, p. 21.

 [42] John Donne and Sir Henry Wotten. Izaak Walton describes Donne as being in the company of Sir Robert Drury. See note 43, below.

 [43] This anecdote, with the variation noted above, was first printed in the fourth edition of Izaak Walton, *The Lives of D*ʳ *John Donne, Sir Henry Wotton, Mr Richard Hooker, Mr George Herbert*, 4ᵗʰ edn. (1675), 29–30; it does not occur in Walton's earlier versions of the *Life* (the first of which prefaced Donne's *LXXX Sermons* in 1640). The dating of Walton's printed version and the discrepancies between it and KA's notes suggest that KA's sources are either manuscript or oral. Her father's will names an Izaak Walton living in one of his houses in Chancery Lane at the time the will was made (National Archives, PROB 11/182; proved 18 January 1640); see Introduction, pp. 21, 33.

Many eminent Dreames has been observed of the Family of the Wottens.[44] As S*ir* Robert Wotten[45] Dreamed of his Nephew. the onely heir of the Family,[46] that he was in the riseing of Whiet in Kent.[47] And dreamet the same agen next night. it being a double Dreame like pharrows. often true. and have much remarkablenes in them.[48] This made him speedily write to Queen Elizabeth to clap his nephew in the Tower and he wud acquaint her of the neccessity for it. She did. and it was found out afterwards. that it prevented his nephew[iii] | from takeing Armes with him: which he profesed his intention was to joyne with him.

Another Dreame found out the Theeives who robed Eatten Colledge.[49] by his sending a letter to the Colledge to know whether the Coll*edge* was not robed by such parties which they could not discover but by the intamation in *th*e Dreame.

Henery a Germaine prince[50] was admonished by revelation to search for a writing in an old Wall which should nearely concern him. He did and found nothing but too words. post sex:[51] that is after six. where upon he conceived his death

---

[44] The following two tales occur in Izaak Walton's *The Life of Sir Henry Wotton*, first published as a preface to the posthumous *Reliquiæ Wottonianæ* in 1651 (unpaginated prefatory pages). However, KA's deviations from the printed version (noted below) suggest that her source was manuscript or oral. See note 43, above.

[45] Izaak Walton attributes both dreams to Sir Nicholas Wotton (*ca.* 1497–1567), Dean of Canterbury. Walton's attribution, not KA's, would appear to be correct, as Thomas Wotton was the nephew of Sir Nicholas. Sir Robert Wotton (*ca.* 1463–1524) was the father of Sir Nicholas and the grandfather of Thomas.

[46] Thomas Wotton (*ca.* 1521–1587); see *ODNB* entry for his father Sir Edward Wotton (1489–1551), administrator.

[47] Wyatt's rebellion, a popular uprising intended to overthrow the newly crowned Queen Mary in 1554, named after one of its leaders, Sir Thomas Wyatt the younger (son of the poet), who owned large areas of land in Kent.

[48] Genesis 41:32

[49] i.e., Eton College. Izaak Walton describes the theft as being of the university treasury in Oxford, as does Robert Plot in his retelling of the dream, *Natural History of Oxfordshire* (Oxford, 1677), 8: paragraph 47 (see Mary Baine Campbell, "Dreaming, Motion, Meaning: Oneiric Transport in Seventeenth-Century Europe," in *Reading the Early Modern Dream: The Terrors of the Night*, ed. Katharine Hodgkin, Michelle O'Callaghan, and S. J. Wiseman [New York: Routledge, 2008], 29). See note 43, above, for KA's possible source.

[50] Henry II, Holy Roman Emperor (973-1024).

[51] KA uses a very slightly larger font to differentiate the words "post sex" from those around them.

[iii] Catchword: from

was foretold to be within six dayes. so he piously attended 6: dayes. 6 weekes. 6: monthes. 6 yeares. And on the first day of the 7th year he was chosen Emperour of Germany.[52]

I had noe fore admonishment to look for the Iewel I found.[53] Yet I found it out of an Old wall, tho by meere accident. What it may certainly[iv] import to me. I cannot surely detirmine. Yet sure I think it nearely concernes me. I wish I may as piously attend a circumspection of my daies as this happy person in the story: 1662:

Story in Bishop Hall of the writing of his Laud found out by a Dreame.[54]

Of the Emperour who when he was a Common Souldier. was told by a cunning woman. when he kiled the Bore should be Emp*erour*: he fel a hunting the Bore. but as soon as he kiled a[v] [continues on fol. 13ʳ]

[12ᵛ]   The Lady Diana Holland Dream'd: a while after the Death of her   [unp]
Mother. the Countes of Holland. that she was Discoursing with her in the Vault where she was interd

Madame Why are you gone so far before. you are so far before I cant overtake and com near you.

Noe Die (said she) IYou will quickly come after onely Your two sisters Susan and Isabel must come first

You have but two steps to come.

It so came to pas her two sisters died first and then she two yeares after. And After she had dined she was took with an extreame shaking. and cold: a week after that died of smal pox. She was discoursing of her Dreame at Diner and was then well./.

About 1663. Anapothecary at Westminster Dreamet that he knocket at his wifes grave: And had noe. ^(no on came.)^ (Answer:) He Knocket a second time His wife came: who was dead. She said to him. Will make roome, and lie close for your Father is a coming. (a son that had been dead also).

---

[52] KA's source is Thomas Fuller, *The Holy State and the Profane State*; see 4ᵗʰ ed. (1663), 292–93.

[53] See note 327, below.

[54] Archbishop Laud's records of his dreams were used against him in his trial; see Charles Carlton, "The Dream Life of Archbishop Laud," *History Today* 36 (1986): 9–15. I have not been able to trace a reference to Laud's dreams in the printed works of Bishop Joseph Hall.

[iv] I have regularized "certanily" to "certainly."

[v] Catchword: great

So a quarter of a year after the pote*cary* had a fit of sicknes. and expected death. He recouerd: that being the first knock: without Answer: He had a second fit of sicknes a while after, and then he died. it being a summons to him endead./.

[13ʳ] | great person in hatred among the people. Whose name was the Bore he was 8 chosen ~~to The~~ Romaine Emperour: see.

The Fathers observe of the Sybels, and other oracles.[55] That they were possesd. with such shakings. and transports. as bereaved them of their reason. But Divine inspirations, and Oracles preserve the harmony of the soule.[56]
The extrordinary manifestations of God to any are commonly very short, As we see in the Scriptures. Either external, or internal. External of Elliahs transfiguration, it was in a Moment: Or Internal, by audible and articular expressions. To Samuel, David, to Sollomon &c oftentimes itis hardly discernable. but by the gracious effects on our spirits. As St Petars delieveranc out of prison, assured him of the truth of that Vision. that God had sent his Angel, and delievered him.
God is not prodigal of these special favours. but for some great designes are they indulged. As I have been assured of some in great darknes of soul have had such Visions of light. as both cleared, and cheared them ever after.[57]
Doc*ter* Gauden was credibly informed that 20 yeares past, a very mild and worthy minister. (mr Lancaster:) That their was heard by him: and all that stood by
[14ʳ] him. so loud and[vi] | sweet a consort of musick, for about half an hower before 9 he died. that the good man owned it, as a signal token of Gods indulgence to

---

[55] KA here begins to paraphrase from the funeral sermon for Ralph Brownrig (1592–1659), Bishop of Exeter (*A sermon preached in the Temple-chappel, at the funeral of the Right Reverend . . . Dr. Brounrig*, 1660), by John Gauden (1605–1662), Bishop of Worcester. She copies and paraphrases from this sermon, inserting brief sections from Jeremy Taylor and John Donne, until the beginning of fol. 16ʳ. Gauden's sermon is based on 2 Kings 2:12, Elisha's exclamation on seeing Elijah taken by a whirlwind into heaven. The text and sermon are clearly enabling for KA, whose selections focus on visions and miracles.

[56] "The Fathers . . . soule": paraphrases Gauden, *A sermon . . . Dr. Brounrig*, 58–59. Gauden later compares the Sibyls to the Quakers, 50.

[57] "The extrordinary . . . ever after": paraphrases Gauden, *A sermon . . . Dr. Brounrig*, 116–117. KA's phrasing, however, indicates a fairly free reconstruction based on other sections of Gauden's sermon; the phrase "audible and articular expressions" comes from a related passage in Gauden, *A sermon . . . Dr. Brounrig*, 8.

[vi] Catchword: sweet.

him, thus to send for him. and with the close of which harmony he gave up *th*e ghost.[58]

Doc*ter* Brundrig:[59] told this story. that a Duch minestar, who was a most plain hearted religious man. who coming from Ireland to England, was cast upon the sea by a storme and floated too howers on the waves, dispairing of life and half dead. lying on his backe. and tossed at the pleasure of every wave. A vessel came by him vnder saile and took him up. which when they were recovering, and relieving him with dry clothes. Vpon the backe of this mans coat was seen a print most perfectly of a mans hand. which by being dry and *th*e rest of his clothes wet, was plainly seen by them all.[60]

If any had told Socrates that he saw a Divine vision, he presently esteemed him vaine and proud. But if he pretended onely to have heard a voyce, or a word. he listened to that very religiously. and enquiered with Curiosity. There was some reason in his Fancy Becaus God dus not communicate him self to the eye to men. but by the Ear. Ye saw noe Figure. but ye heard a voice.[61] said Moses to the people. Now w*ha*t a man pretends he hath herd we can enquier if it agree to Gods word.[62]

[15ʳ] One rule in discerning and judging a miracle: or of a Revelation: is to consider 10 whether it be done in confirmation of a Necessary Truth. Otherwise it may be suspected a delusion:[63]

---

[58] "Doc*ter* . . . ghost": paraphrases Gauden, *A sermon . . . Dr. Brounrig*, 32.

[59] i.e., Brownrig

[60] "Doc*ter* Brundrig . . . them all": this anecdote is taken from Gauden's "Memorials of the Life and Death of Bishop Brounrig," appended to the funeral sermon, 211–13.

[61] KA differentiates "Ye saw noe Figure. but ye heard a voice" from the words around it with a very slight increase in font size (the pronouncement is italicized in Taylor's original text).

[62] "If any . . . Gods word": paraphrases a passage from Jeremy Taylor, Sermon XXII, "Of Christian Prudence," Part III, *Eniautos: A course of sermons for all the Sundaies of the year* (1653), 274–288, here 279. As notable as KA's decisions to extract are her decisions not to do so. This passage continues on the following page in tones rather more damning of her own practice: "if [a man] pretends to *visions* and *revelations*, to a private spirit and a *mission extraordinary*, the man is proud and unlearned, vicious and impudent" (280).

[63] "One rule . . . delusion": paraphrases Donne, Sermon XLIII, "Preached at St. Dunstan's on Trinity-Sunday. 1624," *LXXX Sermons*, 423–432, here 429.

Was not one of my Dreames. the presaigement[64] of blesing to the Nation. As the Dream of a poor stranger did confirme Gedion to goe with the more confidence to his victory:[65]

We are genneraly to receive our instructions from Gods word: and where those meanes are duely exhibited. in his Church. we are to rest. as being sufficient to instruct us without revelation. Yet we are not to conclude God in his Law. as that he should have noe prerogative, nor so to bind him up in his ordinances, as that he never can, or never does work by an extrordinary way of Revelation./.[66]

Elisha beged a portion of Eliahs spirit. of his example and graces: Give Lord thy servant to follow all good examples. And all my life to have my dear Friends. vpright and sincear inclinations and with Elisha to have a double portion of his spirit. But Lord that spirit is not enough. Eliaha was Subject to passions. subject to be too soon a weary of his race he was to finish. Give me Lord thy holy spirit I maj with more courage and constancy. with les dejection and melancholy ster [16ʳ] on my course of life. and not be a weary as Eliaha who was prone to fal[vii] | into 11 wearines of life.[67]

Yet when Eliah: was in his distres in the wildernes. then was it Gods time to shew miraculus markes of his favour, and frequently to send his Angels to him. Neither must he die an ordinary Death.[68]

Text: God who at sundry times, and in divers manners. spake in times past to the Fathers: by the prophets; hath in these last daies spoken to us by his son.[69]

---

[64] i.e., presagement; a sign or indication of the future; an omen, a portent, a foreshadowing (*OEDO*)

[65] "Was not . . . victory": KA's own reflection. Judges 7:13–15.

[66] "We are . . . Revelation": paraphrases Donne, Sermon XXIV, "Preached upon Easter-Day. 1629," *LXXX Sermons*, 233–41, here 238.

[67] "Elisha . . . life": KA here moves onto a prayer that applies 2 Kings 2:9 to her own situation, and draws on Gauden's discussion of that text in his funeral sermon for Brownrig, *A sermon . . . Dr. Brounrig*. KA compares Elijah to her deceased husband ("my dear Friend") and, as Elisha did of Elijah, she prays for a "double portion" of his spirit. Gauden describes the "*dejection* and *melancholy despondency*" of Elijah, who was "sometimes prone to fall not only into *despiciencies* and *weariness* of life, but even to despair" (19).

[68] "Yet . . . Death": paraphrases Gauden, *A sermon . . . Dr. Brounrig*, 34.

[69] Hebrews 1:1-2. KA describes this in her "Table" as "Ser*mon* Why miracles in the Law. Not in *th*e Gosp[el]" (fol. 3ʳ); I have not been able to identify her source. Her paraphrase of this sermon appears to continue until part-way through fol. 17ʳ, where she commences her paraphrase from Featley.

---

vii Catchwords: into wearines

Had God continued to us persons of infalliable gifts. and of extrordinary spirits, as heretofore the prophets and Apostles were. of. it had been a meanes. to take us off. from stud[y]ing and searching the Scriptures. Now God hath left us to hear what his son speaketh, and we are to know the mind of God out of his word. which he hath spoken.

In the Churches infancy vnder the Law, the Saints needed such dispensations of revelations, and visions, and it was granted. But now they are in a better Capacity of finding out the mind of God. By industry, and labour in the ordinary vse of the Scriptures.

Therefore keep to the word of God. and that will keep you from delusiones.

And in things concerning Sence, and Reason, Reason and sence will be your guide that you doe not ere. Now if you neglect the study of the scriptures[viii] | [17ʳ] expecting, and seeking revelations extrodinary of *th*e Spirit, you are beside your busines. For the spirit will never that way lead you into all truth.

The spirit teaches us by sanctifying us through the truth. Sanctify them through thy truth. thy word is truth.[70]

Thus while the sperit sanctifies us through truth. it begets in us a beleeve that it is the truth of God.

It was the Mistery hid from ages, and revealed to us. And all that we have to learn, and enquier is from the Son. to study what he hath taught & manifested to us./.

   Sermon Doc*ter* Featlyes.[71]
Whom have I in Heaven but thee.
If we enquier the disposition of a man. and what a man is. Itis by knowing what he loveth.
So a man may have Faith. and hope. But if not Charity he is never the near.
He may beleeve the truth and be a false man.
He may hope for good things, and yet be bad himselfe
But he cannot love the best things. but he must needs be good. He cannot affect grace, if he have not received some measures of it. He cannot highly esteeme of God. and not be high in Gods esteeme.
Our trust is that we shal not allwayes walk by Faith. and our hope is that we shal one day hope noe more.[ix]

---

[70] John 17:17

[71] KA here begins a summary of key points in Featley's 1613 sermon on Psalm 73:25, "Whom have I in Heaven but thee," *Clavis Mystica*, 537–50. Her summary continues until fol. 19ʳ (and the meditation concludes on fol. 20ʳ).

[viii] Catchword: expect
[ix] Catchword: we

[18ʳ] We beleeve the end of Faith. and we hope for *th*e end of hope; but love noe end 13
of our love. but that it may be infinite.
   Whom have I in Heaven. Consider.
All things vnder the Sun are vanity. Therefore *th*e verity of all things is above the
Sun. There where we shall goe. Endead here we cannot reap the thousandth part
we shall be pertakers of. Here we have but a tast of *th*e Tree of life. a Confused
noise of the Heavenly musick a glimpse of the Sun of rightousnes. Yet here the
soule is refresht, and ravished with these glances more then a constant Gale of
prosperous Fortune.
The world is noe resting place for a solid contentment. Who can aime stedily at a
vanishing shadow. or rest upon the winges of the winde. Such is the comforts of
this life. which are emptines. it self. Therefore whom have I in Heaven but thee.
This speakes to our Faith. that it be resolued on God onely. For true Faith saith.
Whom have I in Heaven but thee to relye on.
And speakes to our Devotion. that it be directed to God onely. True Religion
saith, Whom have I in Heaven but thee to call on.
And speakes to our love. that it be fixed on God onely. True love saith. Whom
have I in Heaven. or in earth. but thee to settle upon.
Noe papist can bear a part with David. Whom have I in Heaven. in this song. For
they have many there to whom they addres their praiers. To saints. and Angels.[x]
[19ʳ] | as one for their diseases. and another Saint for childbirth. and others for several 14
their wants.
Doubtles these monopolies was not granted to Saints in Davids time. Nor the
Fathers had not any knowledg of these new Masters of request in Heaven.
We must know that Invocation is the highest branch of Divine worship:
Papists say we may pray to Saints. because we cal upon the Liveing to pray for
us. And the Saints departed are nearer to God. And if it be noe wrong to christs
intercession to desire the prayers of our Friends in this life. So it cannot be any
derogation to his Mediatorship to call on Saints deceased: Bellarmine braggeth.
that the Hereticks were never able to vntie this Argument.[72] I beleeve him, because there is noe knot at all in it. For to our Friends we desire them to commend
us to God in their praiers. And a duty of christian Charity itis. But to pray to
any Saint theirs noe president in Scripture. from the first of Gen*esis* to the last
of Revelations
When we are come to the love of God.[73] it will ravish us to seek God. and to seek
his face evermore. and whom to desire is the fullest contentment. and to enjoy ev-

---

[72] See Appendix for Featley's sermon, and marginal references to his sources.

[73] KA here diverges from the conclusion of Featley's sermon; her own conclusion which follows is more prayerful than Featley's.

---

[x] Catchwords: as one

erlasting happines. For in God is all. If we thirst for Grace to help us in our time of need. He is so full of Grace. that of his fulnes we all receive. For glory. He is the King of Glory. For Wisdome. in him are all the treasures of Wisedome. For [20ʳ] peace, he is the prince of peace. And | For life, He is the well of Life, and in his 15 light we shall see light.[74] For Joy and pleasure in his presence is fulnes of joy. and at his right hand pleasure for evermore./.[75]

That which is caled Beauty in us.   Is Majesty in God.
Life. with us.   is Immortality.
Strength with us.   is Omnipotency.
Wealth with us.   is all sufficiancy.
Delight is   Fellicity.
Affection. Virtue: Virtue, Nature. And Nature all things. For of him. and through him, and in him. are all thinges[76]

[21ʳ][77]   Observation on my Dream. of Monition.[78]   16

Certainly I may have an expectation, a dependance of something extrordinary, to befal me at the period of that time. When I find stories from Monitions and notices given to some persons, yeares before it come to pas. Yet I have hardly heard of any thing with so much plainnes and certainty, as what I have received: And yet in this certainty I have found a contradiction: that I shal not dye but live. and declare the workes of the Lord.[79] As if that was the meaning, After the being excercised with divers trials and afflictions: that I should continue to declare the workes and manifestations of his goodnes: which hath been in eminent preservations. and most bountiful Blessings. and prosperous succes of my endeavours. in the midst of infinite obstacles, and plunges. often I was encompased. And if it be the Will of Heaven to enlarge my daies as once to Hezekiah was knowne.[80] I beg

---

[74] Psalm 36:9

[75] Psalm 16:11

[76] Romans 11:36 (first part): "For of him, and through him, and to him, *are* all things."

[77] Fol. 20ᵛ is blank except for a cross-reference to one of KA's other lettered volumes, "Book: L: p: 75:" This appears at the top and centre of the otherwise blank page.

[78] instruction, warning or intimation; an omen (*OEDO*)

[79] Psalm 118:17. KA later makes clear that she sees her dream of monition as a "countermand" (fol. 75ʳ) of an earlier dream which intimated that she would live only to the same age as her husband; that is, thirty-six years, two months, and twenty-one days (fol. 1ʳ). See fols. 54ʳ, 63ᵛ, 65ᵛ, 75ʳ⁻ᵛ, 77ʳ–79ʳ; and see Introduction, pp. 16–17, 26.

[80] Hezekiah, King of Judah, was "sick unto death" when the prophet Isaiah "came to him, and said unto him, Thus saith the Lord, Set thine house in order; for thou shalt die, and not live" (words which echo Psalm 118:17, quoted by KA). However, Hezekiah's

of his Maj*estie* a thankful heart. to declare and tel the manifestations of his Love to me. what he hath done for me. w*ha*t great fauour[81] shewed to me a private. to me a particular person.[82] thou hast shewed thy wonders to me as well as to David: [22ʳ] as well as to Kings.[83][xi] | Thy infinite goodnes is my defence, and protection day by day, And surely if thy eye had not been over me, it had been impossible I should have sustained my oppositions. But I have seen the miracles of the kindnes of my God to me. And tho he leaves his children destitute, he dus not deprive them of his gracious help, nor of the safeguard of Angeles

Not unto me o God, not unto my weeke help. but to the Arme of the Lord proceeds my daily succour and my help in time of trouble.[84] That near help, which tho it be invisible to me, and sometimes cannot apprehend I have such aids as endeed I find

When I have litle busines to doe. I prais God for giveing me respit. When I have a great del I prais God for giveing me strength, and assistance. And I beseech him to bles me in w*ha*t I am to doe.

The world may think I tread upon Roses. but they know not the sack cloth I have walkt on. not the heavines and bitternes of my minde Yet my God hath sweetned those bitterneses. Elce the Gal wud have been impossible to take./.

[22ᵛ][85]   S*i*r if you had been a Gentleman, as you pretend to. You wud have   [*unp*] had civiler words in yo*ur* mouth.[86] I ~~have~~ doe not deserve that odious, immodest Character your rudenes was pleased to give me. Besides I should be vnwilling to call a woman of fourescore old. Ancient is honourable: old is despicable. Old belongs. to Old shooes.

---

goodness and prayers are rewarded: he is healed, and fifteen years are added to his days (2 Kings 20:1–6). See fols. 65ᵛ and 75ʳ⁻ᵛ for further references to Hezekiah; also see Introduction, pp. 16, 37.

[81] KA has written "fauour" over the top of another word here; her original word is not discernable.

[82] See Introduction, pp. 27–28, for special or particular providences.

[83] KA reiterates her interpretation of this dream on fols. 62ʳ⁻ᵛ.

[84] Psalm 9:9; Psalm 37:39

[85] This is a borderline case for treatment as an interjection. The meditations on either side are self-contained, but are sufficiently closely related that they could be regarded as linked. See Textual Introduction, pp. 41–42, 44.

[86] It is not known whom KA is addressing in the outburst on this page; however, it seems that she has been rebuked and called an "old goat" for riding in her coach and making a muddy roadway worse for those on foot.

[xi] Catchword: Thy

Old clothes. not to my self. For endead when I am com to the longest date and age. in this world. I hope then to be as young as when I first came in it. shal be entred in to a new Spring. Not to come within the compas of any chandg or decay more./.

Surely I have not deserved in my conversation among men, his most abusive and scandalous speech. I ride in my coach. while I dare to let the way be so bad. for them to walke./ old Goat. the rudest Speech not proceeding from a Gentleman as he pretends. but from a Hinde,[87] a soughter./[88]

I wish him noe more punishment. then to have such a shooe for him to clence. which it was not possible to prevent the dirt lying sometime. til could be took away. which was carried away in carts nothing but water. laded in./.

[23ʳ] Stil Look what God Almighty does for thee. and then thou wilt not regard 18 what men does agen thee. And soe in this time of lonelines. What a prety cherful companion I have. that knowes not any thing of the Clouds and damps of mellancholy. That Gods gracious goodnes ~~appoints~~ allowes me my little Daughter.[89]

I Cant but recite to my selfe my former sweetnes of life. How I had one that rendered me all the love and all the affection a person could possible obliedge his friend with.[90] And God was pleased to give a conclusion of it. Yet instead I have the favour and Love of my most mercifull God. And I cannot but perswade my selfe. I have stil influence[xii] by his desiers for my perfection from him who bore me that regard when he was on earth. Nay I cannot tel but that his love to his relative may not be of a far more excellent nature and effect to me then before. Tis problematical, therefore I dare not be too presumptuous. in the beleeve. Tho some providences and marks have gave me some demonstrations. How ever. I am assured the blesing of Heaven is more then ever ^was^ in my prosperous Condition. And this is the true sanctuary of refuge and rest./. see pag: 85:[91]

---

[87] "A servant; esp., in later use, a farm servant, an agricultural labourer" (*OEDO* "hind" 2)

[88] "Obs. rare. A ploughshare[r]" (*OEDO* "sough" n. 3)

[89] KA's daughter Anne. KA laters wishes that Anne be "defended from the passion of her [grandmother's] Mallancholy" (fol. 93ᵛ).

[90] KA's deceased husband, Thomas Austen.

[91] See fol. 71ᵛ, KA's p. 85, on which she also contemplates her deceased husband's ongoing influence.

[xii] "in-" on the previous line is superceded when KA writes this word complete on the beginning of a new line.

[23ᵛ]   Example of Ioseph to his Bretherin not to revenge   [unp]
It was a lasting rememberance the dread which Iosephes Bretherin was in: As After the death of Iacob: they were affraid he wud retribute their cruelty. shewed him. As with all submission did acknowledge it and beg his Fauour: Ioseph returned actes of loue. and tendernes to them. And stil told them theyr vnkind act was to bring about Gods abundant mercy to be a help to them and to preserue them from Famine and poverty.[92]
See what grace & a spirit sanctified, and trained up in the road and obseruation of providence will doe.
That which the world termes greatnes of spirit cannot doe this. That wil prosequte reuenge and waight for occastion to returne euel actions. with far worse if a power can doe it.
Learne in all the affronts you receive, and vnkindneses meet with to haue Iosephs temper to render kindnes and loue in the blowes of injury,[xiii] in the contumelies of men be really ready to shew fauour and to doe good[93]

The History of Ioseph. is ful of remarke, to view it.
As we cannot but conclude The wayes which Gods prouidenc takes, if ^is^ ful of greatnes and glory. And. by contrary wayes performeth his purpose. How many
[24ʳ] wayes was poore Ioseph distrised with. That there was litle semblance | of the 19 performance of his Dreames: Vnles by Contraries
By Contraries it was a long time fulfiled: In stead of Honour he found diristion[94] contempt and danger. And litle hope of riseing when he was neare a Cruel death.
Then was his chastity assaulted, and instead of Honour brought to a prison by a shameful maner. Appearing to his disgrace.

[25ʳ][95]   Of the Feare of God[96]   21
No man is more miserable then he that fears God as an enemy. Then Duty is intollerable, and therefore of all the evils of the minde fear is the worst, and most intollerable. Anger is valiant, Desier is busie, and apt to hope. (and) Credulity is entertained with appearances of succes. But fear is Dul, and sluggish, miserable,

---

[92] Genesis 50:15–21
[93] Any terminal punctuation here is lost in the binding of the manuscript.
[94] i.e., derision
[95] One leaf, paginated but otherwise blank, is here omitted in *Book M*'s foliation; see Textual Introduction, p. 41.
[96] KA here begins to paraphrase Taylor, Sermon IX, "Of Godly Fear," Part III, *Eniautos*, 114–24. She commences here, 119.

[xiii] jnjury

Book M 71

and foolish. And from henc proceeds obseruation of signes, and of vnlucky dayes. and erra pater.⁹⁷ If men doe listen to wispers of fear, and have not reason, and obseruation enough to confute trifles they shal be affrighted with the Noise of Birds, and the Night Raven. And every old woman shal be a propehtes. And the events of our affaires which should be managed by ~~Reason~~ the conduct of counsel, of reason, and religion. Shall by these vaine obseruations, succeed by chance, by ominous Birds. by the faling of the salt, or the decay of reason, of wisdome, and the Iust religion of a man.

And to these trifling superst[it]ions, may be reduced observations of Dreams, on vnsecure expectation. of evills that never shal happen.

Dreames are without rule, and without reason. They proceed very much from the temper of the body. and trouble of the minde. Tho sometimes from some Daemon good or bad.

The dreaming of teeth. they say, import the los of a Fri[e]nd tho rather it tels of the Scurvy growing. And divers things may point at Diseases. Because the body being out of Frame.

[26ʳ] The fancy may be vexed into a representation of it. Now if the evvents of our Dreams doe answer in one instance, we becom credulous in twenty, and so we discourse our selues into folly and weak obseruation, and give the Devil power over us in those circumstances we can least resist him.

Let the grounds of our actions be noble, beginning from reason and prudence, and measured from the expectation of vseual prouidenc, and proceed from causes to effects.

Let us fear God when we have made him angry, & not be affraide of him when we heartily and labouriously doe our duty.

The 3 great actions of Religion,⁹⁸ are to worship God, To fear God, to trust in him. Now the inordinations of ~~all~~ these, turnes to superstition: The obliquity of trust, The errours of worship, the exces of fear. Gods word must examine all.

First fear is a duty we owe to God, as being the God of power, and justice, the Iudge of Heaven and earth. the avenger of all vnjustice, and oppresion, a mighty God, and terrible, and a sever⁹⁹ hater of sin.

Now fear is the girdle of the soule, the handmaid to repentance. the arrest of sin. Its the bridle to vice and makeing the soule to pas from trembling to caution and

---

⁹⁷ erra pater: an almanac, used for the prediction of fortune. See Robert Nares, James Orchard Halliwell-Phillipps, and Thomas Wright, *A Glossary: Or, Collection of Words, Phrases, Names, and Allusions to Customs, Proverbs, Etc., which Have Been Thought to Require Illustration, in the Words of English Authors, Particularly Shakespeare, and His Contemporaries* (London: J. R. Smith, 1859), 281.

⁹⁸ KA here jumps back to Taylor, Sermon IX, 116.

⁹⁹ i.e., severe

[27ʳ] watchfulnes. and by the gates of repentance,ˣⁱᵛ | Leads the soule to love, and to 23 the Ioyes in God.

And fear is the instrumentˣᵛ to Religion, and the onely security of the les perfect persons. And God sends often to demand it by threatnings, and afflictions & troubles. upon us:

But this so excellent grace, is soon abused, in the tendar spirits, by infellicities, or a sad spirit, And the Devil often takes aduantage, to turn fearful natures to timerousnes, and scruple, to sadnes and suspicion of God, And thus he runs towards heaven as he thinks, but he chuses foolish paths, and takes any thing as he is told, or fancies. But fear when itis inordinat, is never a good Counselor, nor makes a good friend.

And he that fears God as an enemy, is the most miserable and compleatly sad person, in the world. For.

There be some such perpetual tormentors of themselues, with vnnecessary fears. that their meat, and drinke, and all their actions are a snare to them. and every temptation tho resisted makes them cry for pardon. These persons doe not beleeve noble things concerning God. nor thinks how God delights in mercy. Such are either hugely tempted, or hugely ignorant.

Now he that is affraid of God cannot love him. at all, and whom men fear, they hate certainly. and flater readily. and therefore tho the Athe[i]st says there is no God. the scrupulous fearful, and superstitious man does wish their was none.

Tis true in the Law:¹⁰⁰ God vsed his people as servants. and enjoyned many hard [28ʳ] things. intricate,ˣᵛⁱ | and painful, and expensive. In the Gospel. he hath made 24 us Sons, and gave commandements, not hard, but ful of pleasure, and also for profite. to our comfortable well being. And how many blessed promises in the Gospel, and few threatnings.

So that in the Law they feared God as a severe Lord. dreadful unto death. in threatnings. this the Apostle cals, the spirit of Bondage. But we have received the spirit of Adoption, and a Fellial fear. And our Iudg is our Aduocat, and our Brother is our Lord.

  Godly fear, is ever without dispaire.

And to those who raise Doctrineal fears, concerning God, which if they were true, the greatest part of mankind would be tempted to think they have noe reason to love God. As to say the greatest part are decreed to be Damned. And they speak noe good things concerning his name. who say God Commandes us Lawes impossible. That think he will condemne whole nations for different

---

 ¹⁰⁰ KA here begins to paraphrase from Taylor's Sermon VII, "Of Godly Fear," Part I, *Eniautos*, 83–94. She paraphrases this sermon, 87–94.

 ˣⁱᵛ Catchword: leads

 ˣᵛ jnstrument

 ˣᵛⁱ Catchwords: and painful, and

oppiniones.†[101] We must remember Gods mercies are over all his workes. and he shewes mercy to all his creatures that need it. And God delightes to have his mercy magnified in all things, and by all persons, and at all times. And therefore as he that would acquse God of injustice were a blasphemer, so he that suspects his mercy dishonours God as much. and brings upon himself that fear, which is the parent of trouble, but noe instrument[xvii] of Duty.[xviii]

[29^r] We must highten our apprehensions of the Divine power, and his justice, so it passe noe further, but to make us reverent, and obediant. But that fear is vnreasonable, servil, and vnchristian, that ends in scruple, and incredulity. and desperation.

Its proper bounds are humble, and devout prayers. a holy piety, and Glorifications of God. We must be full of confidences towards God. And with cheerfulnes rely on his goodnes, for the issue of our final interest.

For the presumptious let them know. their is cause of fear, because to the most holy and confident his way is narrow. and dangerous. and ful of pitfals. we are tempted, and doe tempt our selues. therefore to him that standeth take heed. lest he fall.

And they may fear, whose repentance is not an entire chang of life; who can never git the Dominion of their vice. They may fear, lest God be weary of giveing more oppertunities. Since Their vnderstanding is right, and their will a slave. Their reason for God, and their affections for sin. Of these our Saviour speaks

Many shal strive to enter in, and shal not be able.[102]

Of our Zeal: and Duty to God:[103]

No man is zealous as he ought, but he that delightes in *th*e Seruice of God. Elce when he prayes, tis as children goe to Schoole, or gives Almes as they that pay Contribution and meditate with the same willingnes. as Young men die.

[30^r] The Fire of Zeal must never goe out. it must shine like the stars, tho sometimes covered with a Cloud. Yet. they dwel for ever in their Orbes. and goe not out by day nor night, and set not when kings die, nor are extinguished when nations change their government, So tho a christians zeal, and praiers be sometimes

---

[101] † in the text here corresponds with † at the same level on the facing page, fol. 27^v, which is blank except for: "*Book* A: †see p*ag* 125: in Miracles of Divine mercy."

[102] This is the conclusion of Taylor's Sermon VII, "Of Godly Fear."

[103] KA here begins to paraphrase from Taylor, Sermon XIII, "Of Lukewarmnesse and Zeal; or, Spiritual Terror," Part III, *Eniautos*, 164–178.

[xvii] jnstrument
[xviii] Catchword: We

drawn backe by importunity of busines. by necessities, by Compliances, Yet stil the Fire is kept alive, it burnes within, when the light breaks not forth./.[104]
see B*ook* C: what the fear of the Lord is: p*ag* 121:[105]
I wil teach you the fear of the Lord:

Obser*vations* of the Last Iudgement: D: Taylor:[106]
Whereas the general sentance is given to all wicked persons. To all on the Left Hand. to goe to everlasting Fire. Itis answered that the Fire indeed is everlasting, but not all that enters into it is everlasting, but onely the Devils. for whom it was prepared. and others more mighty Criminals. As St Iohn in the Revelations speaks perticular who shal be tormented for ever and ever. Also everlasting signifies onely to the end of its proper period. appointed by God.
The blessednes of the Saints is. that they shal indeed be for ever and ever, in immortality.
Whether the wicked shal have immortality. is questiond by the old Docters of the Church.[xix]

[31ʳ] Its certaine that Gods mercies are infinite, and its also certaine that the mater 27 of eternal torments cannot truly be vnderstood. And when the Schoolmen goe about to reconcile the Divine Iustice to that severity, and considers why God punishes eternally a temporal sin. They speake variously, and vncertainly and vnsatisfyingly.
But the Generallity of Christians have been taught to beleeve worse things. And its strang to suppos an eternal torment to those to whom it was never threatned, or ever heard of christ. to those that lived probably well. to Heathens of good lives. to vntaught people, to Young men in their Natural follies.[107]
Their are too[108] dayes in which the fate of all the world is transacted. This life is mans day. in w*hi*ch man does what he pleas. and God holds his peace. Man distroyes his brother, and himself, and governments, and sins, and drinks drunk. and forgets his sorrow, and all this while God is silent, save that he is loud with

---

[104] "No man ... forth": Taylor, Sermon XIII, "Of Lukewarmnesse," Part III, *Eniautos*, 176.

[105] This is a reference to one of KA's other lettered manuscript volumes; see Introduction, pp. 42–43.

[106] KA here begins to paraphrase from Taylor, Sermon III, "Dooms-day Book; or, Christ's Advent to Judgement," Part III, *Eniautos*, 30–43.

[107] "Whereas . . . follies": Taylor, Sermon III, "Dooms-day Book," Part III, 40–41 (she reorders some passages).

[108] i.e., two. Taylor: "two great days" (30). KA here jumps back to an earlier passage from the same sermon, 30–31.

[xix] Catchword: its

Tho many Dreames have come to pas. Yet when persons by an over curiosity have anticipated their desire to know their ffortune it seldome hath been a good successe to them. But they had reason to repent.

It invited Henry the 4th preparation to the holy warre, because it was told him he should not dye, til he had heard Mas in Jerusalem. But he was fain to take his leave of the world, before he expected it, and died in the chamber caled Jerusalem in westminster. You may conclud this prophesie to be begotten by ye Devil. And if he be stopt at one hole, he gives out at another like a ffox:

The Like story of a pope who was told he should not dye til he came to Jerusalem. wch was a Church in Roome. &c: at the entrance of which he was slaine.
And so this equivocating Devill cosend this monk. That he should not dye, till he should find him sleeping between sheets. The wary Monk abstaining all such Lodging. At last by over-watching in his study. the Devil took him naping with his nose Betwixt the Sheet-leaves of his conjuring book.

Hells Alphabet must be read backward, let Satan give an account of his own Cozinage. wch is to save his credit. he takes misticall expressions that in case he should fail in his answeres layes the blame on mens un-

his holy precepts. and that God overrules the evvent. But leaves the desiers of men to their own choice, and their course of life such as they will chuse. But then God shal have his day too. the day of the Lord shal come, in which he shal speake in terrour, and noe man Answer./.[109]

[31ᵛ] In Ap[ril] 1666: a boy was playing at St Andrewes Church: and there was onely [unp] the clarke[110] and he. he heared a voyce say Goe away:[111] he asket the clarke what he had with him he sed he did not speake to him. the clarke as well as he heared it agen say Goe away, they both were affraid and by that time another came into the church and heared it say a 3d time Goe away. soe presently the boy went to clamber up where was a monnument and it fel downe and dashet his braines out.
It was a hollow sound the Voyce./.

[32ʳ][112] Tho many Dreames have come to pas. Yet when persons by an over curiosity have anticipated their desier to know their Fortune. it seldome hath been a good succes to them. But they had reason to repent. 29
It incited Henry the 4ths preparation to the holy warre, because it was told him he should not dye, til he had heard Mas in Ierusalem. But he was fain to take his leave of the World, before he expected it. and died in the chamber caled Ierusalem in westminster.[113] We may conclud this prophesie to be begotten by *the* Devil. And if he be stopt. at one hole, he giteth out at another like a Fox:
The Like story of a pope. who was told he should not dye til he came to Ierusalem. w*h*ich was a Church in Roome.[114] ^see: at the enteranc of which he was slaine^[115]

---

[109] "Their ... Answer": Taylor, Sermon III, "Dooms-day Book," Part III, 30–31.

[110] i.e., clerk

[111] There is a very slight differentiation in size between "Goe away" and the text around it.

[112] One leaf, paginated but otherwise blank, is here omitted in *Book M*'s foliation; see Textual Introduction, p. 41.

[113] "It incited ... westminster": King Henry IV describes this prophecy and his misinterpretation of it in Shakespeare's *2 Henry IV*, 4.3.363–68.

[114] i.e., Rome

[115] "The Like ... slaine": this anecdote, similar to that in Shakespeare's *2 Henry IV*, "has been repeated in different forms, and in relation to different persons," according to Robert Chambers, *The Book of Days: A Miscellany of Popular Antiquities*, 2 vols. (London: W. & R. Chambers, 1832), 131. Chambers relates it to Gerbert, Pope Sylvester II (131–32). It is related to Pope Sylvester III in the *Eulogium (Historiarum sive temporis)*, vol. 1. (London: Longman, Brown, Green, Longmans and Roberts, 1858), 256–67. KA's source is unknown.

And so the equiuocating Deuil, cosend the monk. that he should not dye. till he should find him sleeping between sheets. The wary monk, abjuring all such Lodging. At last by over-watching in his study. the Devil took him naping with his nose Betwixt the Sheet-leaves of his conjuring book./.[116]

Hels Alphabet must be read backward. Let Satan give an account of his own Coznage w*hi*ch is to save his credit. he takes mistical expresions that in case he [32ᵛ] should fail in his answeres. Layes the blame on mens[xx] | Vnderstandinge him: [*unp*] Thus they who are correspondents with the Devil. have need when they have receivd the text. to borrow his comments too.

But men had need take heed of curiosity to know things to come. which is one of the Kernals of the forbiden fruit[117]

[33ʳ] Some Dreames are not to be slited. As that young man who Dreamet he should be slaine by a Lion. w*hi*ch because that Beast did never come in their Country, He was Laughing at it, while he was in the Temple of the Gods. And their, out of a Confidence of this impossibillity. He put his hand in to the mouth. of a Lion. Figured for ornament
a Serpent bit him and he died./

The Lady Margaret Henry 7th: mother a most pious woman (as that age went) and was esteemed in goodnes *th*e next to the Virgin Mary. (.by those who too much adored her) She vsed to say if the christian princes wud vndertake a war against the Turks. she wud be their Laundres:[118]

This Lady had ~~some~~ ^a^ Dreame, gave her a prediction of part of her Fortune: see end History: H*enry* 7: L*ord* Herb*ert*[119]

---

[116] "And so . . . book": this anecdote, which KA repeats almost verbatim, is told from Act 1, line 15 of Richard Brome's *A Jovial Crew; or, The Merry Beggars* (perfomed in 1641, and printed in 1652 and 1661). The play opens with a satirical conversation about fortune-tellers.

[117] "Hels Alphabet . . . forbiden fruit": paraphrases from Fuller, "The life of Andronicus," *Holy and Profane State*, 492.

[118] Camden recounts Lady Margaret Beaufort's pronouncement in *Remaines concerning Britain*, 6th impression (1657), 271. KA does not echo Camden's wording; her source may be variant.

[119] KA's reference here is to Francis Bacon's *The historie of the raigne of King Henry the Seuenth* (1622), which she confuses with Lord Herbert of Cherbury's history of Henry VIII (1649). Bacon recounts that *"When the* Ladie MARGARET *his* Mother *had diuers great* Sutors *for* Marriage, *she dreamed one Night,* That one in the likenesse of a Bishop in

---

[xx] Catchword: vn-

Socrates was of opinion that none who are beloved of the Gods. but have some Revelation:[120]

The Story: of a Templer a burning at Burdeaux.[121] spying Pope Clement,[122] and Philip K*ing* [of] France[123] Looking out at a window at his exceqution. said Clement thou Cruel Tyrant. and Philip K[ing] of France I summon you both to appear at the tribunal seate. to give an account for y*our* cruelty. within a year and a day where I shal answer. for y*our* rigorous dealing. & within *tha*t time both died)

See B*ook* I: pag 260 of Dreames & of prophesies./

[33ᵛ]   Story of Mr Chainy: Near Chattame.[124]   [*unp*]
Mr Chany a Gentleman in queen Elesabeths time when she was at Tillbury:[125]
He spoke words of Treason against her at the spanish envastion
He heareing she wud send for him prepared his pettition. So she sent her pursevant to take him he being a Horse backe while he was pursued. & coming to the place caled the Hope Neare Rochester. He plundged into the sea. & went to *th*e ship where the Queene was. & held up his pettition & swume on horse backe three times round her ship & flung his pettition to her. This extrordinary attempt in the sea drew her to pardon him. And he went backe through the sea. as soone as Landed took his sword & run his horse threw. He was asked why he wud kil soe braue a horse *tha*t not one in a thousand could doe the like. He sed it should never saue *th*e life of a Traytor againe. A bout a year after he was rideing by that place where *th*e bones of the dead horse lay. his Horse started upon *th*e place. & flung him upon the very horses head & broke his neecke./ Vpon his Tombe near Chattame is the picture in stone of a horses head in memory of this remarkable ingratitude.

Pontificall habit, did tender her EDMUND Earle of Richmond (the Kings Father) for her Husband"; see p. 247 (the volume's penultimate page).

[120] A reference to Plato's *Apology*. KA's source is unknown; her earlier reference to Plato derives from Jeremy Taylor (see fol. 14ʳ). Plato's *Apology* first appeared in English in 1675.

[121] i.e., Bordeaux

[122] Pope Clement V, former Bishop of Bordeaux

[123] Philip IV of France (1285–1314)

[124] A change in ink colour for this anecdote makes it a very clear example of backfilling.

[125] Queen Elizabeth I at Tilbury, where she famously spoke to the troops on the eve of the Spanish Armada, 9 August 1588; see Leah S. Marcus, Janel Mueller, and Mary Beth Rose, eds., *Elizabeth I: Collected Works* (Chicago and London: University of Chicago Press, 2000), 325–56.

[34ʳ]   Of Hildegardis./.[126]   31

God first humbles and afflicts, whom he intends to illuminate with more then ordinary grace. And tho she had afflictions God gave her winges, and raised her mounted soule in Revelations. And St Bernard, and the pope allow those Revelations to be authentick. She prophesied of the Mendicant Friers. and divers sins of covetiousnes And of the coming of those vermine into the world who wud rob secular princes of their prerogatives and many things concerning the abuse of the Papal church. She was of the Popes conclave. and Emperours Counsel, to whom they had recourse in Difficultes. Yea *th*e greatest Torches of the church. lighted themselues at her Candle, and Patriarchs, and Bishops sent knots as pased their fingers for her to vntie.

Hildegardis was for certaine a gracious virgin, and God might performe some great wonders by her hand./.

[35ᵛ][127] B*oo*k I: pag 87:   Here ade this to B*oo*k C: 131: or   33[a][128]
                          B*oo*k F: pag 79:

Surely my God is prepairing for me Halcione daies for daies of trouble and Molestation I have found from men. Who considers not afflicted widowes. They take aduantage of them, who has litle help. and gives frequent occasion of more disturbance. My God if it be thy will to consigne me quiet and repose, if not in this life, I am sure in another, for thy promise hath assured it. In thee there is peace to be comforted, tho in the world trouble. And if I must taste of every variety of trouble, in allmost every concernement. And if my neighbours must dart envy and vnkindnes to me. circumventions and Injuries. My God hath strengthened me to this day. Continue thy help in all my Croses. O God of help and Father ful of pity. Amen./.

Salm.[129] When D*oc* Hobson preachet at Twic*kenham*[130]

---

[126] The following is a summary of Fuller, "The life of Hildegardis," *Holy and Profane State*, 36–40.

[127] Immediately preceding is a blank opening, fols. 34ᵛ–35ʳ. Fol. 35ʳ is paginated as p. 32.

[128] KA gives the same page number to both pages of the opening, i.e., fols. 35ᵛ and 36ʳ. See Textual Introduction, p. 42, for discussion.

[129] i.e., Psalm

[130] I have not been able to identify Hobson. KA's sister Mary had married Joseph Ashe of Twickenham; see John Burke and John Bernard Burke, *A Genealogical and Heraldic History of the Extinct and Dormant Baronetcies of England, Ireland, and Scotland*, 2ⁿᵈ ed. (London: John Russell Smith, 1844), 16; and KA refers on fol. 64ʳ to having visited Twickenham six months previously.

My[131] think's this text speakes much to me.
What waight I for. my hopes in thee.
Then why disquieted. Then why opprest.
While in the liveing fountaine be refreshet./.

[36ʳ] †[132]Waight on Gods time for thy delieveranc out of troubles. either in this life, or 33[b][133] by a Freedome by Death.
And learn in afflictions, if God vouchsafe to visit me, to preserve me, in my being, in my subsistanc in him
That I be not shaked. disinherited, devested, of him, tho I be not instantly delievered. Yet this is a refreshing, a consolation, to sit vnder the shelter of the Love of God. And if God doe not presently deliever. know o Satan how long so ever God deferes my delieveranc I will not seek the false and miserable comforts of this world.
Consider afflictions.[134] are the excercises of wisdome. the nursery of virtue, the venturing for a crowne and the gate of Glory.
Afflictions are (also) oftentimes the occasions of great temporal aduantagies. We must not look on them as they si<:> ^sit^ downe heavily upon us. but as they serue some of Gods ends, and purposes. If a man could have opened one of the pages of the Divine Counsels. and have seene the event of Iosephs being sold. to the Merchants. he might with much reason have dried up the young mans tears.
God esteemes it one of his glories, that he brings good out of evil. Bear *that which* God send patiently. for impatienc [continues on fol. 37ʳ]

[36ᵛ]   Of Afflictiones Benefit.   [*unp*]
Great are the riches that are hidden in Tribulation.
Aduersity is sent them. by the Bridegroome to prepare them for his weeding:
Prosperity is often contagious: And vnfortunate
Indulgence abandons us to Contagious prosperity.

---

[131] *sic*

[132] † corresponds with † on fols. 38ʳ and 37ᵛ. This marker indicates the beginning of the "too Last Sides" out of Jeremy Taylor which end on fol. 38ʳ and which are referenced on fol. 37ᵛ.

[133] KA gives the same page number to both pages of the opening, i.e., fols. 35ᵛ and 36ʳ. See Textual Introduction, p. 42, for discussion.

[134] KA here begins to paraphrase from Jeremy Taylor, *The Rule and Exercises of Holy Living* (1650), 153–55.

To a Captive.

Fortune knew noe better way to raise you then by this Fall. You must bid adiew to *th*e resentment which the lose of your Friends cause. That such was the order of the World and disposition of affaires as little losses were to vssher in great aduantagies./.

[37ʳ] | dus but entangle us. like the flatering of a Bird in a net.[135]   34
Therfore Consider when God cutts off my weake Arme of flesh. from my shoulders. tis to make me lean upon him
And becomes my patron, and my guide, my Aduocate, and my Defender.[136] Nay and he may if he will observe wisely shal find so many circumstances of eas[e] and remision, so many designes of providenc and Comfort, that it often happens in the whole sume of affaires That a single lose is a double blesing.
~~And~~ God the great governour of the world.[137] orderes it by the variety of changes, and accidents. and very oftentimes we see. That which was a misfortune in the perticular, in the whole order of things, becomes a blesing biger then we hoped for.
Stand stil, and see how it wil be in the event of things. Let God speak his mind out; For it may be this sad beginning is but to bring in, and to make thee entertaine and vnderstand the blesing:[138]
When a vehement Calamity lies long. I can plead, out of Gods precidents. That this wil not last, David was not ten yeares in banishment. but he enjoyed the Kingdome forty.[139] Queen Eliz*abeth* was 5 yeares in affliction then it did appear God had mercy for her.[140]
[38ʳ] God will if he ses fit. recompenc my howres of[xxi] | sorrow, with dayes of joy. My 35 Yeares of trouble. with those of quiet and delieveranc.

---

[135] "Consider afflictions . . . net": KA's paraphrase from Taylor, *Holy Living*.

[136] "Therefore consider . . . Defender": taken from Taylor, Sermon XXV, "The Miracles of Divine Mercy," Part 1, *Eniautos*, 313–26, here 326.

[137] KA begins to paraphrase again from Taylor, Sermon XXV.

[138] "God the . . . blessing": Taylor, Sermon XXV, 325.

[139] King David of the Psalms, whose flight into the wilderness was followed by rule over Judah and then the united kingdom of Israel (*ca.* 1010–970 B.C.).

[140] The period between the death of Edward VI in July 1553 (or possibly the Wyatt rebellion in January and February 1554; see fol. 11ʳ) and Elizabeth I's accession in November 1558.

[xxi] Catchword: sor-

And tho God strickes, itis lest I should not know him. & againe his hand strokes me that I should not faint vnder his hand correcting me.†[141]
Have I been preserved: in my troubles. As that good man when blowne upon the water, at the mercy of every wave, and yet defended.[142] Have not I been so too, Sunk downe into the Sea of griefe. I was not drowned then. For thy hand o God saved me, I was tosed from one wave to another by vnkindnes, by aspercions, and low all along thy hand held me fast. Thus wast thou pleased to suffer me to be distresed. Yet not forsaken. by thee. Nay I may say for these 6 yeares that are past I have never been off from the waters of peril. from one danger, one violence, one oppresion, one desertment. one Crose or another. And stil o God thou hast converted every allay, every rebuke. to see thy mercy in. to tel me thou hast not forsaken me. Thou o God wilt doe a miracle rather then forsake thy children in their distres: Hast not thou sumed up all thy promises in one. I will never leave thee nor for sake thee.[143] Friends, and estate may, thou wilt never. see *Book* A: 143:

[38ᵛ] 9 Nov*ember* 1664: It pleased God to take a way an honest Servant William 36[a] Chandeler. who had dwelt in my house almost Ten yeares, He served me Faithfully. I trust he is gone to a better service. tho he had some infirmities. I hope christ hath forgiven: A Long faithful servant is a breach in a Family. I beseech God to assist me in every Alteration. In the Cenes[144] of this world.
He was buried 11: Nov*ember*:[145] Aged 38 yeares. Foure Nightes before he died I Dreamet I saw him fall downe dead before <:>us.[146] ~~Tho~~ And I did see him die. Tho when I waket I hopet he wud not die. And he comeing downe *th*e night before he died and thought himself pretty well.

Death came upon him in the space of 3 howeres when before that he thought he might doe well. But After the minister had prayed with him. and he setled w*ha*t he had to his friends. he died all the way. And was apprehensive of every

---

[141] † corresponds with † at the top fol. 36ʳ; these bookend a passage which is referenced with a further † at the top of the otherwise blank fol. 37ᵛ (unpaginated), where KA has written:

these too Last sides out of Doc: Taylour.

of presidents of Gods way for our help:

We are apt to beleeve the first part of *th*e Covenant blesings and mercies, But not the second part which belonges to us, resignation and obediance.

KA's "too [two] Last sides" are fols. 36ʳ and 37ʳ (and the beginning of fol. 38ʳ). Fol. 36ᵛ is a later insertion.

[142] Acts 27:14-44, Paul's shipwreck. See also note 402, below.

[143] Hebrews 13:5; Deuteronomy 31:6.

[144] i.e., scenes

[145] See fol. 2ʳ.

[146] KA has written "us" over an earlier word that is now unreadable.

decay. His Coffe left him. Noe ses he. I shal bid you good night. The L*ord* Iesus receive all yo*ur* souls. Then after began to sweat. Now the work is done. and ½ an hower after died. Speaking to the last minute./

[39ʳ]   Vpon paying for the fal of Mr Riches house.   36[b]
May I as readily receive loses with patience as thy bounty with gladnes. The Lord hath gave me above my expectation or desert: I must look for accidents, wh*i*ch can have noe foresight of me to prevent.

Surely after all the croses and disappointments of this world At last I shal find rest. and *tha*t shall be turned in to joy: Ecc*l*esiastes 6: 28:

If the Lord takes away: or accidents, and impositions falls out extrordinary upon me. Let me remember. as before how I have received plentifully, and vnexpectedly: wh*i*ch is a help to bear, the burthens my estate gives a necessity to at this time, as &c: Well does a many disaduantages look upon me this year. (and the subtile evading of S*i*r T: R:) the stabing downe of the house. &c: in such a time when I have a great building to doe. Thus it pleases God to appoint it And yet I may look a litle further, and there I shal see, before a 12 month is out. How many aduantages, what plentiful additiones will accrue by Gods favour to us. Let future expectation ballance these seeming and present inconveniances. Then satisfy thy self. if I live I shal have enough. If I die If I had all the world and all the wishes and accomplishement of every desier. I shall not have cause to need any of those thirsts. and vast finet[147] ambition

My God I beseech thee let not the Troubles I meet with make me a weary of my race I am to goe on.[148] but strengthen[xxii] |

[39ᵛ]   :27 Nov*ember* 64:   37[a]
Thy seruant I may discharge my Calling, and doe the work thou putst in my hand.

And Lord sanctify the afflicitons thou has laid upon me. o Lord sanctify all that thy hand hath seen good to excercise thy <s̶.̶.̶.̶d̶> ^servant^ with. And prepare me Lord by all thy scourges, by all thy providences, for that great mercy and blesing thou art making ready and preparing for me, wh*i*ch thou art providing For thy great blesings in this world, or for great and etternal Glories in a better. <.̶.̶.̶> Is the surest:

<———————————>[149]

---

[147] i.e., finite

[148] Isaiah 40:31

[149] Several words (approximately seven) have been scored out in a dense, circular, continuous pen stroke, rendering them unreadable.

---

xxii   Catchword: thy

Lord fit me for thy mercy. Lord prepaire me for thy favour and blesing. Lord sanctify me for thy selfe. And for the accomplishing thy gracious will in my Saluation. And then come Life, or then come Death. I am in the hand of God. And that hand of Love will Crowne me/ Amen./.
Lord if it be thy will. say itis enough. to thy servant my dayes. and yeares of sighing; and enter not into Iudgement with thy servant for before thee noe flesh can be found acceptable./.[150]

[40ʳ] My God grant I may begin that triumphant duty to praise thee on Earth. which shal be performed to all Etternity by thy Saints and Angels.   37[b] †[151]
Thy mercy of Creation to me is great. but the blesing of preseruation is greater. O Let me magnify and bles thy name for that great mercy and blesing to me: Surely with David thy mercies are more in Number then I can count./.[152]

(† writing this pag: 37: makes me think I am in the 7th year of my widowhood:) (and in the 37th year of my age. this *November*: Last: 1664:[153]

I wish I may rightly vnderstand of things. and consider my Condition may be happy if I wil help to make it so. For surely I must put in my helping hand, or God wil not aid me with his.

And let me consider whether itis not possible to be happy without a second marriag: I here St Bernard til a great Queen she was as ^more^ honourable in her widow condition, as by being a Queene.[154]
Tis vnhappy in this world. If we have riches. So hard a matter to vse them well. Either too saveing: or too spending. And they are ordered so. that vnles you are rather Frugal then the contrary, they wil not stay with us. but put the owners to hard neccesities. sometimes ^as^ Henry 8

[40ᵛ] If the benefit of humaine Learning and knowledg, can bring such aids to the [*unp*] vnderstanding and Iudgement of persons: What a far blesseder condition is it

---

[150] Psalm 143:2

[151] The reference is to the parenthesized text further down the page.

[152] Echoes Psalm 139:18

[153] Thomas Austen died on 31 October 1658 (fol. 1ʳ), so KA has just completed six years of widowhood and entered a seventh in November 1664. Similarly, she is aged 36, and so is in her 37ᵗʰ year. She meditates on turning 37 on April 30 1665 (fol. 77ʳ); and see fols. 78ʳ–79ʳ. See also note 79, above, and note 329, below.

[154] Bernard of Clairvaux, letter to Melisande, Queen of Jerusalem: Bruno Scott James, *The Letters of St. Bernard of Clairvaux* (London: Burns Oates, 1953), 347–48. KA's source is unknown.

to be daily. supported and directed by the aid of Heaven. by the assitanc of his mercy to me./

Wise Sollomon he tels me true.
There is a time for all things due.
A time to spare. a time to spend.
A time to borrow. time to lend.
A time of trouble. time of rest.
A time there is to be opprest.
A time of Folly. Time to be.[155]

First:/[148] Lord lend me thy supporting grace.
May sustaine me through my race.
Through out my Lonely pilgrimage.
Thy strong supportance doe engaige.
Help me when my emergincies
Doe daily multiply and rise.
My Life is stuck about with feares.
My best fruition's stroud[157] with Teares.
Thou'st tried me lord, hast tried me young.
Hath exercis'd me very long.
Yet let it be a longer date,
If that I find thy love, not hate.
Thou seest o Lord, what sighes arrise
And I am apt to beg suffice.
If it appear vnto thy will
My often sighings, mayn't refil./
O stay thy hand if sinners may implore
And let thy soveraigne balsume, Lord restore.
My often vncomposd, afflicted mind
And look to that same rock which has been kind
That hath refreshet me. that hath sent reliefe
When sinking in the burden of my griefe.[xxiii]

38

---

[155] These lines are based on Ecclesiastes 3:1–8. See fol. 59ᵛ for KA's later expansion on these lines.

[156] KA numbers almost all of her poems in her left hand margin. See Introduction, p. 39.

[157] i.e., strewed

[xxiii] Catchword: Report

[41ʳ] Report distinguishes of w*ha*t griefes are. [*unp*]
    Lean ones, deplor'd. fat sorrow's find noe care.
    That Looking glas is false, for Heaven can make.
    Fortune to Tremble, and earths Ioyes to quake,[158] ./.
        My blessed Lord. I find thee stil
        My safeties hold, and my high Hill.
        Tho sighes may discompose a while
        At the conclusion vse to smile.
        When was I ever most. beset
        That Heaven his favour did forget.
        Lord keep me that I maynt presume.
        On easy love, lest it consume.
        May thy (refreshes) guard) ^revivements shield^ dispaire
        I may not Mantl'd be in care.
        Thy gracious pleasure does invite
        ~~We should not~~
        To be refresh'd, with due delight
        Infuse that tincture most divine
        That) ^Thy^ joyes may vanquish my repine/.

        See pag 56[159]

[42ʳ] I know o Lord thou canst glorify thy name, in the distruction, and extirpation of 39 me and mine Yet if it may stand with thy pleasure, magnify thy goodnes in our preseruation, and continuanc a while to serve thee And build up my children to Honour thee. Let them be a Family thou mayst delight to save them and deliever them from the many dangers and accidents. from their Enemies and from the devises of supplanters to them

        To my Child*ren*:
The Almighty Bles you all. with his divine blesing. and bles my blesing. and that my hearty desiers may Confer to your welfaire and Heavenly ^spiritual^ and earthly prosperity. And think when you receive my blesing that you receive that of yo*ur* Dear Fathers also. (I representing him al)

Lord imprint every day more in me and my children. The markes of thy Bounty that we should receive so much, and deserve so litle./.

---

    [158] This comma appears to have been added later, when the indented lines of verse were added. KA has not scored out her former terminal punctuation.

    [159] Page 56 is fol. 56ᵛ, a prayer for protection and deliverance in her troubles.

[43ʳ]   To my S*on* T*homas* A*usten*:   40
A Fellow of a Colledg is made up of pride and vnmannerlines. (in divers of them)
And they that are fellow commoners, learne those ill habites.
I repent me of nothing more I made you one. I had better have took the good
Counsel of Doc*ter* Wille. not for the chardges, as the divers dangers is in it
What makes noble men to be so extremely Civil but being vsed from all men to
receive a great respect by obseruanc and keeping their hates off in their presence.
Which dus not exclude theirs by their dignity above others: but Civility and
good breeding obliedges the same answerable returne: As the L*ord* Manchester
to Cos*en* T: R: put off his hat all the time he had busines to my Lord.
And truly in my observation this very rude Fashione creates abundance of pride
in Colledges. Either all Lordly. Nay Kingly. or elce vassals. and s[l]avish. in the
Royalty of Colledges
And certainly for the ill breeding and vnaccomplishments in Colledges, inforces
Gentlemen of quallity to send their sons to Travil. to learne Civillity and sweet-
[44ʳ] nes of deportement. For by the early[xxiv] | habit of prid, and surlines and stoutnes.   41
of carriadg. they hardly ever forget it while they live.
I suppose that Fashione Commenc'd for a good end. That the leaders of youth, by
their gravity might make an obediance in youth.
Yet I imagine Civility and Ceremony was in the first rudements,[160] scarce come
in to that time. And most sure there is a greater share of politure and Civility
knowne in the commendable breeding of Gentlemen then was at that time when
Colledges first was founded.
This custome in my weeke opinion may be diclined as the introduction to rudenes,
to lofty and conceited carriadg, and w*h*ich renders yo*u*rself in y*ou*r own esteeme
far better then y*our* correspondent.
Tom: w*ha*t ere the Fashione is. I wud have yo*ur* demeanour other wayes. And tho
you may goe scot free. Hat free. be not so rude in y*our* carriadg. but if a Beggar
puts off his hat. give the like. And now I see the rise and orriginal of Person Wilsons surly nod. from his prestine preheminence:/
Be conversant in Civil Law. I have heard say it wil fit you for Common Law. and
is the foundation of Law by so much reason in it./.

[44ᵛ] You are very happy S*i*r you have ~~had~~ received yo*ur* first Education in the Vniver- [*unp*]
sity, Tho it be for breeding Gentlemen, some w*ha*t a clownish place, And exacte-
nes, of Demeanour is not to be expected, But you have had a supply for that. being also so happy to have had a Conversation in the Court. Which has redeemed
you from anything which rellishes of that Nature, Yet I am of oppinion they who

---

[160] i.e., rudiments

[xxiv] Catchword: habit.

have noe other then Court breeding. come not to be principaled neither in Religion. nor sollid Learning./.[161]

There is nothing I adoar more in this world then Ingennuity,[xxv] And an ingennious spirit is seene in all thinges.
What is Ingennuity.[xxvi]
I take it to be dexterity and aptenes to vndertake all things readily, with life and apprehention, with Iudgement and sollidity, as suites with the vndertaking. And for the proper deriviation of the word I am not a schollar to know from whence it comes./

[45ʳ]   Vpon Sis*ter* Austens vnkindnes to me vpon all occasiones.[162]   42

My punishment. is for that sin. But surely Bro*ther*[163] I did not mind my own interist at all. Noe nor my Relations, that I rejected her my relation. But thy Fortune, thy aduantage, thy reputation I aimed at. Altho all was crost. And thy Fortune wud have been as great, and my contentment much. And the vnworthy aspertions to me removed. and had not bin to appearance/
And the vnhappines that attended on her my Friend might ~~not~~ have bin. prevented.
But it was not I: For God appointed, she that now persequtes me, to be aduanced by me. ^an instrument^[xxvii] and to try hur ^hur^[164] humour how she would behave her self, how she would manage her prosperity. It twas to try my humour too how I would receive the Contumelies of one I had been instrumental to raise. And to give me the relish of an enemy when I expected. a Friend. and perhaps deserved as to them. (tho they think other wise.) Yet not from my God. he raised them out of his wisedome to be my Scourg. blesed be his name.
And to my relation as an aggravation to her greater vnhappines that shee had been happy. this was for her good at conclusion too. And as Mr Raworth said this [45ᵛ] day, The happines[xxviii] | of this world, is not so much as we expect. Nor the evils 43[165]

---

[161] For later references to Tom's education at Oxford, see fols. 82ᵛ, 99ᵛ, and 114ᵛ.

[162] "Sister Austen" is Susanna Austen, the widow of KA's brother-in-law John Austen, who died in 1659. See note 373, below, and Introduction, pp. 11–13.

[163] KA is addressing her deceased brother-in-law, John Austen.

[164] "hur" (i.e., her) in the original line has been created by writing over "my"; the inserted "hur" serves as a more legible clarification.

[xxv] Jngennuity
[xxvi] Jngennuity
[xxvii] jnstrument
[xxviii] Catchwords: of this world is not so

so great in aduersity, we need be so much affraid of: A poor Condition. God dus afford contentment, as well as rich./.

[46ʳ] Dec*ember* 5t[h]: 1664 vpon Robin Austins¹⁶⁶ recovery of the smal pox. and Coronal Pop*ons* son Iohn diing of them. a Youth of a very forward growth. their ages
the same. Pop*ons* 3 yeares for growth more.¹⁶⁷

2d How does thy mercies stil renew.
    How does thy benefites pursue.
    My child lay sicke. while darts of death.
    Was ready to exhale his breath.
    A dangerous infectious Dart.
    Might have seized vpon his heart.
    Expeld his vital powers in haste.
    And early in his none age¹⁶⁸ waste.
    His slender life. then could not pay
    His offerings by a longer stay.
    His life was in the twilight Sky.
    Nor knew he not thy praise most high.
    O let him live and praise thee who
    Dost ade more daies. and life renew
    Why was mine spar'd, and one so strong
    Whose lively health, Judg'd to live long.
    A Verdant Youth, in's growing spring
    The prime of all the schollars. Him
[46ᵛ] A Iewel in his parents eye
    And this so lov'd a youth ^<⸺> did^ dye.
    He strong by nature, and mine frail.
    Was spar'd, the other did exhail.
    Was it his sin, or my ^own^ desert,
    Made mine to live and him to part
    O noe my Lord. with ^(my)^ handes (I doe) vphold.
    It was thy will, nor dare be bold

---

[165] KA begins here to give some versos separate page numbers, but this does not become entirely systematic until fol. 56; see Textual Introduction, p. 42.

[166] KA's second son, Robert Austen.

[167] See also fol. 54ʳ. This poem is anthologized in Jane Stevenson and Peter Davidson, eds., *Early Modern Women Poets (1520-1700): An Anthology* (Oxford: Oxford University Press, 2001), 314–15.

[168] i.e., noneage: youth, early stage of growth and development (*OEDO*).

To search thy secrets. or Ask why
My week Son liv'd, a strong did dye.
Thy glory, and thy mercy too,
As well in death. as life in sue./

    Meditation on my death[169]
When thy stroak comes. yt wil dissolue my breath
And shal Annihilate me vnto death,
Let thy Eternal pity on me streame
And by my sauiours Merits me redeeme
Tis he hath paid the Ransome of my sin,
Elce I, deplored I, had ever bin,
Condemned to the prison of dispaire
Nor been released by my effectes of praier.

[47ʳ] In Vaine my verse, in vaine what cou'd envoke,   46
Could ever give me the least Dram of hope,
But in the vnion of that Ransome pade,
My Bleeding soul, to Ioyes shal be Convaide
Here rest my heart, in this assured Balme
My God holds forth, all Miseries to Calme
Th'empetious[170] Tempests here I find to beate,
Shal everlastingly find their retreate,
O fit me Lord, And me prepare to come
Where Mercy'il be vnfolded in a sume
A sume that brings perfection, brings repose,
Soe Make it Lord, When this dark light shal Close.

[48ʳ]   Discourse to: L: vpon the Newington Barrow[171]   47
My Lord when the King had this estate in his enterist it was of such a trivial value, as he Iudged it not considerable at al. therefore parted with it.[172] In earnest

---

[169] KA does not number this poem, and it is in the same variant black ink as the unnumbered poem on fols. 4ᵛ–5ʳ, "On the Birds Singing in my Garden."

[170] probably derives from "empester / impester": to entangle or encumber (*OEDO*)

[171] This is the first time in *Book M* that KA meditates explicitly on the estate of Highbury, or Newington Barrow, the paternal inheritance of her eldest son, Thomas, which is a recurrent focus in the remainder of her meditations. See Introduction, pp. 9–11.

[172] The Crown had conveyed Highbury to Sir Allen Apsley in 1629 to offset costs that Apsley had incurred in victualling the Navy. See Introduction, p. 9.

Sir six and thirty yeares to com is the age of a man.[173] Nor dus a man live a man longer then that time. Subduct his first and his last time, where he actes the part of two children. And the next stage after his first child hood: put into the scale of his life. where he is guided by irregular passions and desiers. by folly and want of an experiencet Iudgement. to guid and command himself. And thus he runs in his vngovernd time. to one vice or another. as he can hardly redeeme himself from ruine, either he is the bond man of a Vsurer. or of his Tyrant appetite taken in the Fetters of a ruinateing love. So that til he has relinquishet his vice. and makes vse of that refined facculty Reason He is noe Man.

About ~~which time of~~ ^the commencement of these^ 36 yeares. gave me my birth[174]

I have ~~been~~ growen full into the world with many yeares. And tho *Sir* the Lease was an old one then (to ye) It is made young againe to us. So can not I be.

[49ʳ] And now this Lease becomes new to us. It wud have bin the same if the revertion 48 had not been parted with to

My L: I hope we shal reap the Harvest at last of a long expectation. An expectation. that every one could not stay for. onely a good Husband. Let us not receive interruption of this at last. which has tried the virtue of our disposition. And I hope we shal be better able to keep it when our Family have lived in credit for this 100 yeares. without it./.[175]

Of Ho*nour*: Contraries.

Contraries, and transcendants have a relation tho by opposition one to another: As I have found by good experienc, the succes of two thousand poundes. hath been the growth of most of my Fortune.[176] So I desier never to find the contrary.

---

[173] The discourse on these pages is concerned with the expiry of a thirty-six-year lease period that the Crown had imposed on the estate when it was conveyed to Sir Allen Apsley. See fols. 76ᵛ and 103ᵛ; also see Introduction, p. 11.

[174] KA was born on 30 April 1628 (see fols. 40ʳ and 77ʳ; and see Introduction, p. 6).

[175] On the facing page, fol. 48ᵛ, KA has added the following: "We are not com to the Fruition of it at this time. being stil in Lease." This addition is made in the middle of the otherwise blank page, level with the end of this last paragraph (the lack of "Fruition" relates to the "Harvest" in this last paragraph). See KA's meditation "On that day Highbury came out of Lease. Mic*hae*lmas 1665," fol. 103ᵛ.

[176] KA received £2000 "for her owne vse & by her to be disposed of at her pleasure" on the death of her mother in 1648 (the will of Katherine Rudd / Wilson / Highlord, National Archives, PROB 11/205); see Introduction, pp. 8 and 13. It is interesting that she

as by the Contracting a great debt upon an estate, will eate and devoure up a bigger estate then I have.

If I could have a Fortune could entice a person of Honour.[177] Yet I am not so in love with it. to be ready to part with that I know the getting of. And know for w*h*at extravaganc it was sold:

[49ᵛ]   Of Honour.   [unp]
I esteeme Honour not any thing worth, vnles it be well guarded with wealth, that it ravil not out to a degree, farre meaner then Yeomandry is. So that the Fortune I Iudge to be the real Honour. And the Title is the ornament, the embellishing of that Fortune, w*h*ich makes it look a litle brighter to dazle common eyes.
And if the costlines, and splendor of my Title eates up my estate, I shal rather degrade my self of it, by a privacy: Then degrade me of my real supportation, or Contrive vnworthy detaininges of any persons money, whereby I am made most really contemptable.

True Honour[178] consists not so much in those preferments and titles of the world, which for the most part are vaine like it selfe, But in holy wisdome, grauity and constancy which becomes a *chri*stian, either in well doing or in comely suffering The honour of worthy actions brings not only peace of minde, but makes the face of Goodmen to shine:[179] p: 18: Gaud~[180]

Book I: pag: 12: of Mediocrity: and of Honour:

[50ʳ] perhaps I may change my Condition[181] After I haue answered some disignes.   49
Then shal I not ame at Honour, (tis quiet). tis costly to maintaine Honour in all its curcumstances, nay and tis scarce Honour if punctilioes is not kepet up. Beside I some w*h*at dislike it. Since I haue a president before my eyes. what the costlines of honour. lost w*h*at I bought.

---

begins this meditation with reference to her inheritance of "pin money" along the female line, as she goes on in this meditation to repudiate the notion of remarriage.

[177] i.e., a suitor

[178] A change to a blacker ink and more spidery hand indicates that a new meditation begins at "True Honour" and runs until the end of fol. 50ʳ.

[179] Echoes Ecclesiastes 8:1

[180] This may be an abbreviation for "Gauden" and, if so, may refer to John Gauden's *A discourse of artificial beauty, in point of conscience between two ladies* (1656), in which Gauden cites scripture that "urge[s] against painting the face" (p. 18).

[181] i.e., remarry

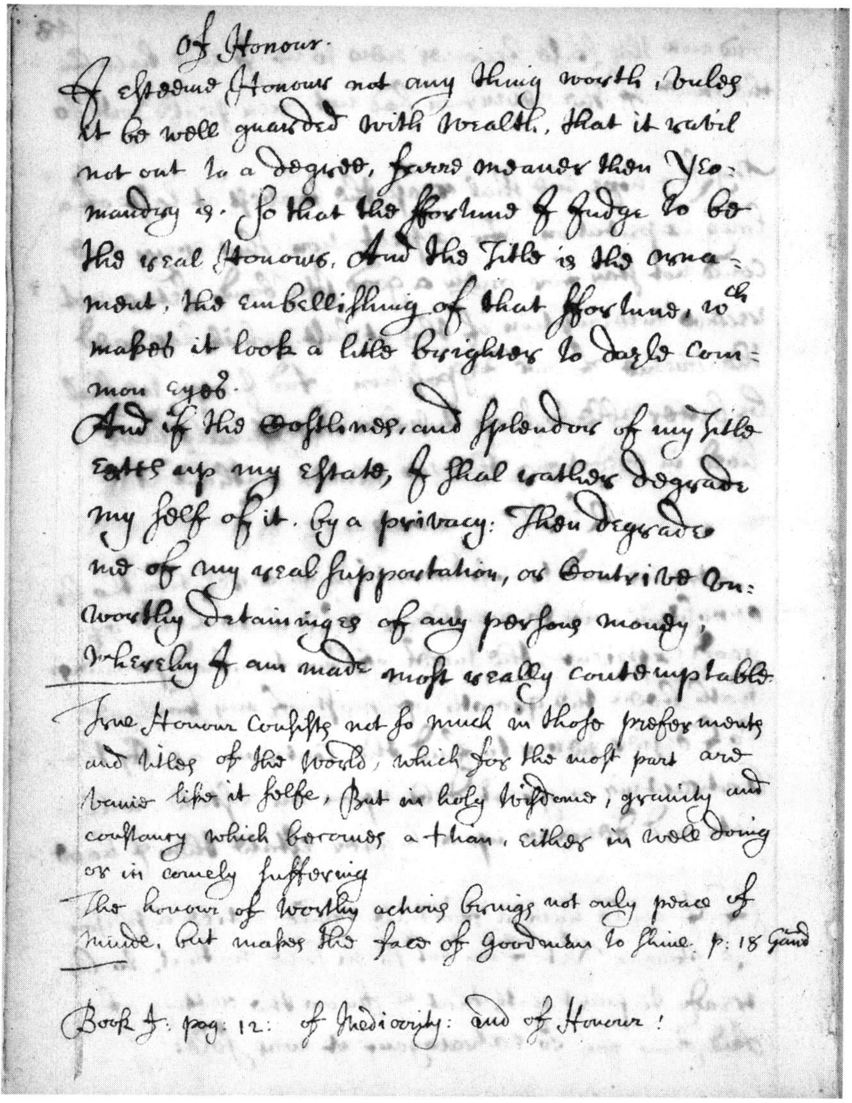

Of Honour.

I esteeme Honour not any thing worth, unles
it be well guarded with wealth, that it rubb
not out to a degree, farre meaner then Yeomandry is. So that the fortune of Iudge to bee
the reall Honour. And the Title is the ornament, the embellishing of that fortune, w^{ch}
makes it looke a litle brighter to dazle Common eyes.
And if the Costlines, and splendour of my Title
eates up my estate, I shall rather degrade
my self of it, by a privacy: Then degrade
me of my reall supportation, or Contrive un-
worthy dètaininges of any persons mony,
whereby I am made most really contemptable.

True Honour Consists not so much in those preferments
and titles of the world, which for the most part are
vanie like it selfe, But in holy Wisdome, gravity and
constancy which becomes a man, either in well doing
or in comely suffering

The honour of Worthy actions brings not only peace of
minde, but makes the face of goodmen to shine. p: 18 Gaud

Book I. pag. 12: of Mediocrity: and of Honour!

Figure 6. *Book M*, fol. 49^v. See Introduction, pp. 18–19.
©The British Library Board, Additional Manuscript 4454.

Neither is it riches I want: Heauen has gaue already most bou[n]tiful. Tis a person, whose soule and heart may be fit for me is the chief riches to be valued. Yet since this is more dispencable in men. not so much to consider termes: And hath a reflextion of disrepute when womens inclinations are steered all by Love. A Rich woman must not marry with a person of meane Fortune./

Surely Mediocrity is the happiest condition we can obtaine.[182] And yet that is so disposed. As the Lazy man comes not near it. And the Active man stayes not at it but climbes far beyond it: Til he paces all the degrees, from competency, to superfluites. And from thence Ambition tempts him with Titles, and emenency. And Yet he may be as happy by a sweet peace without goeing up those additional steps. which creates obligations
&c: see Book C: pag: 50: The ill effect of Honour p: 73: & pag. 21: In *that* book: Arguments for it: Man is made to grow: p: 63:
Book <.>   Book. C:[183]

[51ʳ]   1664:   50
I observe w*ha*t a Long and healthy age my Grandmother Rudd lived above 80.[184] and Mr Smith of Ald͞ Bury 90. and Person Wilson. about 80. all lived in the city and did not love the Country. Their diet was temperat their excercis lithe.[185] a souftly pace. ever went. Not put nature scarce ever in any Violenc. by over striving or heating w*hi*ch makes a faintes often times. ^& a decay.^
Yet I attribute the chief part of this long life to the quiet of their mindes. never engaiged in any thing disquieted or disorderd that peace within them
How ~~did~~ ^was^ my own Mothers strong nature worne out by too much stirring and walkeing. And the many cares and busneses w*hi*ch a great Family gave occasions to her. That Nature. was spent. w*hi*ch in likely hood by indulging to retirement. wud have prolonged. The distractions of the times wherein she lived gave her many discomposures. and crosses. by abuses.[186]
D*ea*re Mother thou hadst a great estate. and a great burden too./.

[51ᵛ]   To my Children   [unp]
Let the example following divert y*ou*r wishes and your aimes at the estate of Friendes

---

[182] KA later evokes Ecclesiastes 4:6 in relation to mediocrity (fol. 112ʳ).

[183] These are references to KA's other manuscript books; see Introduction, pp. 42–43.

[184] KA's maternal grandmother, Anne Rudd (named in the will of Austen's mother Katherine Rudd / Wilson / Highlord [National Archives, PROB 11/205]).

[185] agreeable, mellow, pleasant (*OED*O).

[186] KA's mother, Katherine Wilson Rudd / Wilson / Highlord, died in 1648. See the Introduction, pp. 7–8.

Book M   95

Your Vnkle Feeld[187] had an Estate of £800 p*eran*n*um* and noe children. Soe that y*ou*r Fathers Mothers and her Sister Mrs Duffeild had expectation of his estate to come to their children. When he died he left to sisters younger son an estate of revertion after his wife. Durhames fel to your Vnkle Austen.[188]
Yet my obseruation took notice That if he had not left him any thing it wud been better.
First £2200 it cost the widows life. And soe much in Finisheing it. That had the purchas & Finishing money bin layd out on any new purchas wud haue come to asmuch: And tis thought might haue preuented his Mͬ
Suspend all craueing and expectation. Goe on in y*ou*r own way of industry. And be the raiser of your Fortune. and leaue the rest to God. and he will doe better then your own projectes can

[52ʳ] These two last weekes, have been weekes of discomposure to me, of troubles.   51
Lord carry thy servant through every week of danger. And dus this week to be-
gin with accidents too: assist and keep me. Sprinkle Lord with thy blesing all my actions if it be thy will. howeverwith patience and discretion to governe my self in all *tha*t shal befal me./.

             Vpon Lending Mr C:ͬ money:[189]
His abominable rudenes for my kindnes to him. I may learne a lesson from. Have I lived in the towne for many yeares, with that vngrateful person. and Iudged him a man of Credid. therefore was deluded to lend him Money. And now he hath it, dus he contemne & vpbraid me. and defy w*ha*t I can doe. Nay is he ready to Answer the Law to my face. and like a Knave tels me I have neither bil, nor bond from him. Surely as I was excercised in my first afflictions with those try-als, and dejections. to be instructions to teach me piety and hollines to cast my dependenc on the God of comfort to ^be^ stayd by his consolations.
Now for this last year. I have had crosses from men have knowne the affaires and dealings of ~~men~~ ^them^ That things hath not gone smooth and easy. full of rules
[53ʳ] | and divers crose emerginces. From these I am to be instru[c]ted in. And as I   52
have found to this day. all that hath fallen is for my good. so may these several exigents. if I wil take them by the right handle. They are to instruct me in wis-dome. to render my experianc of the world. fuller to me then without them: And either to prevent for the Future. or to give a remedy in them.

---

    [187] i.e., great uncle; their father's maternal uncle

    [188] John Austen, KA's brother-in-law, who later bequeathed the estate to KA's son Thomas in the event of his own daughter's death (see Introduction, pp. 11–12). See also fol. 111ᵛ.

    [189] The identity of "Mr C:ͬ" is unknown, unless this is the "Mr Cruse Cheate" re-ferred to in KA's list of expenses between August 1664 and Michaelmas 1665 on fol. 99ᵛ.

I am not to be of so easy a credulity to think I shal not be deceived. when I may find. too many persons are made ful of circumvention. I am also to put more regard. more enquiery. and Cautions in my dealings.
And thus I may be glad I have met with some to prevent more./.

[53ᵛ] 3d/ On the Death of my Neece Grace Ashe. 4 years old.[190]   [unp]

Sweet blooming bud
Cropet from its stud
When growing up
Vnto faire hope
Thy preety sweetnes time hath hid
As soone as showne we are forbid
To Gaze vpon that Louely hue
On which Times shady Curtaine drew

Yet when we know
The best maynt grow
In this dark vaile
Where ills stil Aile
The great disposer sets them free
Whose Better Character doth see.
And earely in their Noneage[191] place
Where their chiefest part wil grace./.

[54ʳ] On the Death: of Mr Franceis Duffeild my Husbands Cosen Germaine/[192] 53
Died December 18t 1664.
of smal pox: aged 35 at Medenham.

How many Young persons are dead since I had my Dreame gave me intimation of mine.[193] And when I related the time to them, it appeared very short: ~~And~~

---

[190] KA's younger sister Mary married Joseph Ashe of Twickenham in or before 1650 (*Orphans' Finding Book 1643–1661*, fol. 49ʳ [Corporation of London Record Office]). See Burke and Burke, *Extinct and Dormant Baronetcies*, 16, who do not list Grace among their children, presumably because she predeceased their record-taking.

[191] youth, early stage of growth and development (*OEDO*)

[192] i.e., cousin germane: first cousin. The son of Thomas Austen's maternal aunt (see fol. 51ᵛ).

[193] A dream, predating *Book M*, which KA believes has intimated to her that she will live to exactly the same age as her husband; see note 79, above.

Whether I shal finish up my Course then I know not.[194] This I am sure, They have theres. who did not think should be so soone, As my worthy Friends. my Bro*ther* Austen,[195] (My Granmother,[196] Onkle Rudd.[197] (tho they two were almost ripe, their Yeares did neccesaryly obliedge them to Look from this world. to another.) Then followed my Bro*ther* Wilson.[198] Sis*ter* Richard Wilson a beautiful young wom*an*: And of acquaintance. Doc*ter* Broke: Mr Chillingworth. Ric*hard* Morecroft. Mrs Cordivel. Cosen Sara Foulke. and her 3 children. died within half a year one of another. And Williame my servant.[199] My Cosen Duffeild *th*e Darling of the Family, a Lusty[200] proper man. wel and dead. in a week, (about that time Coronal Popons son died.)[201] His Father full of infirmities of age and sickenes not come out of his chamber in 3 yeares. And he must dye before death comes. in his sorrowful affection for his most hopeful son. Mrs Young of Kingston. a lusty person dead: And I am liveing. These may be preparations to me. I may make my self ready. And if my part is next to be acted. I may not shrink by fear, But learne to render up my self to *th*e Almightys pleasure.

[55ʳ] O this day in the multitude of thinges I am a weary.   54
Yet then I cast my eyes on this 68 salme 28: vers revives me ^againe^ Thy God hath sent forth strength for thee: [202] And surely by a supply of that asistance of heauen my wayes shal be established with blesing.
Then being supported through my wearines. My strength (with David) will I ascribe vnto thee.[203] For thou art the God of my refuge: He verily is my strength and my saluation. he is my defence so that I shal not greatly Fal.[204] Fal I may, But then the Divine loue will bear me in his Armes. It shal not be a Fal to ruine me.

---

[194] See fols. 62ʳ, 63ᵛ, 65ᵛ.

[195] John Austen; see Introduction, pp. 11–12.

[196] KA's maternal grandmother Anne Rudd? See fol. 2ʳ.

[197] Presumably not the "A Rudd" recorded on fol. 2ʳ, whose death was not until 11 November 1668.

[198] Perhaps the "Bro[ther] R:" whose death is recorded on fol. 2ʳ and, if so, perhaps KA's brother Richard Wilson.

[199] William Chandeler, died 9 November 1664; see fol. 38ᵛ (also fols. 2ʳ and 99ᵛ).

[200] full of healthy vigour (*OEDO* 5)

[201] See fol. 46ʳ.

[202] Psalm 68:28. KA's wording of these two verses from Psalm 68 follows *BCP*; see Introduction, p. 30.

[203] Psalm 68:34; KA uses this verse for her inscription on fol. 114ʳ.

[204] Psalm 62, esp. verses 2, 6–7.

Therefore will I make stil this repittition of this Ioyful Succour I meet with in my extremities. God truly is my strength and saluation, my defence so that I shal not fal.[205]

Nay I may assuredly beleeve as long as God is with me I shal not fal. So fall as to be dejected. or dismaied If I Fall by Heauens Tuition I shal then rise to a blesed exhaltation and fauour

That I may be held by his loue Meditate on t*he* 62 salme of placing affiance[206] in him and drawing it off from all false retreates and wrong succours./

Stil learne of David: He was as valiant as euer drew sword. Yet in patient bearing and forbearing, he went beyond all men before him

[55ᵛ]   On my troubles: in 1664:   [*unp*]
My troubles may be above the strength of Nature, Not above my spiritual strength, is of high Ioy to me.
Lord if it be good in thy sight Let not this rugged world allwayes disquiet me, allwayes render crosses & vexation to me. Give me the oppertunities of serveing thee, from the perturbations and proseqution of Covetious[207] Men.
My Saviour Give me that peace which thou promisest thy Chosen that my heart be not troubled./[208]
†[209]

All tho our life is miserable, and extremely apt to be stroued[210] with sadnesses. in every condition & curcumstance of it. (as Doc*ter* Taylor most fully relates. in a perfect resemblance)[211] Yet heres the refuge for a christian. Which I have often found. I will fly unto my God. vnto that God which hath performed all things for me. And I trust will not leave me now. but stil his favour will shine upon me in this Time of peril./.

†[212] This 5th May. 1666 my multitude of busines & of crose affaires I doe renew that pettition that my God wud strengthen me & wafte me ouer this ocean where I am[213]

---

[205] Psalm 62:2 and 7

[206] faith, trust; Psalm 62:8 "O put your trust in him alway (ye people)."

[207] i.e., covetous

[208] John 14:27

[209] The reference here is to the text so marked, further down the page.

[210] i.e., strewed

[211] Jeremy Taylor. I have not been able to trace KA's specific reference here.

[212] The reference here is from the marked point earlier on the same page.

[213] This is a clear example of KA returning to one of her own meditations at a later date and writing further. See Introduction, pp. 5 and 42.

[56ʳ]   To obtaine a Sweet Nature   55
The beginning of a gracious disposition, is to be quallified with Ioy. The Fruits of the spirit is Ioy, long suffering, gentlenes, goodnes.[214]
A chearful disposition is the fitest to serve God and pleas him. Also the most acceptable for a Comfortable Socciety. Cheerfulnes is ready to forgive errours. tis ful of love. and Love can pardon a multitude, You may observe in some Young persons. who are of a cheerful nature, of w*ha*t sweet complying tempers they are of. And when age comes with infirmities, that Ioyes are vnpleasant. w*ha*t sowre peevish dipos[i]t[ion]s arriseth in the temper of men and women.

To spend time
Consider how to spend my time, Not trifling away, but with method, vsefully, and comfortably, And to waigh the howeres of the day, to divide them in several studies. imployments. In Devotion, in Sobernes. In educating my children. In History, in a portion for retirement: In seecking knowledg: Tis observed. the ignorant man is compared to a Beast: But he is far worse then a Beast. their nature is to be ignorant: Tis mans fault if he be so./.

[56ᵛ] Ian*uary* 28: 1664:[215]   Troubles.   56[216]
Remember David And all His afflic*tions*:[217] Remember thy Servant, and all her afflictions to: And if it be thy will, to say itis enough: Thou Lord knowes how to deliever the Godly out of temptation
O my God make me fit for thy gracious Conduct, and then I shal com within thy promise of defence.
O my Lord bepleased to deliever me from temptation. Thou knewest my Saviour, how many wayes we are beset, with snares and dangers in this life. And therefore did place this pettition, in that holy compendium of our continual prayers to thee. (Deliever us from) ^Lead us not into^ Temptation.[218] ^free me^ From the perplexitys of troublesome men. who makes aduantages of accidental cassulties

---

[214] Galatians 5:22

[215] i.e., January 28 1664/5

[216] KA here begins to number versos separately and systematically; see Introduction, p. 42.

[217] Psalm 132:1

[218] Matthew 6:13, *BCP* (KA's "holy compendium of our continual prayers to thee"), sig. B3.

February 10th[219]
My Gracious Father help thy servant out of *th*e multitude of encumberances that dus beset me round. I thought my troubles grew to an end, now my 6 years is near at conclusion,[220] But low I find them rather augmented, one perplexity arrives close to another, without intermission to over come one, before I find another. Thus it hath been with me formerly, as soone as one was past. another came. But now I know not how to doe any, so many assaile & Crowd in upon me together. O my God let my heart smight me, w*ha*t are the sines lye hidden and vnrepented of. that thy displeasure is so many wayes upon me.[xxix]

[57ʳ] †[221]Make thy Face to shine upon thy servant, save me For thy mercies sake.[222] 57
Make me to heare Ioy and gladnes, that the bones w*hi*ch thou hast broken may rejoyce.†[223]
O that my heart might be a humble heart. That tho I am in intricacies, my sins deserve far more, Blessed Lord sanctify w*ha*t is upon me, And give me Courage and prudence, Wisdome and patience, to over come them to thy Glory. Then shal I lay thy delieverances, or supportations. either to ease me, or Free me. Which o my God as may be most to thy will and thy Honour. I shal lay them on thy Alter of prais, and thanksgiveing, all the dayes of my life

make thy Face. &c
†[224]

---

[219] i.e., 10 February 1664/5. Sir Allen Apsley's creditors petitioned the House of Commons in February 1664/5 for the ownership of Highbury and Galtres (*Journals of the House of Commons*, 3: 594, 612), and KA comments on fol. 60ᵛ, "It came to pase that on the 9th of feb*ruary* I was appointed to be that day at the Com*mittee* of Parlia*ment*." See Introduction, p. 10.

[220] KA passed the end of her sixth year of widowhood in October 1664, and hopes for a deliverance parallel to Job's. See fol. 40ʳ (and note 153), and Introduction, p. 16.

[221] † at the beginning and end of this short passage seems to indicate that it should operate as a kind of refrain. A catchword from the bottom of fol. 56ᵛ connects directly to the phrase, "O that my heart. . . ."

[222] Psalm 31:16

[223] Psalm 51:8

[224] † indicates a repetition of the refrain written at the top of the page. The date, 10 February, appears at the same level as the cross-reference marker on the page, but appears to relate to the entry below, apparently a second meditation on the same date.

[xxix] Catchword: O. It connects in this case with the passage of text after the "refrain" in KA's prayer, "O that my heart. . . ."

Book M   101

    10 Feb*ruary*[225]
How dus God Almighty comfort me. that he relieveth the Fatherles and widowes,[226] then when crose men burden them with the waight of perplexities, the Father of pity will bring them out of their power:
I hear the prophet Dav*id* say. the way of evill men shal be turned vp side downe.[227] Those projects which they think establishet with assurance, shal be leveled and turned to the ground, And the top of their expectation to faile. And the lord will save such as be of a clean heart. of a contrite spirit. The Lord will Raigne in his compassion for ever; even thy God o Sion to all gennerations.[228] praise yee the Lord. o prais the Lord while I live that hath been the help of the afflicted and hath been so to every genneration / See Salme. 6: & 7:th

(Now is :Mr Rich. Mr Symons. ~~Syd s<cr>oop~~ ^The parliament^[229] Mrs Pelhams vnjustly takeing aduantage all upon me at once./.[230]

[57ᵛ] I here David pray to be delievered. from men which are thy hand o Lord.[231] And 58 surely I am the more satisfied That when I find troubles from men. That it hath pleased thee to make them the instruments of rebukes to me, by this allay they can not smight me more then my gracious Father permites. for my Good. And tho evil men give offence. Yet woe be to them by whom they come. O God make me a passive sufferrer farr rather then an active doer of injury, And I beseech thee o God to forgive them who doe me wrong: For this Is my Duty to pray for them who despightfully vse me,[232] I am commanded to be in charity with them, I pray God make me to be so, and to overcome my passion, which ~~by~~ ^t^hies^e^ ^parties^[233] most despightful vseage creates in me. And ever to cast away revenge./

---

[225] i.e., 10 February 1664/5
[226] Psalm 146:9
[227] Psalm 146:9
[228] Psalm 146:10
[229] KA has written "The" over the top of "Syd" and has begun to write "parliament" over the top of the other, semi-legible, word. She has then written "parliament" clearly above the overwritten words.
[230] This appears to be a later addition, written into a small space at the bottom of the page.
[231] Psalm 17:14
[232] Matthew 5:44; Luke 6:28
[233] KA has made these alterations in a different ink, perhaps when re-reading. She has changed "by his most despightful vseage" to "these parties most despightful vseage," making clear that she is not attributing "despightful vseage" to God.

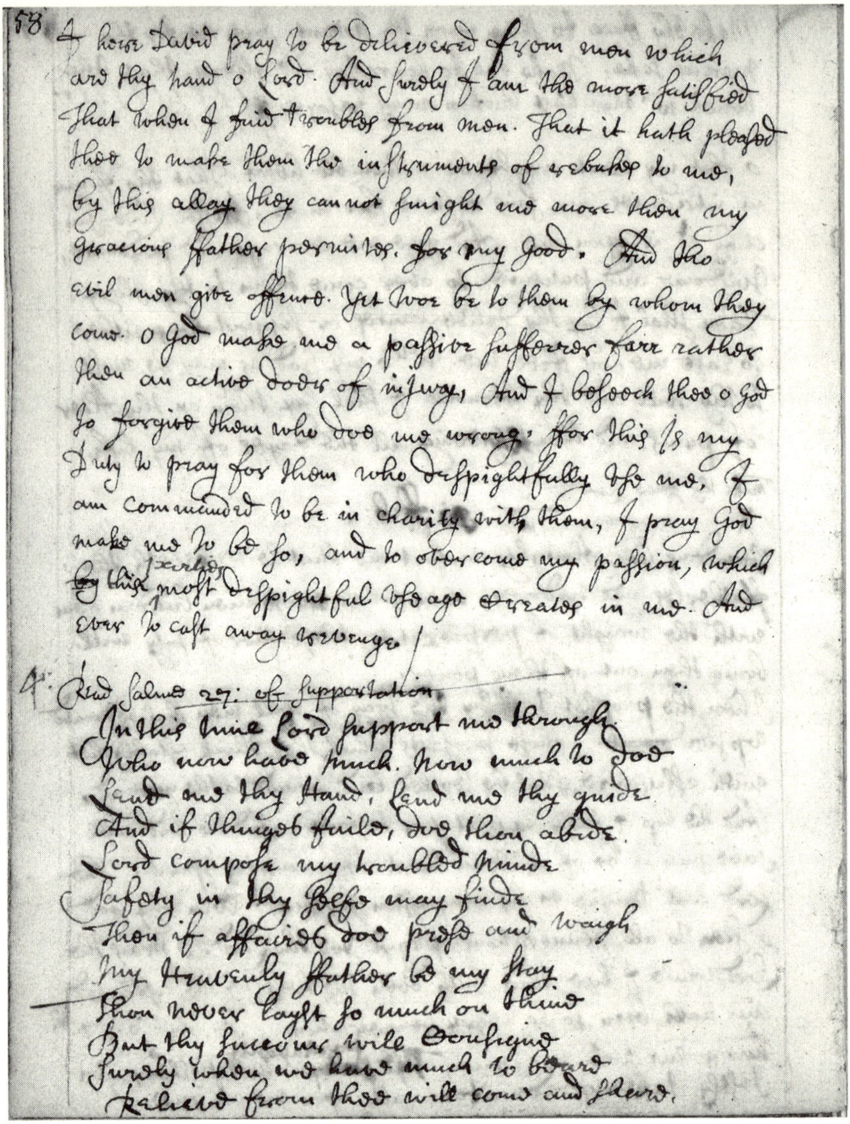

Figure 7. *Book M*, fol. 57ᵛ. See Introduction, pp. 30–31.
©The British Library Board, Additional Manuscript 4454.

4: Read Salme 27: of Supportation[234]

In this time Lord support me through.
Who now have much. now much to doe
Lend me thy Hand, Lend me thy guide
And if thinges faile, doe thou abide.
Lord compose my troubled minde
Safety in thy selfe may finde
Then if affaires doe prese and waigh
My Heavenly Father be my stay.
Thou never layst so much on thine
But thy succour will Consigne
Surely when we have much to beare
Relieve from thee will come and share,
[58ʳ] Then pity me Thou Heavenly aide
And be my shield now I have praid
Now stormes of difficultes arrise
Give me Wisedome, make me wise
And that which is my part to doe,
Assist with blessinges doe endue,[235]
I'have often found thy shining beame,
Then Come and help in my extreame.
My strength is not compos'd so strong
But subtile violence will wrong.
And in this world shall be a prey,
Vnles the aid of widdowes stay
Vnles thy blessings doe concur
Shall find all comforts to demur
And since thou wilt acceptance find
When we quiese a quiet mind
Such meek deportement to thy will
In every accident be still
For then noe crosse can intervene
Where condescends[236] to thee'are seene

---

[234] Verbal echoes of Psalm 27 are scarce in the poem that follows, but the poem "develops the theme of dependency that follows the psalm's declaration, 'The Lord is my light and my salvation; whom shall I fear?'" (Raymond Anselment, "Katherine Austen and the Widow's Might," *Journal for Early Modern Cultural Studies* 5 [2005]: 15).

[235] supply, endow (*OEDO*)

[236] i.e., condescents: assents, compliances (*OEDO*)

Not Crose. nor trouble can arrise.
If thou beholdes me with thy eyes.

5 What need I fear, what need I hope,
This terrene[237] Stage, has litle scoape.
The ills we doe enduear not long
Its Flatering bliseses[238] are not strong
Are like the water, like the wind
Such is the fleting joyes we find
Are like the sand, or like a cloud
So finet[239] blises find a shroud./:

[58ᵛ] 6: And is this day, this day ^now^ is closed[240]   60
So shal my life be once reposed
And all the tumults that invade
A time will come shal overwade[241]
They need not scare me or affright
They'r onely sent for one short night,
As Fleeting Air, as winged Time,
Troubles, and life will quick rejoyne.
Suppose my life, it be a shade,
This shaddow the Almighty made.
And hath appointed out my dayes.
Whether For short, or longer staies,
Vnto his Glory I resigne.
What ere I am, And what is mine./

Vpon: February 14th <............................> † I.[242]

---

[237] belonging to the earth or to this world; earthly; worldly, secular, temporal, material, human (as opposed to heavenly, eternal, spiritual, divine) (*OEDO* a. 1)

[238] *sic* (blisses)

[239] i.e., finite

[240] The line's scansion suggests that "now" should be a replacement for "is" rather than an addition to it.

[241] to wade across (water) (*OEDO*)

[242] 38 lines of verse, occupying the remainder of fol. 58ᵛ and all of fol. 59ʳ, are scored out with a circular penstroke, to the extent that the verse is unreadable. The date of 14 February, just legible at the beginning of the scored out lines, suggests that it is a version of the poem that follows (fols. 59ᵛ–60ʳ), or at least a poem on the same topic. For the cross-reference mark within the scored-out title, see fol. 62ʳ.

Book M   *105*

[59ᵛ] Vpon Courtiers at *th*e Com*mittee* of parlia*ment* striving for Highbury: *th*e 14th   61
Feb*ruary*: that I was there. 1664[243]

7: Wise Sollomon he tells me true
    There is a time for all thinges due
    A Time to spare, a time to spend
    A Time to Borrow time to lend
    A time of Trouble time of rest
    A time there is to be opprest[244]
    Such is this time now men of power
    Doe seeke our wellfaire to devoure
    Confederated in a League
    By an ~~oppresive~~ ^vnjust and^ Dire †intrege.   †intrege[245]
    Envy thou base incroaching weed
    Never did any Noble deed.
    We cannot be sequer[246] for thee
    O thou most treacherous quallity
    Noe time in this same world ~~seque‹..›e~~ secure
    Alive nor dead, a hold have sure.
    A shovel throwes us from our grave
    As envy pluckes from what we have.
    Tis better farr on Heaven to place
    Where we are Freed from envyes chace
    Noe thiefe noe supplantation can
    Dispoile w*ha*t is the best of man
    Nor of thy favour most great Lord
    In our huge straights dus aid afford.
[60ʳ] Since I have seene the Lord to six   62
    Most saddest Yeares[247] my heart Ile fix
    And while I move vpon Earthes Stages
    Fly to that same Rocke of Ages
    All Widdowes Fall, all Orphanes bow
    To our great God, that Smiles allow.
    When in your plunges, your distres

---

    [243] i.e., 14 February 1664/5

    [244] Ecclesiastes 3:1–8. See fol. 40ᵛ for an earlier version of these lines.

    [245] This clarification is necessary because KA has overwritten an error in the original text.

    [246] i.e., secure

    [247] For the significance of a six-year period to KA, see Introduction, pp. 15–16.

When powerful wrong contractes you lese
Fly to heavens sure help alone.
For Heaven will hear when men heares none /

Men never think their wifes may be
Neccesitate by missery
Or their children be a prey
When them selues are gone away
I not resented widdowes teares
Before I was distreased with feares
This retribution doe I find
To meet with all the world vnkind.[248]

My sin for give. let pitty flow
And comfort vnto sad hearts shew
Most gracious Heaven relieve sad hearts
Be healing Balsume in their smartes.
O Heaven send downe thy Ful reliefe
Who art the help of all in chiefe./

[60ᵛ]   My Dreame on 2d: of January 1664:[249]   63
I dreamet I was goeing to a weeding.[250] and took my leave of my Mother, then I went vp a high paire of Staires and came into a Roome where was a long Table in *th*e midle at the vper end sat my Husband. a discourseing with a Gentl*ema*n in a Gowne. siting at the side of the Table. I Looket upon them and went downe, as I went downe a few stepes I saw my Husband agen. I kised him. and asket him how he could come downe before me since I left him siting. He told me by a Backe staires. So downe I went. And then I forgeting my muffe. I went up *th*e backe staires for it. But I had not gone up aboue 8: or 9: stepes but I waket.
This ran in my minde divers dayes afterwards. and I concluded. the First paire of staires signified to me to the end of Ian*uary* and the second was so many dayes in Feb*ruary* and then something wud fall out to me. And indeed I was troubled that some vnhappy aduenture wud come. as I in dreaded every day. wishing February out.

---

[248] These lines are related to those that follow, despite the line space KA leaves between them. See KA's reflection on fol. 57ʳ that God "relieveth the Fatherles and widowes"; see also Introduction, pp. 16–17.

[249] i.e., January 1664/5

[250] i.e., wedding

Book M 107

It came to pase that on the 9th of february I was appointed to be that day at the Com*mittee* of Parli*ament*:[251] And when I came into the Roome it was the same as I saw in my Dreame. the situation of the Roome the same with *th*e Table. And as soone as I cast my eye on S*ir* Iohn Birkenhead.[252] I was confident he was the very same man I saw my Hus*band* with.

[61ʳ] This busines was a weeding: for it was a Contract. a^xxx | Confederacy to take 64 away our estate. And I shal noe more be of that opinion gennerally observed in Dreames that a weeding foretels a bur[y]ing. and a bur[y]ing a weeding. But that itis danger of Conspiracy against one. as This was to us:[253]

And certainly something might concerne S*ir* Iohn by my husbands seeming to divert him. that if he acted in so Iust a matter it wud not be well to him. And by my Hus*bands* siting at *th*e vper end of *th*e Table. as if he wud be his judge.

It proved a very troublesome time to me. For I was sicke of an exceeding cold in my head maded me to be allmost Deafe and dumbe. and goeing to West*minster* about 6 times. I was exceeding ill. and more vnfit to contest with such a busines then ever I had been before. God haveing continued my health all wayes before: That now it was a huge burden. And how subtilely carried they their designe by resolueing the comm^ity^ they chose shud make w*ha*t report they pleased to the par*liament*:

The 11 of Feb*ruary* My son was very ill. in so much I had that day the tidinges he was in a Consumption, and very dangerous, by a Cake of Fleame backet at his stom*ach*:[254] That day also was discovered to me w*ha*t potent traines[255] was laid to git his estate. And my own faintnes and weeaknes. became. insupportable
           my nied:

If the Lord dus not help me I shal be like to them that goe downe to the pit.[256] This day that I have feares of the Lose of my Son. of the lose of ~~my~~ his Land

---

[251] See note 219, above.
[252] See note 309, below.
[253] Squeezed into space at the end of this line is the following:
    ^By my muffe goeing for yt I was to be Laped warm
    as it fel out. went in muff. & veluet hood & mantle.^
[254] KA's eldest son Thomas, whose inheritance of Highbury is at contest.
[255] train: a course of action. See also fols. 61ᵛ, 65ʳ, and 91ʳ.
[256] Psalm 28:1

[xxx] Catchword: con

[61ᵛ]   Meditation   65
If the Lord is not on our side, now men rise up agen us.[257] I if the Lord takes not our part. now that we have great opposeres. They will swallow our estate up quick, while their many devices are intended to overthrow us.
Help me o lord, now I am helples. now I am weeke by distempers of body. be strength to my body, be supportation to my minde. Endow that with Fortitude and submision. And be pleased to send thy Angel and deliever me. Vouchsafe a Conducting guardian Angel to defend us. Thou didst send an Angel to disco<m>feit Vaunting Sanacrib.[258] The Almighty can also frustrate the snares and traines laid by our vnjust oppressors. if it seemes fit for his glory. Or if our aduarsaries have the vpper hand. the Almighty can convert *th*e lose receaved for our greater gaine. And sanctified aduersity is better then Fortunes. where heaven denyes it.[259]

Sure if they take away our estate. three worlds would heare of it. Heaven, Earth, and Hell. Hell wud Gape, Earth wud Complaine and Heaven wud Iudge.

Flie sinne, for sharp revenge doth follow sinne.
    And wicked deeds do wrathful doomes procure,
If God stay long eare he to strike beginne,
    Though long he stay, at last he striketh sure./.

[62ʳ] While I am distreset with Feare.   66
Grant thy favour smile and chear.
While troopes of Discomposures rise
Gods Former Love may fill my eyes.

Heaven can Light my Candle. Heaven can make my darknes to be light.[260] by his sweet and blesed refreshment to my ^soule^
†[261] I could not be at home the 14th feb*ruary* to rejoyce in *th*e favours of God in preserveing me in 6 yeares of troubles.[262] I waighting on the Commite. but I may have another day may give the relation of it.

---

    [257] Psalm 17:7

    [258] 2 Kings 19:35. Sennacherib, king of Assyria, who had been threatening Hezekiah.

    [259] See Introduction, p. 17, for "sanctified affliction" (Keith Thomas, *Religion and the Decline of Magic* [London: Weidenfeld and Nicolson, 1971], 81).

    [260] Psalm 18:28

    [261] The point to which this mark refers is unclear, but its correspondent mark may well be that in the title to the scored-out verse on fols. 58ᵛ–59ʳ. That title also includes the date 14 February.

    [262] See note 341, below.

Certainly the Conclusion of this last 6t yeare I had such a~~<-->~~ accumulated troubles, and a many incumberances. many businesses. with a weeke disposed body to goe through. That if heaven had not in a most special. most eminent manner supported me. it had been my death. So that I was nigh unto death, and my weekenes and indisposition continued many dayes.

Now it hath pleased God I have pased that time wherein I thought death might have been presented to me I hope it will please him to comfort me according to the dayes wherein I have seene evil and the yeares of my Trouble. That ^as^ I doe not yet dye but live. so as I live, I may declare the conducting love I have found from my God.[263] He hath been a Sun and a shield.[264] and noe good thing he wil with hold from them that trust in him.

[62ᵛ] O that I may live to tell the singular providences of God to me. That all widdowes and orphanes. all Fatherles and Friendles may put their trust in God. may set their hope in him, who hath been in my ready defence in the yeares of my distreses. then when *th*e water floudes were ready to drowne me./[265]

On 25th: Feb*ruary*: 1664:[266]

8: Make me my Lord even this time see.
How much thou hast defended me.
This yeare. three monthes. Five yeare beside
Thy supreame favour was my guide.
Blessings on blesings did bestowe
Love in the Cup of trembling shew
Lord if thou hadst not sometimes smiled
My Feares had rendered me exhil'd
The many waves did overflow
Sometimes I thought thy favour slow
In those disconsolated yeares
So often strewed with sighes and feares
Then came thy aide and succour downe
And was my Light, my life, my Crowne
[63ʳ] None but Heavens all seeing eye
Could lay ^cast^ my discomposures bye
His sweetly moveing providence
In sore afflictions was my Fence.

---

[263] See fol. 21ʳ and note 79, above.
[264] Psalm 84:11
[265] Echoes Psalm 69:2
[266] i.e., 25 February 1664/5

Did lay their billowes stop their rage[267]
Did my oppressiones Storme aswaige
Blest succour how hast thou consign'd
Revivements when in grief confin'd
What shall I render to my God and pay
For his conducting and defending stay.
Etternitys it self's too small
To reckown up thy mercyes all
And to repeate my tongue is dumbe
Noe Figures Audit up the sume
O noe my Lord, theyr higher farre
Then the deep Centor to the Starr
None but Arch Angeles can declare
Thy Ample glories what they are.
When thou hast made me like to those
And this same band of death disclose
I shall triumph then with the skill
In high perfection praise thy will
And in thy Hierarchy I shall
Innumerable acts extoall./

[63ᵛ] Vpon my Dreame. the 20th Oct*ober* 1664: when I Dreamet I saw 4 Moones in 69
a clear Sky:
    Meditation
9: Will Foure Moones more my Fate declare?
    Waight I in hope? or in Dispaire?
    Dus life or Death my date vnfold?[268]
    I know not Lord. thou art my hold.
    Which state is fittest Lord for thee
    To that most willingly agree.
    If through the pavement of *th*e grave
    Heavens providence more beauty have
    My God I doe submit and know.
    More glory vnto me will shew
    Then this fraile life can contribute
    When pleasures to our hearts most suite.
    The meane time Lord prepare my heart

---

[267] See note 402, below.

[268] KA believed she would live to the same age as her husband, a belief "countermanded" by her dream of monition recorded on fol. 21ʳ. See note 79, above.

Book M

    For what thy ~~purposes~~ ^goodnes shal^ impart.
    For what thy purposes intend
    In Embassaige of life, or end.
    Addorne my Soule and beautify
    That chiefest part; I may comply.
    O fit me Lord, to dye or live
    To doe my Duty while I breath.
    Then weelcome life. or death each one.[xxxi]

[64ʳ] If thou entitle me thy one.
    If thou convert this litle sand
    To stand the shoke[269] of thy command.

    I dreamet I think it was about *the* 20th August 1664. the last night before I came from Twickenham[270] That my Father Austen and my Bro*ther* Aus*ten*[271] was partners at one Game at Cribage. and my Husband and I: and as soone as the Cards was dealt, my Hus*band* sed he wud deale againe. I was vnwilling. & sed I had a good Game, For I had three Ases: & I sed that was six;
    And this I thought intimated to me Six monthes. And some thing wud happen. W*hich* now *that* six monthes is past. I think *that*. and my 4 moones Dreame related, to ~~that~~ our estate of Highbury w*hich* then was caled in to a most dangerous question. by persons who <was> ^is^ ready to doe w*hat* they please<d ⟨...⟩> ^if^ the special providence of God ^doe not^ prevented them:[272]
    That troublesome busines might wel be compared to a game at Cards. wherein my Father Aus[ten] and all of us have been concerned in *the* takeing care of and defending. ~~And it pleased God that on *the* ..th of~~ February: 64: ~~I . . .. had hope it was ended~~ [. . ..][273]

[64ᵛ] Our Aduar[s]aries doe see our cause is so apparently right. ~~as I hope~~ ^and yet^ they will <⟨...⟩> essay to vex us more. ~~which~~ I beseech God if it be his pleasure to divert their vnjust pretent[i]ones.

---

   [269] i.e., shock?
   [270] On fol. 35ᵛ, KA writes a short verse on having heard Doctor Hobson preach at Twickenham.
   [271] KA's father-in-law Thomas Austen and her brother-in-law John Austen, both of whom are deceased.
   [272] KA has changed the tense of this sentence from past to present.
   [273] The text has here been struck through with a looping circular penstroke, the date "February 64" being left. There are then two further lines of text, not indicated here, struck out with the same looping circular penstroke.

   [xxxi] Catchword: if

I Dreamet a while before. I had thiefes came to my bed side. And there was my Husband came & gave me two Ringes. One His Fathers Gold Sealed Ring. the other a Diamond Ring of his Brothers.[274] And his Father was in the entery. but did not come in, And <st.> thus I was delievered from the Thiefes.
And when I waket I hopet I shud have the better of my Fathers estate. of Highbury:[275] & of my Bro*thers* estate of the Red Lion. now at. this time w*hich* I am in Law with by my sis[ter] Austen:[276]

I have had these two yeares in my house. an vnfaithful seruant. And when I: found out his knavery, was forced not to acquse him of it, but to keep him. while my vrgent occasions was pased, yet he at last discovered, told me he must be goeing into his own Country in 3 dayes, and could not stay. Then when my other man had broak a bone   :and could not stir in many dayes to doe anything.

[65ʳ] on   Their reporting our busines to the parli*ament* the day they were riseing. 72
Now I am sure this is the time all my Monitions to me tended:[277] This. is the time of the greatest trouble for outward concernes of estate, I pray God it may be my time of trust and reliance in him
I am in the hands of potent men. Men skilful. to distroy of subtil men, who lay traines[278] to ruine *the* widow and Fatherles. But stay, I am in the hands of a gracious God. Can disappoint their projects, and suffer them not to goe further then his pleasure.
And let me be assured that pleasure of heaven. if I and mine depend in him, can make our outward loses of this world turne to our greater gain. in another. And let us be encouradged. that God is able to give as much succes to our remayning estate, as if we had that too. Of this I may be sure from my experience God hath blest me with succes and prosperity in my estate, as to all men it may appear a wonder, As if I had that estate in my possesion, they wud deprieve us of, to mens vnderstanding could hardly encreas to more
Therefore will I commit the event of it to heaven. For he will dispose for the best. Therefore in patienc I shal endeavour to posses my Soule. And then heaven wil

---

[274] KA's father-in-law Thomas Austen and her brother-in-law John Austen again feature in her dream. Their estates are the sources of the properties over which KA is engaged in legal action.

[275] Highbury, the estate of her father-in-law, Thomas Austen. See Introduction, pp. 9–11.

[276] The Red Lion, the estate of her brother-in-law, John Austen. See note 373, below, and Introduction, pp. 11–13.

[277] See, in particular, fol. 21ʳ "Observation on my Dream of Monition."

[278] See note 255, above.

bles us. And I shal magnify his name, whether we have it. or whether we loose it. for thy mercy hath. and will enduer for ever.[279]

[65ᵛ]   Meditation, on.

10: I now have pas'd those yeares did waight,
From intimation of my date,
Might then expire, I now march on.
Longer in life, more time to run.
As Hezekiah was repreiv'd.
I yet of life am not bereiv'd.[280]
Another space is lent to know
What I to my Creator owe.
His noble acts my tongue relate,
Beyond all time, beyond all date
His ancient favour, ads his new
Before Heavens firmament he drew.
His love to Mankind, in that Streame
He did descend his gracious beame.
On me vnworthy that high grace,
Most eminent in six yeares space.
Those minites which I could not tell
In each of them did care excell.
And all my time his grace was found.
But in Aduersity 'twas Crown'd.
Tendered with peculiar love
When I sat sighing could not move
Or make recovery in my lose.[xxxii]
[66ʳ] I was vpheld in Every Crose.
What are the Stories I can tell
Higher then Mountaines, or Seas swell
From Earth to Heaven, is not so high
As my Gods providences spy.
So Great a God should me behold
In all my pathes, cannot be told.
Noe words I have that can indite
Or while a Mortall can recite

---

[279] Psalm 136, refrain
[280] See fol. 21ʳ and notes 79–80, above.

[xxxii] Catchword: I

That his Great Glory should espy
And save a worme, not throwe her by
Low men wud spurne, and when they tread
Not value it but leave it dead.
And yet, High Heavens, descendes stil flow
Lord how much Mortals ever owe
To thee their Saviour in their greif
Thy vioals[281] powers of full reliefe
What can I render vnto thee
But that which floweth stil to me
From thy influence, from thy Rayes.
Implant divine, Etternal prayse
That I may pay thee what is thine,
For surely any thing of mine
Is most vnworthy to present
To thee all pure, all excelent

[66ᵛ] Infuse o Lord that Spirituall flame 75
That I may offer thee the same
But still I fear while I am dust
That heat abates, and is vnjust.
Will Loose its waight, and cannot shine
Thy praises forth, till made divine.
Fit me by all thy Dealings past.
For thy high Ioyes shall ever last.
And when I'me made a perfect soule
Shall perfectly thy praises roule./ Amen./

Here joyne those 4 Leaves out of parch*ment* booke. of meditat*ions* of praise. be-*ginning* Oct*ober* Last 64./.

[67ʳ]   Ap:[282]   76
11: Come all my thoughts, awake, awake,
And Trophes of his praises make,
Come summon forth his acts of praise.
How his rich conduct freely stayes.

---

[281] probably "vials," in reference to Revelation 15:7, "seven golden vials full of the wrath of God" (see *OEDO*, n. 2)

[282] Perhaps an abbreviation for "Apostrophe." KA's knowledge of Donne's sermons is clear; it is possible that this poem, with its imperative verb forms and repetition, echoes Donne's Holy Sonnet "At the round earth's imagined corners."

From secreet Cavernes of my brest,
Tel, o Tel how heaven gives rest.
I faine wud of his Glory sing
My soule is narrow cannot ring,
Tis circumscrib'd, and is confin'd.
I ready onely am in mind.
Affection and my Will is bent
My God accept of my intent.
For Nothing elce I have to pay,
I dedicate my heart to stay.
And what I cannot Lord expresse
Vouchsafe to read it out by guese.
Noe character of humaine Art.
Soe high a subject can impart
Or while we fly on winged Time
Itis impossible to clime
Th'immense perfection of thy name.
(Stupidity must here refraine.) or
Stupidity can never Frame./

[67ᵛ]   On, report at parliament:/   77
For this Complaint of oppresion, God hath punishet the Land Formerly, in the great Callamities which fell upon the times, And surely if they pursue, and commit the same Crimes, of vnjustice, and Injuries to poore men. And especially to acte violence on widdowes and orphanes, how will their cries and greviances perce the eares of Heaven, who will hear and Iudge their cause, against an vnjust Nation./. O God hear thou in Heaven thy dwelling place,[283] and have mercy upon us,

O Lord direct thy Servant. o lord assist thy Servant/ In this so waighty concerne I have to overcome. I am week as a child to Contest, with my potent Aduarsaries. Yet I have an Allmighty God (and a Iust Cause.) who I trust will defend me. One day I shal be delieverd, from these inquietuds from these Molestations, of Law. and trouble, when it pleaseth God. the which I have beene in compased with.
~~Surely if they take Highbury from us, what a happines I continue ^a^ sing^le^ life. My Sons welfaire may be reestablishet againe. by Gods blesing for ^on^ my industry. for him./.~~[284]

---

[283] 1 Kings 8:39, 43

[284] This section is struck through with diagonal lines.

[68ʳ] O Heaven be thou the Iudge, of our just Cause. Who ever has a hand in our overthrow. o Lord forgive them all. And send some Marke, some impresion upon them, in mercy, whereby they may aske thee forgivenes.
O God that hast heard the sighing of oppresed widdowes. of helples orphanes heretofore here me at this time./.

Meditation:
O merciful Father. Let me never forget thy testimonies of Conduct. Let them be perpetual assurances thou wilt not forsake me
And what a mercj^,^ful ^Full^ off allay and mitigation,[285] that God did not lay the triall and hazard of our estate, at my First Widdowhood.[286] But hath forbore to six yeares. Shewing me six yeares of his blesing, and tender care over me. greater then the affection of parents, or of any relative. Surely by this sweet method of his correction to me, not laying more upon me then he enabled me by degrees to Bear. Let me stil be satisfied that as my God hath mingled mercy: and protection through every chastisement. will in this also. And here I will acquiese. Not ceasing either my praiers, or industryous dilligence, that if it seemes good in this sight of God. to lend us that pleasant and fruitful Canaan. to posses to his Glory./[287]

[68ᵛ]   1665./
Surely when I consider the pasages of my widdow state, w*h*at a blesing I am to be thankful, I made *th*at resolution to continue seaven yeares.[288] for *th*e perticular esteeme to my D*eare* Friend.[289] And that I have continued almost to that time. And certainly if my sons estate be taken away, I shal begin to take a new Lease of seaven yeares more. if God Almighty spare me so long, For the good of my son, for his wellfaire and resupportation. Noe, noe, Fortune, noe selfe enterist I hope shal prevaile on me for his prejudice. If his estate doe hold he wud not much know my kindnes, If it faile, my love, my affection, my zeale, my honour shal be expressed both to him, his D*eare* Father, and worthy Grandfather,[290] who have a deep obligation ever imprinted in my memory, respects and endeavours. Thus Friends are not known til aduersity, Yet happie itis not to have aduersity to try the generosity of Friends, But to have noe Friends in the Croses of the World is a double Callamity.

---

[285] KA has changed "what a mercj, full of allay and mitigation" to "what a mercyful allay and mitigation" or *vice versa*; her final intention is not clear.

[286] i.e., when KA was first widowed, 31 October 1658.

[287] Canaan is the Promised Land into which the Israelites are delivered, here an analogy for the possession of Highbury and the promise of heaven. See also fol. 76ᵛ.

[288] See Introduction, pp. 15–16, for the significance of seven years.

[289] KA's deceased husband, Thomas.

[290] KA's son, husband, and father-in-law (all Thomas).

| Book M | 117 |

The Lord continue to this poore destitute Family Friends. and above all Friends himself, the vnfailing Friend./.
Let us stil observe that, which can never be too much observed, how Divine providence never failes the innocent./.

[69ʳ]   Meditation   80

12 Six bitter Gusts, blew for six Yeares.[291]
   A Heavenly hand bore through those teares,
   The Clouds of sorrow and griefes storme,
   By Heaven's support receive'd noe harme:
   Rebukes are Bracelets doe enchaine,
   Vs fast to Iesus, and obtaine
   His saveing pity, then when griefe
   Dus represent us smal reliefe.
   We come into his shelter most,
   When strong oppresive repine[292] boast,
   God is not deaf, will surely pay,
   Revenge, who innocents[xxxiii] betwray
   O Lord incline to save that dust
   Who builds on thee, our (stay and)^(onely)^ trust./

O God tho my enemies seek to take aduantage upon my week and destitute and helples condition A woman without Alliance of the Family to help one. Yet o God help me & make me overcome those bands that doe environe me.
They Curse when any Friend speakes for me. & band[293] & threaten them with a Court displeasure But my God can wound with an Arrow suddenly, & sudenly can be removed<.> O God how doe they seek to git by violenc & oppresion. vnder pretence to gratify the kings friends. by such rigour and extortion. surely he that helps those *tha*t can*n*ot help: themselues. wil disapoint there devises/

[69ᵛ]   In Answer to one. why not marry to ease me. of my burdens.   81
O noe Cosen Mariadg should be peaceable. and not stroud[294] with thornes and incumberances. I doe not know w*ha*t regrets might have bin by it. Tis sufficient

---

[291] For further meditations on a six-year period and its significance, see fol. 76ᵛ and note 341, below; also see Introduction, pp. 15–16.
[292] i.e., either repine (discontent, complaint), or rapine (plunder, pillage, robbery).
[293] to join or form into a band or company; to unite, confederate (*OED* v. 4)
[294] i.e., strewed

[xxxiii]   jnnocents

I am able to bear with patienc my self the lose of an estate. becaus biger afflictions And if my children should find lose in their estates. by Gods blesing should be able to make a supply. to them in their great disapointments. Which I could never doe by ingaiging my self away from them
                You might be kind to them also.
O noe I can not vnderstand it. And as I am able to make requital to them without studying designes of Entreaty and commiseration for them. when I have parted with my enterist can render a Compensation./

[70ʳ] Many women have had great Afflictions. Yet sometimes I think, mine out goes them all. But then I turne on to'ther side. to the Favour and conduct of my Heavenly Guardian: his sweet converting every rebuke to a blessed love token.

Was there ever an estate had so many troopes of enemies as ours have, And it may pleas God. their very multitude. and divers enterists. may overthrow one another. And *that* they may conduce[295] to our safety.
My God thy name I bles, that gives me peace, thou art my sure support. These Croses come from thee for my good:

My poor sisters[296] is sorrowful; full of affliction. (she that is far better then I.) Yet her's appeares to present consideration sooner at conclusion then mine have bin. ^Yet^[297] She is like to pas, before she sits quietly downe. with some disrelishing disturbances. And then it may pleas God to give her refreshments. and take off her Fetters./

I pray God grant his peace may fil my heart. and posses my soule, w*h*at ever the men of the world disposses us off: Let my heart be filed with thee, posseset with trust and dependance, with Faith and assurance in Christ, Then wil this disposition be assured peac in all the Callamities that can befal me. or mine.
If we have thy peace o God. tis a peace and Ioy which passeth all vnderstanding[298] (but w*h*at are filed with it)

[70ᵛ] This Divine peace. w*h*ich Gods childrens have in their bosomes, will allay the tempests and inquietudes of this life. It will give Anchor in the violences of vnjust actiones of men.[299] This is the peace my soule above all desieres, Fare rather

---

[295] aid in bringing about, contribute to (*OEDO* v. 5)
[296] *sic*
[297] The insertion seems to apply to the clause following.
[298] Philippians 4:7
[299] See note 402, below.

Book M   *119*

then to be invested in peaceable possesiones, to posses thee. God the Father of ^peac^ God the son the prince of peace, God the holy spirit the[300]

Vpon the interruption of Highbury.
Blesed be the Lord that hath given me a rebuke in this so near Expectation of ours.
And if the monition I received tended to the Death of our estate in stead of me, His name be blessed.
I have found the sweet favour of my God. in all his sharp stroakes. And the result of this will be converted for the best, Let the event be seemingly displeasant

26 March 1665. at *the* Sac*rament*
The Light of Heavens Divine providence hath hitherto been my Splendor, my Luminiary, Therefore shal I not doubt in the darkest Eclipses of this World, he will stil be my assured confidence. This day o Lord I have beged at thy Alter of mercy, for a renewed supportation from thy power, And then let the issue of thinges be w*ha*t they can, if I have thy light to lead me I am safe, even in the midst of all my enemies:[301]

[71ʳ] O God Strengthen my Vnderstanding. and Iudgement, and patience, And if thou hast stroud[302] my way with Thornes, Yet those thornes will be Roses, if they be stroued by thee: Nay if all my way is hedged with Briares and Thornes, if they grow up by thy appointment, for my good, And if I depend on thee, wilt preserve me from being scratchet and tore by them, They are to make me Causcionary and watchful. not to dismay me. For while I am vpon this vail of tears, my breath-g>^ing^ must be sighes. O my God speak peace to my soule, while men doe detraction, and Injuries to us. Let me not baulke any way, thou hast chaulked out for me, stil goe on with Courage w*ha*t ever the difficulties are.
O let me glorify thy name in all the pathes of thy providences. Is the vnfained desier of my soule, Come life, come death, come aduersity. or prosperity. stil I may serve thee, and performe thy will.
Begin: This discourse: p*a*g 33: ending. 39: Begines at pag: 56: to 84:[303]

84

---

[300] This meditation breaks off here. The following meditation, "Vpon the interruption of Highbury," is in slightly smaller and narrower handwriting, suggesting that it is a later addition.

[301] Evocative of Psalm 43:3

[302] i.e., strewed

[303] These references may well be to her own pages in *Book M*, fols. 35ᵛ–41ʳ and 56ᵛ–71ʳ (this page), all of which focus broadly on her "troubles" and providential interpretation of them.

By the perpetual changes we see in this world: God will prepare us for those durable constancies, we shal find for ever in the next./.

[71ᵛ]   Out of a poeme of Doc*ter* Corbets: to his Friend: 85
when she might be a widow:[304]

And as the paphian Queen by her griefs show'r
Brought up her dead Loves Spirit in a Flow'r:[305]
So by those precious drops rain'd from thine eyes,
Out of my dust, o may some vertue rise!
And like thy better Genius thee attend,
Till thou in my dark period shalt end./   See pag: 18:[306]

Certainly if there was such a story of *tha*t Queens grief which brought the comfort of her Lover to her. I may also beleeve some virtue is derived to me from the spirit of my D*eare* Friend.[307] And that That embleeme did convay an influence to me, w*hi*ch my mournful laments, and meditationes drew. Not onely Heavenes Comforts, but his intilligence also:/

O Heaven that has been my guardian, and sent me assistance to a miracle, Leave me not now in this incumberance on me. And I shal resolue to sanctify ^to^ thy great Majesty by all thou dost afford me, and to make them (by thy grace) Laders to clime up to my etternal possesion. I desier thy blesing. They may not Anchor my affections and love on *th*e sandy Foundation of this worlds instability, but serve for a farr more noble intendment.
Make me Lord to know, Why I should live. the end it tends to. And how I should live. that I may be wel instructed. informed, and directed. how to performe *tha*t end w*hi*ch is commanded, By my Creation, my Redemption. o thou holy spirit my
See pag 170[308]

---

[304] KA attributes these lines to Richard Corbett (1582–1635), Bishop of Oxford and of Norwich, and coterie poet. They are, however, from Henry King, "The Legacy" (lines 31–36), which was published in his *Poems, Elegies, Paradoxes, and Sonnets* (1657; 2ⁿᵈ edn 1664). See Introduction, pp. 32–33, for KA's attribution of these lines.

[305] Venus (whose birthplace was believed to be Paphos in Cyprus) is the "paphian Queen," mourning the death of Adonis. Out of her tears, mingling with Adonis's spilt blood, the anemone flower sprang; see Ovid, *Metamorphoses*, X.

[306] See fol. 23ʳ, KA's p. 18, where she has contemplated her deceased husband's ongoing "influence" (and on which she has cross-referenced this page).

[307] KA's deceased husband, Thomas

[308] Page 170 of *Book M* would be fol. 114ᵛ, but KA does not paginate that folio. The reference is likely to be to another volume.

[72ʳ] Sanctifier, Sanctify thy servant to dischardge thy will./ 86
The Last week I attended a Friend of mine, (Cosen Birkenheads Wife. Mr Priers Daughter)³⁰⁹ to her grave. And when I recollect my distemper w*hi*ch began in Feb[ruary] last about *th*e beginning, and continued til the midle of March.³¹⁰ By a violent cold in my head. took away my hearing, my speech, my eye sight. and vappours flew up almost continually, as dessed³¹¹ me in *tha*t manner, I had scarce the benefit of my vnderstanding. This Cold and illnes meeting with troublesome busines *th*e more discomposed me. That I could not tell whether my occasions I had augmented my illnes, or my illnes made my busines so tedious to be endured. And comeing upon *that* time I sometimes had the perswasiones I should dye at. And yet the Lord was pleased to let my Glas run longer, and give a final stop to this sweet good woman. adorned with the graces and true humble virtues of a christian and a Wife. The orriginal of her illnes onely a cold in her head. caused the same effectes as fell to me. in my head: Yet Death became in Earnest to her. and after 3 or 4 dayes the sicknes was contracting at her outward sences. in 2 or 3 dayes more grew violent by convultions, w*hi*ch deprived her of her life. The 3d of Apriel: 1665:/

God hath spared me. and my two sons All three. haveing felt severe effe[c]tes of the sharp winter: And how many gone, and witherd as gras. And their places know them noe more³¹²

The 5t March 1664:³¹³ My Bro*ther* in Law S*i*r Edw*ard* Cropley died.³¹⁴ The same month Litle enfant Rowland Walteres. And, S*i*r Tho*mas* Bides Eldest son of 13 yeares: The 21 Ap*ril* Aunt Wilson :Aged 79: died mother to Cos*en* Samvel Wilson

[72ᵛ]   Of New*ington* Barrow:³¹⁵ hazard: 1665:/   87
If there is such a power can take away that w*hi*ch the Lawes of the Land dus affirme to us. I know noe other remedy, then to prepare my self to work for my liveing, for I must expect all that I have may be gone: And I bles God I shal be able to doe it.

They cannot take away the peace and content of my mind, and that disposition to dispose of my time in a peaceable contentment:

---

[309] It is not clear if there is any connection to Sir John Birkenhead, described on fol. 60ᵛ.

[310] KA is here describing her illness of February–March 1664/5, when she was attending the Committee of Parliament at Westminster. See fol. 61ʳ.

[311] dess: to pile up in layers

[312] Psalm 103:15–16

[313] i.e., 5 March 1664/5

[314] KA's youngest sister, Martha, had married Sir Edward Cropley, second Baronet (John Burke, *A Genealogical and Heraldic History of the Commoners of Great Britain and Ireland*, 4 vols. [London: Henry Colburn, 1838], 4:142).

[315] i.e., Highbury

Gods care hath been over me, and it will be over me stil I trust./

How many Enemies have I to contest with all, And how many parties to satisfy. and to behave my self obliedging too. Direct me my God./

Lord how are they increased that trouble me? Many are they that rise up against me.[316]
Lord hide thy servant from the Insurrection of vnjust men. Who whet their tongue like a sword, to divide and cut away our Iust estate. They encourage themselues in an evill matter, and lay snares by a secreet combination. But thou o lord art a sheild for me, My Glory, My Riches, and the lifter up of mine head against them all:[317] So *that* in thee I will not be afraid if they multiply to tenthousands that set themselues against me round about. If thy gracious providenc arises and [73ʳ] saves me:[xxxiv] | Then am I sure of thy best blesing: And lead me o Lord in thy rightousnes. because of mine enemies,[318] Make thy way straight before my face, Thy Way of the Wise Providence let me vnderstand, which can convert the Victory my opposers may have to see thy favour leaves me not, To excercise my Faith thou wilt be a refuge for the oppressed, a refuge in times of trouble;[319] Let me ever trust in thee, since in all ages, Thou hast not forsaken them who depends on thy promises. and seekes thee with a true sincere heart./. read 27 Salme./.

What shall I say of my foregoeing Felicities. I found of that Ioyful intimation of my soveraignes restoration in a Dreame.[320] B*ook* K: pag 207:[321] And shal it be that my Lord and Kings comeing in must prove a fatal blast to our Estate. It cannot be. Yet if we are condemned by his Cleere Iudgement (and not by the violence of our craveing Aduarsaries) I submit. Since he is returned in peace I sacrifice life and Fortune. And Let that blesing on a Dying Nation Take all that I can offer.

[73ᵛ]   Of Eng*lish* and Duch Quarrel: 1665[322]
I pray God compose an agreement, and Vnione betweene both Nationes.

---

[316] Psalm 3:1
[317] Echoes Psalm 27:6
[318] Psalm 27:13
[319] Psalm 9:9
[320] i.e., the restoration of Charles II, 1660
[321] See fol. 97ᵛ for a further dream recorded in Book K.
[322] The second Anglo-Dutch War, which was declared in May 1665 and concluded at the Treaty of Breda, 21 July 1667.

[xxxiv] Catchword: Then

Tis pity. that honest industry. should receive a. punishment. And tis also vnworthy That, That Nation should prove a Viper. to eat out the boweles of the Mother which has feed and nourishet it. The english nation haveing bin the instrument of the Duches subsistance, and greatnes. (And) How did they in their deplored condition When the Spaniard governd them vnder bloody Masters. who made spoil of their people, ~~insulting over~~ ^by^ the Cruelty did by Duke D'alua. who braged he had excequted eighte[e]n thousand by the hand of the common excequtioner.[323] And Yet it was their opinion they did not vse cruelty enough. Then it was they made their misserable Laments knowne to Queen Elizabeth (who was the Ballance to turne the Scale of Europe) she adheard to their partie and delieverd them from the Spanish insultement.

O ingratitude well mayst thou be termed a monstrous vice. Now prosperity hath out worne those humble submisions, and received benefits. Now you vnworthy Nation are become Injurious and insolent to your obliedged benefactors. who created you./.

On the battel at sea: Iune 1666:[324]

Every one in these sad encounters prayes & desieres a perticular prosperity: One that the Hollander & French prevaile, And we that the English: My prayer is that a vniversal victory may be obtained. and that all parties may be ready to comply to amity & detest the fury of blood & slaughter of Mankind.[325]

[74ʳ] Vpon Gods giveing me health.   90

Surely o God when I was attended with discomposeing infirmities. and had a Multitude of occasions. I complained with a kind of dispair, I could hardly overcome what was vpon me. Well might it be very burdensome, for when we consider the waight of sicknes, tis the greatest affliction of Nature. and when attended with another waight of difficult Matters to negotiate. In a season of Sharp weather. was an accumulated heap of Tryals. from these God hath gave me a suspencion. and restored me to my health. hath exceedingly assisted me and delievered me (tho for a time) out of the perplexities and made my way easy to me againe. and laid aside those agitations of my minde

---

[323] Don Fernando Álvarez de Toledo y Pimentel, 3rd Duke of Alba (1507–1582), who governed the Spanish Netherlands between 1567 and 1573, and executed thousands of people. KA's source is Fuller, "The life of Duke D'Alva," *Holy and Profane State*, 509.

[324] The Four Days' Battle, 1–4 June 1665

[325] "Mankind" is written on the bottom of the next folio, fol. 74ʳ (across a single opening). The following lines have also been added to spare space at the bottom of fol. 74ʳ, and are clearly related to the end of this meditation (although a slight change in the thickness of the ink suggests they may have been added at a later date): "How shal we hide our selues vnder those stormes of Callamity, and Scenes of these miseries of Mankind. but vnder thy winges o Lord./"

praised be the God of my help:
read 7 Salmes caled the Hallelujahs. before 119:[326]

[74ᵛ]   :Vpon my jewel:/.[327]   91

Surely in *th*e sparkes of this Iem I can see the sparkes and shinings of Gods love dart out to me.

O that I may waight at his Alter, all the dayes of my life, and pay my vowes which I have made to him when I was in trouble.[328]

And tho I have pased that time I expected some issues of Divine providence wud perticular attend me, and be explained to me: I may stil waight, and stil learne to be assured, as a propitious hand hath bin my attendant. all the yeares of my afflictions

And in a most supporting maner at *th*e conclusion of that time, when sickenes and opposition meet together; (And then I was defended):

O that I may find the same protecting guard in every remaynder Moment of my life, Then shal I not onely find This Embleeme as an Ambassador of peace to me formerly, but in the future too:

Nor let me think my observations have bin vaine and fruteles. Not significant and I vseful to me, The issues all along hath bin gracious. And the event ful of the good pleasure of my God: And God hath spared me my life. And gave a Coun-

[75ʳ] termand that he wud spare it. That he wud excercise me with | afflictions, for the 92
tryal of my submision and reliance on him. *tha*t with Iob I might trust in him.[329]

And it may be God hath a further end to serve of me, ~~And~~ that I should live to praise his name as Iob and Hezekiah did.[330] Altho Satan endeavourd to make the Faith of the first to faile: And Death brought ill news to the later. God was glorified in both:

And as Isack lay at the Alter.[331] So did my life lye a Sacrifice at the Will of my God: And if it had pleased him to take it away; my children lay almost helples; and their Fortunes at the Arbitrary Will of enemyes, and incroachers: This was

---

[326] The Alleluia psalms are the twenty psalms of the Hebrew psalter in which this acclamation occurs, Psalms 104–6; 110–18; 134–35; 145–50 (see Robert F. Taft, "Christian Liturgical Psalmody: Origins, Development, Decomposition, Collapse," in *Psalms in Community: Jewish and Christian Textual, Liturgical, and Artistic Traditions*, ed. Harold W. Attridge and Margot E. Fassler [Atlanta: Society of Biblical Literature, 2004], 7–32). KA is most likely referring to Psalms 112–118. See also fol. 77ʳ.

[327] See also fols. 12ʳ, 76ʳ, 92ʳ, 108ᵛ–109ʳ for this "providential jewel."

[328] Psalm 66:13–14

[329] KA's dream of monition is a countermand of an earlier dream; see fol. 21ʳ and note 79, above.

[330] See note 80, above, for Hezekiah.

[331] Genesis 22:1–13

Book M   *125*

to try my Faith, ~~and~~ To surrender them and my self. to him ^To hide^ the Blesed guardian of orphanes. To him *that* hath spared my life for his glory, To him *that* could have raised ^up^ Isackes. out of *th*e dust vnto Abaraham.

To that most merciful God. that hath chastened me sore, but not given me over vnto Death by its waight. That hath countermanded I should not dye but live, and declare the workes of the Lord:[332] Let my heart o God be fited and set in tune to chaunt the actes of thy favour shewed me, And to bring forth the fruits of amendment of life, since thou hast enlarged a Longer date to it: Nor was Heze-
[75ᵛ] kiahs death foretold | to him by a plainer demonstration then I had: For w*hat* 93 could be more certaine. to perswaide my self of the reality; then the agreement there was of my Husbands age. and mine to be the same. at the periode of the time Limited to live:[333]

So was the Counterintimation the same. as to Hezekiah. Nay I received it by a wonderful providence ascertained to me in the words the prophet David Spoake: corresponding to those of *t*h*e* pro*phet* Esay: which were sent to hezekiah.[334]

Has my God lengthend out my threed of life; and am I to tel his wonderful workes. that others may see them as well as I:[335] Open my lipes o God. and my mouth shal shew forth thy praise,[336] Direct me I may spend my time, thankfully and vsefully, Yet since itis not in the power of man to direct his way,[337] not in the ability of my frailty to ~~set~~ exalt thy goodnes. Not in my ^weeke^ Courage and Constancy to ^goe over^ over come the Briares and thornes. the snares and temptations of this life. w*h*ich if we pase over them with patience and courage, with meekenes and resignation with acquiesment and addres. then we come nearest to the Commands of God. O thou the helper of the destitute instruct me. to those ends. / see book: I: 89:[338]

[76ʳ] Some persons may think me void of ordinary vnderstanding to make so much 94 of a Trivial thing of so smal extern value.[339] Yet it cannot invalid my eminent

---

[332] Psalm 118:17. KA is here referring to her dream of monition, fol. 21ʳ.

[333] KA believed that she would live only to the age that her husband did (see note 79, above); that is, thirty-six years, two months, and twenty-one days (fol. 1ʳ). This is one reason that she attributes significance to seven years of widowhood, as she was twenty-nine years old when widowed. See also note 341, below; and see Introduction, pp. 15–16.

[334] Psalm 118:17, which echoes and inverts the words of Isaiah to Hezekiah in 2 Kings 20:1–6. See note 80, above, for Hezekiah.

[335] Perhaps an echo of Psalm 107

[336] Psalm 51:15

[337] Echoes Proverbs 16:9

[338] "O thou . . . see book: I: 89" has been added to the end of this page in a different ink.

[339] i.e., the jewel; see note 327, above.

esteeme. For sure I may very well place that Embleeme as a Hand tha and Figure that relateth and expreses. Aduersity. and prosperity.[340]
In aduersity that therein a Divine hand wil send me relieve and supportation. strength and patience
It lookes at prosperity too. Notwithstanding so many occasions of incumbent expenses. so much. as If all that I had coming in might been to the defrayment I had not bin accounted prodigal.
But to my own admiration how it could be, have I bin bleset with bountiful encreasing portions in the midst of obstacles.
Much of this in the beginning was insinuated to me. But the event declares plainer. And as I have pased extrordinary troubles and greviances. as w*h*at woman more. and goe through with so litle outward dismay or did not seek a shelter by a second marriag.
Also for blesings w*h*at woman. nay or man can tel the like. (^with^out Marchandize help. or a Trade). as I. But not to me: But the great God hath done it./

[76ᵛ] (Perhapes) ^who knowes. but^ God in his providenc sent me 6 yeares of trouble 95 to prepare and fit me for the bountiful and prosperous blesing God was makeing ready for me and for my son.[341] An estate that might well be six and thurty yeares in waighting for.[342] and six yeares in Learning how to receive and entertaine the blesing to enter into *t*he land of Canan a rich soile flowing with milk and honey:[343] siluer and Gold: And to me who had once the Interist to Injoy it longer then I shall. God thought fit to put me bye. But hath provided for me another plentiful Fortune. O that I may know how to be sufficiently thankfull and know how to manage so great favours of Gods providence:/

[77ʳ]   See Medi*tation* in Parchment book. P*ag* 73: on my 36t yeare: 96
    This on my 37th Aprile 30th 1665: being Sabbath day:[344]

God Allmighty hath bin pleased to ade another year to my life. and made my 36 now thiurty seaven. yeares. And tho those yeares are paset ^Wee know^ time

---

[340] See KA's later meditation on prosperity and adversity, based on John Donne's funeral sermon for Sir William Cokayne (fol. 91ᵛ).

[341] KA meditates repeatedly on a six-year period of troubles, to be followed by deliverance in the seventh, a belief in which she associates herself with Job (see Job 5:19). See, for example, fols. 62ʳ, 69ʳ, 99ᵛ; and especially 102ᵛ–103ʳ; and see Introduction, pp. 15–16.

[342] The lease period on Highbury coincides with KA's thirty-six years of life. See note 173, above.

[343] Exodus 3:8, 17; Exodus 13:5. See also fol. 68ʳ and note 287, above.

[344] i.e., KA's birthday is 30 April 1628

pased, lookes like the Arrow that is flowne, like the simillitudes of swiftenes, frequently recounted: And though my yeares ^are^ gone And I can never more recall a day backe againe, much more a year: Yet o my soule every day resolue with the Salmist.³⁴⁵ to bles thee (o God): And every year for this patiente forbearance of me, for thy bounty, for thy tender providence over me, Therefore wil I praise thy name for ever and ever.

And as in that 147th Salme of the recital of Gods acts of munificence to David: so in the last Salme but one.³⁴⁶ in one of those victorious Salmes of praises which crownes the whole book.³⁴⁷ He incites to give praise for our birth. Let Israel rejoyce in him that made him. Let the children of Zion be Ioyful in their King.³⁴⁸ Nay and let my soule and my body too, Every Faculty of soule. every member of my body, sing vnto my God that hath made me. (and) Where of this day is the annual ^com^memory^ation^ of my birth and being Blesed be my God he hath done soe much for me, whereof I am glad: O that the high praises of my God ever be in my mouth,³⁴⁹ ˣˣˣᵛ | that hath lent me another year, Ending upon his day of praise. Nor dus it onely finish up this last yeare. This day which my redeemer hath celebrated for his praise. This day is the commencement of a new year to me. which as it represents my birth. my comeing into this world. so let this new beginning, incite my liveing well, and vsefully in the world. whereof I now am incorporated into it by so many yeares past, and am become an obliedged person. to performe those duties commanded from my Creator, To my soule my body. to my perticular relatives and General.

Not Let me be troubled o God. my yeares spin so fast away, and are increased to more then halfe the age of man,³⁵⁰ which how few arrives to this account pased. and how fewer number to that which nature in some have attained: of this later date, noe Art, noe certainty, noe assurance, no positive demonstration can make out to me, for another year. Noe they cannot command the cassualties, the Constellations of one day, of one hower to be confined:†³⁵¹

My Conclusion to this meditaiton shal be. with panting desiers. That every day of my life may | redound to the Glory of that Great God who^se^ ~~hath~~ I am (by his grace) and who hath made me. Then if my time is concluded sooner or later,

---

³⁴⁵ The Psalmist, David
³⁴⁶ i.e., Psalm 149
³⁴⁷ Psalms 145–50. See note 326, above.
³⁴⁸ Psalm 149:2
³⁴⁹ Psalm 149:6
³⁵⁰ i.e., 70 years; KA is now 37.
³⁵¹ Dotted lines here indicate a link to the passage at the foot of fol. 78ʳ, dated 30 April 1666 (that is, one year after the current meditation).

ˣˣˣᵛ Catchwords: that hath

I know it shall be in the most proper and seasonable time finished when it comes by his appointement who hath all times in his hand,[352] who hath my perticular detirmination in his keeping. To whom be the glory and honour of all his commiserations. to me. and of this year pased. On this day of his praises, bles the Lord, and for ever more praise his name./[353]

~~Within the Compas of a yeare I could reckowne that~~ The one and thurtieth year of my life, was at the First year of my Widdowhood: And now the 37th yeare of my life: is in the seaventh year of my Widdowhood:

†[354]This 30th of A*pr*iel 1666: in the recital of the dangers this year. I may well ade and apply to that obseruation of the last year:[355] For the cassaualties I haue pased in this is a clear demonstration to me That it was not possible to foretel w*h*at might be, or to preuent the dangers depending on us. O God we cannot: It belonges to the glory of thy prouidence our delieuerance is wrought by thee.[xxxvi]
[continues on fol. 79ʳ]

[78ᵛ]   To rejoyce in God: a Duty in all Conditions   99
My God let me be assured, w*h*at ever ruged path thou hast desingned and dictated for me to pas if I trust in thee thou wilt make that hard way pleasant.
If I doe not trust in thee I shal be consumed.
O Lord posses my heart my affections with that cheerful disposition of Ioy w*hi*ch thou requierest and Commandest. to deport my self in every estate always to rejoyce. And tho Sin is bitter, and hath a waight to sinke into the greatest sadnes. Altho afflictiones are grevious, and w*h*at is grevious must be displeasant. Yet since ~~of~~ o my Saviour thou dost afford so gracious a remedy for sinners thy most pretious bloud to absolue and reconcile to thee. Since in our greatest suffarance in this world, in our most sharp rebukes. thou dost afford Faith and patience and hope. how can it but their must

---

[352] Echoes Psalm 31:15

[353] Echoes Psalm 149:3

[354] Dotted lines here indicate a link to the point on fol. 77ᵛ, indicated. The additional meditation which begins here continues on fol. 79ʳ, suggesting that it was added to blank space after the meditation on fol. 78ᵛ.

[355] KA appears to meditate on her birthday each year; see the heading to fol. 77ʳ, which refers to a meditation in another of her books in 1664 ("on my 36t yeare"). See Introduction, pp. 5 and 42.

[xxxvi] Catchwords: And in

needs be Joy. Joy in the forgivenes of our sines. Ioy thou dost convert Sorrowes of this life to fit us for a Crowne of glory.
A ^true^ christian has these two groundes for his Joy. and that he is of the true Faith./
Who was a greater Sinner then St paul:
Who was a greater sufferer then he. And w*ha*t Saint did ever exceed him in his Ioyes in christ./.

[79ʳ] And in that day of my near dissolution, was thy ready safeguard found. I now can ade another reccord of the fauour Heauen allowes to me. To bles his name for this yeares mighty preseruation to me and to mine. Low death was stroud[356] all the way before me, accidental and epidemical. We haue bin rescued from *th*e raging pestilence *tha*t deuoured thousands. We are suruiveing Mounuments of Heauens perticular Loue.
Let me and mine make it a birth day to us all. Growing in Obedience, growing in thankfulnes. Or if we doe not those heapes of Mortality wil rise up and be our condemnation. We might haue bin part of their admonition. They now are ours. O God giue us Grace to improue all thy monitions. My perticular delieueranc from apparent death. and from Contagious plague. Let us Remember how emenintly thy fauour hath bin our hiding place. 100

[79ᵛ] May. 20 If the parliam*ent* takes away our estate. who are to sit in Iune next:/[357] 101

Blesed Alderman (Highlord)[358] How doe I revere thy memory, who wast the Foundation in a great part: of my second and later Fortune; (My own Fathers being the happy instrument to raise me to my Marriage without other assistance:[)][359] Yet by Gods prosperous blesing by the second addition I received.[360] will make repaire if the violence of vnjust persons bereive this Family w*hi*ch I am grafted in,[361] of w*ha*t is their Iust due, and Honourable expectation. If they take away 40ty pleasant Feilds from us. Situated in a Fertile Soile.[362] We have about 40 Considerable Houses placed in an aduantagious ground. standing in a plot of

---

[356] i.e., strewed

[357] i.e., June 1665. See fol. 84ᵛ; and Introduction, p. 11.

[358] KA's stepfather, John Highlord; see Introduction, pp. 7–8.

[359] KA's father, Robert Wilson, provided well for his orphaned children; see Introduction, pp. 6–7.

[360] KA's description, below, and later references make it clear that this "second addition" is "the Swan my buildings," referred to on fol. 90ʳ; see note 426, below, and Introduction, p. 13.

[361] KA's family by marriage, the Austen family.

[362] See "On the Situation of Highbury," line 1 (fol. 104ʳ).

the same likenes as *tha*t Land is. I may well esteeme it parrallel in situation to it. That Land hath Feilds of each side a rode, or Lane, And this hath houses of each side a Lane or street.

Let our enemies doe their worst. I cannot but infinitely wonder (how) God Almighty onely makes exchange. to us. both comeing in their profits out together:[363] My building may be perfected at Mic*h*aelmas next. when Highbury was to come to our possesion. (if we should hath both given to us. surely it wud be a blesing bigger then (we were fit for.) or) we could receive.)

[80ʳ] Fortune doe thy worst, I am not in thy power. Not in the hands of hab nab[364] of 102 thy blind Lottery. that cannot distine any thing to the wertuous. Noe I am in the hands of an especiall providence, w*h*ich differs as much from thy gifts. as Virtue dus from wice. as truth from falshood: This shal truly satisfy me, as w*ha*t I have did come by the blesing of God: so w*ha*t may be lost comes by his permistion too. I shall not murmur nor procure Curses who ever is the possesor of w*ha*t was ours. that a blast and Caterpiller may deuoure it.[365] Tis sufficient He that wrongs the Fatherles, the Widowes, and oppreses innocent persons. Heaven has made Lawes from *th*e worlds Creation, and since that time. (From the Cruelty to Abel) hath bin enforced by all the wiolences commited That noe true prosperity is intailed to vnjust attainements. I may be sure that a litel w*h*ich the rightous hath, is better then the proud reuennues of Vsurpers.   †107:[366]

O Heaven give me thy especial grace, w*ha*t ever my Condition is. I may demeane my self with sobriety and patience. I may see w*ha*t thou hast bountifully bestowed on me. may retard all vnevennes of spirit. may vanquish that vnquiet temper of revenge. and molestation, May Conquer all weakeneses of passion, all [80ᵛ] clamors of discontent. and the frailty of my sex.[xxxvii] | knowing God is my Aduo- 103 cate. God is my portion and my inheritance.[367] Not onely my Etternal, but by his exceeding blesing my temporal also. to the wonder of all Spectators:

O that I may have that true charity, not to pray against my enemies but for them. Since God is ready of himself to hear oppresed persons. Tho they make noe Colliques,[368] tho they vent noe sighes, tho ~~they~~ noe teares of distresed orphanes water the groundes which the power of violences commandes away. God will hear in Heaven. and o *tha*t he may hear to convince the wrong doer. of that

---

[363] See fol. 109ᵛ for this hope as a miscalculation.
[364] hab nab: get or lose, hit or miss, succeed or fail (adverb, or quasi-noun) (*OEDO*)
[365] Echoes Psalm 78:46
[366] See KA's p. 107 (fol. 82ᵛ).
[367] Echoes Psalm 16:5
[368] i.e., colloquies

---

xxxvii Catchword: Knowing

most hanious sin of oppresion, (The sin and scourge of all ages.) that Our thuirsty craveing aduarsaries may not violate justice, and ^devoure^ that w*hi*ch the Iust Lawes of purchase hath assured ^vn^to us:
O that God may hear to convince the wrongdoer in to a reconciliation to himself: And how ever they succeed in this world, it may not be a snare to their Family. or ruine to their etternal estate./

Lord now I walke in the midst of trouble doe thou revive me. Stretch thy hand out against the vnjust purposes of my enemies and let thy right hand save me.[369] Thy gracious providence that in many former triales hath bin merciful to me. o now be merciful to thy poore Creature./[370]

[81ʳ] Vpon 25 May 1665. the receiveing a writ to goe to trial at the shut[371] of Sister 104 Austen agen me for the compasing[372] the Red Lion to her. And to make me pay £600 her husband hath tied that estate to pay it with all.[373] A while after, I was reading the 120 Salme. In my distres I cried to the Lord and he heard me.[374] And doe these words relate any thing to me in this occasion. Is a shuite of Law? properly a distres? Truly it might have bin a great distres if it had bin all that we have. Yet while we have so many pretenders to take away far more then that, dus encreas a biger regard to this And while itis one of those troubles w*hi*ch ^Iob reckowns^ springes out of the dust.[375] may come within that Comprisement: Since itis from those persons which a few yeares since was in confederacy & amity with me. from them w*hi*ch could the testatour[376] who confered a present enterist to them knowne their persequting vnkindneses. they could not have excercised their ~~anger~~^will^. But it must suffice me he could not discerne how

---

[369] Psalm 138:7

[370] See Psalm 138:7–8

[371] i.e., suit (lawsuit)

[372] compassing: contriving, devising (*OEDO*)

[373] KA engaged in extended wrangling with Susanna Austen, the widow of her brother-in-law John Austen, over the Red Lion, an estate in Fleet Street in the parish of St. Dunstan's in West London. See fols. 45ʳ, 64ᵛ, 81ʳ–83ᵛ, 108ʳ, 109ᵛ, 111ᵛ, and 113ʳ; and see Introduction, pp. 11–13. National Archives, C10/96/1 is a Bill of Complaint from KA against Susanna Austen regarding the Red Lion and the sum of £600 which is owed in legacies to family members and associates. The document is, however, dated May and October 1666 (it is misdated May 1665 in the National Archives catalogue); it therefore relates to a later stage of the dispute on which KA reflects here.

[374] Psalm 120:1; KA begins this text in a slightly larger font, differentiating it from the text around it.

[375] Job 5:6

[376] KA's brother-in-law, John Austen.

they wud be injurious.^xxxviii^ Neither can they discover who will rise up here after to be their molestation. These troubles, these enemies they spring out of the dust and we cannot discerne them. Yet tho we cannot see them, he that orders and disposes for the good of his children dus know of them. and if we learne to salute the Chastisement it wil be a beneficial one^xxxix^

[81ᵛ] Now surely tis by this way holy David prescribes me if I wud have a blesing in my distres tis to cry to the Lord that he may hear me and order it to his Glory. 105
In my distres I cried to the Lord and he heard me.[377]
My God hath heard me in my many former distreses. That were ponderous and waighty. And if he brings new[378] how may my Confidence depend my God will order it for the best how ever it succeed.
Verse : : Not without ground may I continue my praier with David. to be delieverd from a deceitful tongue.[379] Who hath made more faire promises to doe good to this ^our^ Family then he: (Winstanly):[380] and by flatering words deluded me into a Frindship to serve some avaritious designe. which lasted but a litle while. And now breakes out into open treachery. and Injustice, encroaching all that he can to his Family which is the propriety belongs to the Right of another. invading the enterist of an Orphan,[381] and I may say robing the dead, and the concernment of three persons in their graves. (viz: H: H: B:)[382] The liveing think they see them noe more and therefore may doe as they please: I know not how to dispute it. Yet for my part I am affraid of my actions and therefore Iealous they may be such as all may behold them. And I am sure the God of Heaven sees all.

[82ʳ] The CXXI: Salme:[383] tels me what I shal find if I lift up my eyes to the hills: 106
whence cometh all my help: a help that will not suffer my feet to be moved if I stand in his wayes. a keeper will preserve me when I cannot see, to defend my selfe. And in the shades of darknes will be Light. in the heate of day be my shelter. In all those perils and evils which is for his glory. which is for my benefit. he wil preserve my soule. out of them: For temporal delievarances they are not

---

[377] Psalm 120:1

[378] i.e., new distresses

[379] Psalm 120:2

[380] Susanna Austen's father, James Winstanley, formerly the steward of Highbury for KA's husband. See Introduction, p. 12.

[381] KA's son Thomas. See fol. 83ᵛ, below.

[382] I have been unable to determine the identities of these three people.

[383] The paragraph which follows paraphrases Psalm 121. KA has progressed directly from a meditation on Psalm 120 to a meditation on Psalm 121.

---

^xxxviii^ jnjurious

^xxxix^ Catchword: now

comparable to his gracious supportations through those dangers. & temptations to be sustained:
I wud faine know upon this Trial my Sister & her Father[384] hath with me whether with a good Conscience and vpright intentions they can lift up their hearts for a blesing for the succes. I dare not Iudge. it a Self acquseing act. I shal have that Charity to my sister in Law. (tho can not have to her Father by reason of his protestations to doe all the offices of love and Frindship to our Family. When his actions speaks a ruine to it). For her. her Iudgement may be falsely informed: and her duty wrongly inforced.
I shal construe it an errour in Iudgement./
O God pardon the mistakes and vnkindneses in her. And forgive also the errours in my actions, in somethings when I doe ill. I think them wel, and am not ready to see their depravity. so run into them with a Consent./.

[82ᵛ]   On the trial:[385]   107

My heart desiers to resigne the events of this world to Gods blesed pleasure. O God give me more patience. more resignation and Charity. More of those humble graces of submision and obediance. For these will defend me ^and^ regulate me from murmuring and envy. at w*h*at she[386] hath. or may have:/ The issue of their pretentions is now at hand. They may have more from us, and their desiers may be granted. Let me not have les of thy favour and protection. nor my son.[387] And how happy I hear this day from his Tutor of his sobriety and temperance[388] Rather o God let him loose all that this world can give then loose that or thy grace to carry and fit him to a Heavenly inheritance.

† pag 102:[389] It is possible to be wronged, & defeated & put by his right by Injustice, fraud, or a strong hand
Isah: 10 Woe unto them that decree vnrightous decrees. and that writ grivious thinges w*h*ich they haue prescribed. to take away the right from the poor, that widowes may be their prey, & that they may rob the Fatherles.[390]

---

[384] Susanna Austen and James Winstanley.
[385] The trial with Susanna Austen over the Red Lion (see note 373, above).
[386] Susanna Austen
[387] KA's eldest son, Thomas
[388] For KA's son's Oxford education, see also fols. 43ʳ–44ᵛ, 99ᵛ, 114ᵛ.
[389] See fol. 80ʳ (KA's p. 102). This passage has been added to blank space at the bottom of fol. 82ᵛ, which is otherwise only half-used.
[390] Isaiah 10:1–2

[83ʳ] The 30th May: the day before the Trial.[391] 108
O thou Natural vice of Envy: How ready to be filed with it. Especially to a Compettitor. To one of Yesterday started up in our Family to intercept a faire Fortune from us. How ready wil this ill temper carry us out to disrelishes to prevaile more and more: by evil wishes and desieres.
But o thou spirit of sanctity, spirit of peace and *th*e Dove posses and fil and governe every disposition. drive away all rancourous and swelling grutches[392] from me. Let me truly say Thy Will be done in all the affaires of this World.
If their designe is bad, I may the better hope for succes. Yet itis not the first time a good Cause was knowne to suffer.
But Yet My God. If I sin not against thee by my takeing Offence at the victory my vnkind disturber may receive. She can have noe triumph over me, Nor I can have noe lose./.

[83ᵛ]   On the succes to us. of that shuite.[393] 109
The Iudges this day have sentenced for us.
And such is the long progres and Art of Law, That after twelve Termes formality and busines to excercise that trade. The Case was dispatched by six Lawiers & the Iudges in a quarter of an hower.
Yet surely I may conclude if that vniversal Iudge above had not at the beginning prevented. They might have obtained their desier. But far may it be from me to rejoyce in the Death of that enfant[394] The real esteeme to her Father denies it. And I hope noe evil desier in me was to her. for I was ready to deliever those writings w*h*ich was her due. when *th*e Granfather[395] came and demanded them the day before she died. and I had promised him he should have them when he se~~s~~ ~~t~~ sent for them. But before that time came a messenger brought word of her Death. Thus by the prevention of a few howeres. The obtayning the Lease w*h*ich was the ground of the quarrel remaynd in my hands. And the Law presently decided. That the Lease was fit to continue with me for the preservation of his enterist to whom it did belong./.[396]

---

[391] The lawsuit with Susanna Austen over the Red Lion (see note 373, above).
[392] i.e., grudges
[393] i.e., suit (lawsuit); the lawsuit with Susanna Austen over the Red Lion.
[394] John and Susanna Austen's daughter, Katherine; see Introduction, p. 12.
[395] James Winstanley
[396] KA is here refering to the title and lease documents for the Red Lion, which she refused to hand over to Susanna Austen; the first Chancery documents relating to this dispute date from 1662 (National Archives, C10/78/1). See Introduction, pp. 9–13.

[84ᵛ] Iune 16: 1665: on L: Barks shuite³⁹⁷ with me for H*ighbury*³⁹⁸ 111
    Meditation
13 Thy Favour most great Lord thy favour shew
   Then will these^my^ frequent troubles over blow
   Then will these molestations which I find
   Turne to a peaceful harbour in my minde.
   Noe perturbations ever can remove
   My chief affections from thy sublime love.
   Come then my Lord, and sanctify what falls
   A Low submision fites me for thy Call's.
   So shall all Crosses weave into a Crowne
   If thou my Iesu stiles me for thy own
   O doe not leave me when I am deprest
   With humaine deluges, in thee have rest.
   Noe weight so heavy But can make it light
   When thy supportment beares me in the fight
   And Strong temptations then with all its darts.
   Not wound my soule when thy bright aid imparts.

[85ʳ] 14 What makes me mellancholy. what black cloud 112
   Dus intercept my peace, dus me inshroud.
   And entertaines me with the shades of night
   Is all thy splended favours darkened quite
   Where is the signal ~~markes~~^smiles^ did oft display
   In great Ecclipses, joy did reconvay
   Those radiant markes^~~signes~~^, which when I sat alone
   Did seeme a Heaven, so much glory showne.
   And am I now inveloped in feare
   And former ravishments forget to heare
   O God my sin, Tis my diclining Soule
   Flies from thy Alter. To the world's dus roule.
   A Leethe Stupefaction from that snare
   Creating much vnnecessary care
   Restore me ~~Iesy~~ Iesu: that live saveing balme
   That^as^ these discordancies may ever Calme.

---

   ³⁹⁷ i.e., suit (lawsuit). I have not been able to establish the identity of "L: Barks."
   ³⁹⁸ See fol. 79ᵛ; and Introduction, p. 11.

[85ᵛ]   Not to doubt of a God: 113
Let us not be startled by the variety of Religions and opiniones in the world. But let us a beleever that hath God and christ and the holy spirit. Goe on in a firme assurance of Comfort, and not doubt of his religion. That the ground is tradition and Education. For ^by^ the lively and infalliable assurances of the Almighties succours and assistances. of his favour and tendar regard over them who flye to him for refuge. May Convince of the truth of such Religion. Which I have found. As well as Abram and Isack: As well as David: and St Peter and St Paul. As well as Ester and Iudeth and Deborah./.

One troubled his Frend was like to Dye. Answerd
To dye is not to be lost. our conversation & vnion hereafter will be more entire and inseperable.
But S*ir* to live to serve God.
There is noe comparison betwixt a Saint and a Sinner

[86ʳ]   On the sickenes.[399]   114
15
O let me fly to thee, vnto thee still,
A Rocke. of shelter in approaching ill
Such have I found thee, my great God supreame
In seaven Long winters thy light was my beame
To guide my way, and poize[400] me in my straight
Paphed[401] in obscurity, a ponderous waight
Still was thy glory such a staf of rest
As every accident became the best
I cannot be dismaed when have thy guard
Itis a Convoy in what seemeth hard.
Itis a ship, tho rolling on the waves
Steeres to a harbour and avoides its graves.
My part on providence to Anchor still
Nor can these billowes of this world be ill.[402]

O God Send the voyce of joy and health in those sad dwellinges that have it not. And Continue joy and gladnes in those dwellings w*hi*ch yet have it./

---

[399] This is the first of KA's many meditations on the Great Plague outbreak of 1665–66. See Introduction, pp. 31, 35–36.
[400] i.e., poise: ballast (*OEDO*, v. 4b)
[401] KA's meaning here is not clear.
[402] Echoes Psalm 107:23–30. See also fols. 38ʳ, 62ᵛ-63ʳ, 70ᵛ, 109ʳ, and 112ᵛ.

[86ᵛ]   On Sickenes.

O God thou hast excercised thy servant long in Sorrowes. Yet thou hast more Darts. the Darts of Pestilential death. which if it be thy will deliever us from.
That putrid disease which infects the Air. and makes the Air breath death and mortality on us.
Which in its nature dus health and refreshment.
O God direct thy servant where I should be. and where my children for their safety.
O God Give us thy grace. and thy grace wil give us thy glory.
Stay thy hand o Lord And let not thy Iudgments be disperced in the Air. That every breath we receive may not be a distructive breath./

Here is a time of Tryal of our Faith. of resigning my self to God. Hath not God bin a hiding place and sequrity to me in almost 7 yeares of my solitarines. Surely in this publick distres I am encouraged to trust in him to fly to him. God can make this place I am in to be a <G>oar[403] a defence to me. Yet I must know that in this world all things fals alike to all men

[87ʳ] the plague is the more emediate hand of God then any correction. O God let me not thinke to shun thy hand. but that it can find me out in all places. nor let me dread thy hand. Since this world is a weeping place. and Ioyes are in the next.

Dus this present time of Genneral Callamity threaten los of our lifes. And then the lose we may receive from men wil not be sighed for.
Surely if Gods eminent providenc doe guard us from the distroying Angel.[404] And from the vsurping Devil of this world. And that he bring us to confidence agen after terrour. O God Let us not think we have Cut the winges of our temporal aduarsaries or of Death. For God can bring us as long as we are in this life to conditions ful of vncertaintys and we shal be insequer and tosed on the point of danger til we doe arrive at that everlasting haven of peace./

The Lord have compassion on these Multitudes of people that are took away ^dayly^ in whole Families and sweept by troopes to a sudden grave. Exchange their toilsome condition in much mercy Then will they be happier then if they were transfered to be Kings and Princes in this world./[405]

---

[403] KA's initial letter here is atypical. Possibly "Goar," i.e., gore, a stop in a river (*OEDO* n. 4; obs).

[404] 1 Chronicles 21:12

[405] This last paragraph is added in smaller handwriting, apparently at a later time.

[87ᵛ] Gods time of delieverance is the best, the most seasonablest that. he chooseth. 117 From that Sharp temporal Callamity of Plague and Pestilence. And so is that time the fitest when he rescues from opresion of men.

I know not whether I or mine shal escape this trial, this Genneral Scourge. Surely if we doe not. their will be a period of a Long Contention.
Yet the Almighties hand is not shortned but he can save.[406] and redeeme us from a violent disconsolate death. And when his time is come we can be freed from this Rod of oppresion hath bin on our Family these many yeares
And that hath layn upon my backe by all *th*e Violence my aduarsaries could invent by might. and by aspercion. makeing me a Fanatique That by such forged pretentions the readier might devoure the prey. God in his good time can give us dismision from:

[88ʳ] And the rod of the wicked shal not rest vpon | the Lot of the rightous:[407] Noe 118 oppresion: *th*at makes a wise man at his wits end: shal not ~~have it~~ last alwayes. because of the extremity it reduceses to. Trust in the lord & waight patiently is *th*e Salmest direction.[408] See Exod*us* 12: 41: At the end of the 430 yeares even the self same day. All the hosts of *th*e lord went out of the Land of Egypt: ~~Yet it was 30 yeares more then what~~ Abraham had ^bin^ told him in a Dream: Gen*esis* 15:13:

[88ᵛ]   91: Salme: 12: Iuly: 65:   119
I wil say of the Lord he is my refuge, and my forteres
My God in him will I trust; Surely he shal deliever thee from the noisome pestilenc[409]
If a thousand fal at thy side and ten thousands at thy right hand it shal not com nigh thee:[410]
O L*ord* God: now that we fear thy Iudgements *th*at is among us And as it lies now we are affraid: That ten thousands may fal on our right hand: and a thousand on my side by me.[411] How Lord can I think my self better then they. But that thy dreadful scourg wil find us out. also: But o my God if it be thy wil accecp[412] of my contrition. and create such an affiance[413] on thy merciful compation that we may be delieverd and that we may rejoyce and be glad in thee all the dayes of our lifes.

---

[406] Isaiah 59:1.
[407] Psalm 125:3
[408] Psalm 37:5, 7
[409] Psalm 91:2–3
[410] Psalm 91:7
[411] Psalm 91:7
[412] i.e., accept
[413] faith, trust (see note 206)

Spare us o lord. Spare thy people, whom thou hast redeemed with thy pretious blood. & be not angry with us for ever:[414] Spare us good Lord. And commit us to the Chardge of thy holy Angels to stop the currents of danger to us.[415]

My God set thy love upon us. and then thou hast promisd to deliever us: If we know thy name: know thy all powerful Majesty: know God our Redeemer Know the holy Spirit the comforter in our Sorrowes: And know to call upon thee: and then shal we find thy ready answer to us. To be with us in trouble.[416] and | we shal be delieverd either temporally. but most surely from eternal destruction: David composed this 91 Salme when 70000 died in 3: daies:[417]

My God:
16 Whose all suficient mercy I have found
And by whose brightest glory I am Crown'd.
That Lofty favour and refulgent Light
Stil be transparent in dispairing Night.
And while environed with sharpn'd Arrowes
Of Fierce Contagion, send thy saveing Carrowes.[418]
Tis thy peculiar hand and strechet out dart
Tis thy preventive balme can sheild my heart.
Noe Antidote from men that can prevent.
Onely that providence divenely sent./.

My God grant I may not be taken with these worldly enjoyments. which if I have the greatest fulnes. cannot render me a full satisfaction
disvnite vntie and divorce my affections from the love of what ever thy blesing hath lent me. And tottally attract them on thy Glory, on thy Will./

Iuly: 30: 1665:

O Lord in mercy spare this slender Family in this populous Contagion. And remove thy dreadful Iudgements. which hang over our heads. That Hangs over the City, Over the Country. over the Kingdome. Over the Towne I am in Over my

---

[414] *BCP*, from the introductory portion of the Litany

[415] Psalm 91:9–13 promises the charge (protection) of angels to those who have made the Lord their refuge. The fittingness of this Psalm must have been encapsulated for KA in its tenth verse: "There shall no evill befall thee, neither shall any plague come nigh thy dwelling."

[416] Psalm 91:14–15

[417] 1 Chronicles 21:10–14

[418] carrow: gambler (*OEDO*). KA seems to be using it here in the sense of saving providential acts (see the following four lines).

House. And is not yet by thy especial providence[419] in my House. Yet who am I or mine. better before thee Then the meanest Beggar. or then those whom thou hast taken whole Families away: Be entreated o God to give a Cessastion to the distroying Angel: to stop the rigour of the Callamity.

Salme 76:[420]

Thou dost cause Iudgement to be heard from heaven,[421]
<⸪> He shal cut off the spirit of princes. He is terrible to the Kings of the earth./.[422]
The remaynder of thy wrath. (O God doe thou restraine, For delieuerance: Vow vnto *the* lord and pay thy vowes./[423]

The rightous hath hope in his death.[424]

[90^r] May not the thoughtes of Death dismay me.   122
Or be troubled if God take me away from my possesions I have expected to enjoy. (Noe). For remember Christ Iesus came not to redeeme me for them. Not for temporal possesions. But for etternal inheritances. W*hi*ch I hope by his merits to be pertaker of: Such as eye hath not seene, nor ear heard. of.[425]
For Highbury, and for the Swan my buildings,[426] may they never posses my desiers. or swallow my heart.

[90^v] O my God that hath kept me all my life time. keep & defend me in this temp-   123
tation now.[427] When a person of a most subtil insinuation, of a most complying temper. Of Frequent oppertunities seekes all the aduantagies to take my affection. By acts of readines & assistances to me. And by his helpful officies of preseruation. to my health. in the time of this great danger. Doth by all wayes That a great experiance. diveing into my temper and inclination. and deep contrivance can possibly act.

---

[419] See Introduction, pp. 27–28, for special or peculiar providences.

[420] In the following four lines, "lines from four verses of Psalm 76 [are] rearranged and altered to add force to the plea for deliverance" (Anselment, "Katherine Austen," 16). Psalm 76:8, 12, 10–11.

[421] Psalm 76–8

[422] Psalm 76–12

[423] Psalm 76:10–11

[424] Proverbs 14:32

[425] 1 Corinthians 2:9

[426] For "the Swan my buildings," see also fols. 79^v, 100^r, 105^r, 109^v, 112^v; and Introduction, p. 13.

[427] Revelation 3:10

I bles God I earely see at what all his addresses and wining flatering discourses tends too.
O God doe thou shield me as with a Garment,
And give me a Cautious prudence to behave ^& acquite^ my selfe (That I may not doe a dishonourable Folly. To sully and disparadge the Faire prosperityes of my life.
May my Carradge, (in this intervene.) Be watchful, resollute, and yet not contemptuous. or vngrateful. But if he doth obliedge me by kind offices. such as a Friend may receive. That I may returne civility and a faire requital
[91ʳ] And not give so great a satisfaction. as the reward of my selfe, and all my estate. 124
For that which I am in a Capacity Civilly to requite by a lesser reward.

Most vnhappy women. how many are yo*ur* snares and traines[428] laid for you. I noe more wonder how soone you are wone to another affection. There is a Iust cause you should designe your selues with *th*e most discretion you can. to prevent the dangers may vnworthily surprise you in the race of a long widdowhood.

My. retreat is to fly to my ever watchful Guardian in Heaven. And who can be safe without that Special aide, ~~providence~~ which I depend on in all my surprisements: and will not leave me if I goe not From *th*at Father of my spiritual and temporal conduct./.

114:[429]   see 131.[430]

[91ᵛ] The most remarkeable points I have observed out of all the workes of Doc*ter* 125
Dun. I doe refer to two points. Which are prosperity. and Aduarsity.
& Not withstanding ^that^ great aduersity and Crosses attend us in this world. we are not to slaken our duty of industry and vsefulnes in the course of our race. Afflictions have a most excellent virtue.
And industry is established by a strict command of honouring God in vpholding his workes. and doeing his Will. These have an instances in ^~~† Courts~~^[431] the President[432] of S*ir* Williame Cockym.[433] To whom God gave two great Lights.

---

[428] See note 255, above.

[429] KA versifies on God as her "Rocke of shelter" on her p. 114 (fol. 86ʳ); although that poem is entitled "On the sickenes," its topic is connected to her meditation here.

[430] KA meditates again on the folly of remarriage on her p. 131 (fol. 94ᵛ).

[431] The cross-reference scored out here matches with that at the foot of the page, where "Courts" are also referred to.

[432] i.e., precedent

[433] Sir William Cockayne (1559/60–1626), merchant and Lord Mayor of London.

the Sunshine of prosperity and the Mooneshine of affliction.[434] Honour and Fortune crownd his industry: Croses and troubles did the same to his Graces. which fited him for his highest and etternal Crowne./[435]

†[436] Ad<...>s: Aduarsity and prosperity: both conduce for good: And the place of riseing: and *th*e place of falling. is most at Courts: &c: see: pag: 13: book: C: pag–26: book: I:[437]

[92ʳ]   Tho*m*as   126

I purpose to leave you My son^[438] my great Iewel. and a greater then that my provedential Iewel.[439] I confes I present a temptation not to priz the first before the other. since reason demonstrates that more valuable. before the other. litle rarity which must have its worth imposed by imagination and phancy. by effects of the minde. by constructions And I am sure when you goe to a Gold smith The one is a Iewel. the other a peble. one *th*e ornament for an eminent person. The other noe higher then a jem for a child. Yet could I D*eare* son impres in thy Fancy some resemblances of mine. The value and esteeme would hugely transcend the first. Well I give them both to thee. in the one look on my Fortune. to this world. In the other. as an Embleeme of a more lasting riches. And if I enjoyne you any thing. keep that which I chiefly regarded. and know it was once a meanes to ease me ^in^ many stormes of trouble and to mittigate a violent griefe./

[92ᵛ] To my Son Thomas. if he lives to enjoy the blesing of His estate.   127

D*eare* Son. Now you come to posses a comfortable estate. Thinke not that you must entertaine and wellcome it with the thoughts, that itis flung upon you by the hands of Fortune. for if you have noe farther considerations. Fortune will put on a paire of Winges and fly from you. Iust as *th*e Goddes Fortune in old Rome. and their other Gods. who could Fly away to their disaduantage. and transfer their Favours to others.

---

[434] Allusion to Genesis 1:16

[435] "Not withstanding . . . Crowne" loosely paraphrases Donne, Sermon LXXX, "Preached at the funerals of Sir William Cokayne, Knight, Alderman of London, December 12. 1626," *LXXX Sermons*, 816–26, here 824–25. For a discussion of this sermon's appeal to KA, see Introduction, pp. 17–18.

[436] This cross-reference matches that by the scored-out "Courts" higher up on the same page. KA appears to have changed her mind about an insertion, locating her material instead at the foot of the page.

[437] References to other of KA's manuscript volumes; see Introduction, pp. 42–43.

[438] This caret appears to refer to the title ("Tho*m*as"), which may have been added after the first line of text was begun.

[439] See fol. 74ᵛ and note 327, above.

You have a further Duty: By Reccollection and Gratitude. You are not to thinke tho yo*ur* Father and Grandfather are out of sight, and out of yo*ur* knowledge. that your respects are canceled You must know an honour and duty is to be performed to the Ashes of yo*ur* most worthy Father from whence your being sprung. and who did surpase confering nature to you while he was with you by an ardent affection for your Education. Also you are to pay a Gratitude to the memory of yo*ur* honourd Granfather. whose industry and Iust quallifications provided a faire possesion. And in him to the Former predecessors who brought a blessing to him, and from them all derived prosperity to you. One part of Duty is performed: by a Civil prudence, by a Free Charity. and by an industrous oversight. That you may rather commendabley augment. Then riotously or carelesly impoverish. or diminish. Their estates descended to you. And tis eassier and with lese panes. to spine the Web out Longer. Then to ravele it out. I say with Les paines Since where is prodigallity and vicious demeano*ur*. | is more study to Fling an estate away, Then there is prudence to carry and manadge it with virtue, and vsefulnes. to all the intentions and purposes, of Nature, Liberality, and Reputation. Their is more trouble to provide for pleasure. Because there is so great dissatisfaction in t*h*e lest intermision of pleasure as it must be carried on with more sollicitation to create that vannity. and keep it to the hight.

And we may observe to keep up those virtues. of Liberality. ~~of~~ and to be vseful and Noble, to serve one self and others too. and to arrive at honour. is by way of augmentation and enlargement of our Pattrimony: w*h*ich enables to performe any Lawful designement./

To my Son Robert Austen.

This Lesson is related to you: To revere Your Predicessors. in yo*ur* heart. Nor can I be perswaded it wants a notice. or goe without a blessing. but that very much we doe receive by a reverent memorial and respectful regard. And you are to looke backe to the springes of your Fortune. And tho they have glided by yo*ur* worthy Father and Grandfather Austen. Yet for asmuch as yo*ur* estate came perticularly from my portion from my Good father yo*ur* Grandfather Robert Wilson: And my vnparraleled Father in Law. Ald*erman* Highlord tis fit you pay a Homage to their Memory and Merit.[440] This is practised by imitation of their virtues by enjoying yo*ur* blessings by thankfulnes to God that bleset you with a good[xl] | possesion from virtuous honesty. and praise worthy industry

It may be a president[441] to command the same good endeavours and Faire quallities in you. And if they obtained it by their own Faccullty of industry, (assisted

---

[440] See fol. 79ᵛ; and Introduction, pp. 7–8.

[441] i.e., precedent

[xl] Catchword: pos-

by Gods blesing.) What may you then doe. by a reddy help and supply from two Foundations.

I dictate[442] this lesson to you of prudence Since I know itis so acceptable to our great Patteron.[443] And its contrary Careles profusenes the orriginal of all the vnhappines that attends to ^on^ our selues and posterity in this world.

To my Daughter Anne Austen.
Nor are you my daughter to be left out in this Duty.
Look you with Honour on those predecessors mentioned
And take along with you. yo*ur* Granmothers. have yo*ur* Granmother (Anne) Austen's virtue and goodnes. Yet may you be defended from the passion of her Mallancholy. and bare with more Courage the encounters of endeard separations which must neccesarily attend us. her too great love occasioned much vnhappines to her by it. And Remember my D*eare* Mother. Yo*ur* Grandmother. (Katherine Wilson, Highlord,[)][444] Take industry from her and me. And as I have practised virtue and imployment. (I hope to be vseful in my life) From my Deare Mother be you an exsample and patterne to yo*ur* children. And in this I shall conclude to

[94ʳ]   my wishes.[445]   130

You all my three Deare children. ^ That the blessings descended to you from the integrity and worthines of all yo*ur* predecessors be a blessing to discend in channels. to yo*ur* Children, and to many gennerations: And if you doe yo*ur* parts by leading a commendable and vseful lifes. and that you set vertuous exsamples: God will to every Genneration continue his Favour. Who is the Fountaine of all blessings and happy Contentment here, and. who has better blessings to crowne our low and weeke endeavours with. Which that to all you and youres may obtaine is the vnfained prayers. and blesing of yo*ur* affectionate Mother.

---

[442] Presumably in the sense of *OEDO* 2: to prescribe (a course or object of action); to lay down authoritatively; to order, or command in express terms. Not in the sense of oral dictation; the hand here is the same as that throughout the manuscript, presumed to be KA's own.

[443] pater, patron or pattern: a reference either to KA's deceased husband or to the divine.

[444] For KA's mother, Katherine Rudd / Wilson / Highlord, see Introduction, pp. 6–8.

[445] The caret in the first line of text on this page indicates that this title has been added as an insertion.

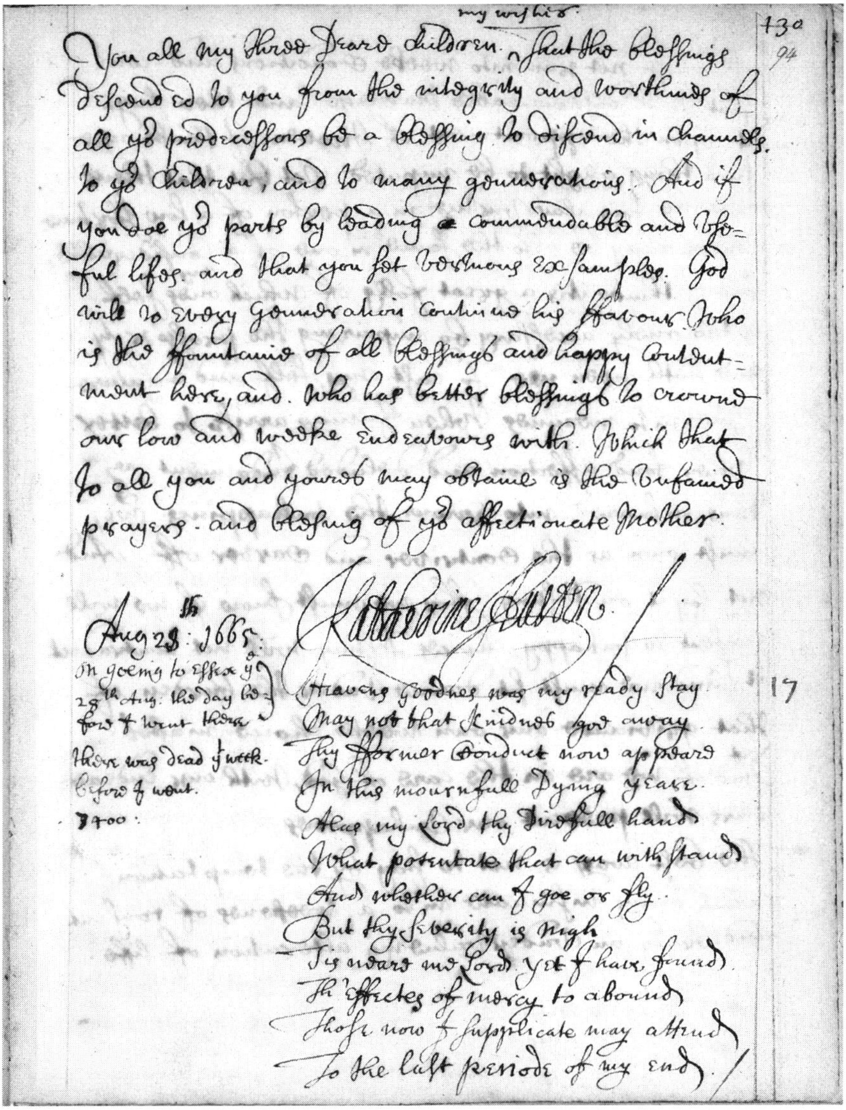

Book M   145

my wishes.

You all my three Deare Children, That the blessings
Descended to you from the integrity and worthines of
all yo~r predecessors be a blessing to discend in chanells
to yo~r Children, and to many gen~rations. And if
you doe yo~r parts by leading a commendable and Use-
full lifes, and that you set vertuous examples, God
will to every gen~ration continue his favour, Who
is the ffountaine of all Blessings and happy Induct-
ment here, and Who has better blessings to crown
our low and weake endeavours with. Which that
to all you and yours may obtaine is the unfained
prayers and Blessing of yo~r affectionate Mother.

Katherine Burton

Aug 28: 1665.
in goeing to Essex ye
29th Aug: the day be-
fore I went there
there was dead y~t week
before I went.
8400.

Heaven's goodnes was my ready Stay
May not that kindnes goe away
Thy former Conduct now appeared
In this mournfull Dying yeare.
Alas my Lord thy Dreadfull hand
What potentate that can withstand
And whither can I goe or fly.
But thy Severity is nigh
Tis neare my Lord yet I have found
Th'effectes of mercy to abound
Those now I supplicate may attend
To the last periode of my end.

Figure 8. *Book M*, fol. 94ʳ. See Introduction, p. 36.
©The British Library Board, Additional Manuscript 4454.

Aug 28th 1665:
on goeing to Essex
the 28th Aug: the day
before I went there
there was dead *that*
week. before I went.
7400:

Katherine Austen./[446]

Heavens Goodnes was my ready stay.   17
May not that Kindnes goe away.
Thy Former Conduct now appeare
In this mournfull Dying yeare.
Alas my Lord thy Direfull hand
What potentate that can withstand
And whether can I goe or fly.
But thy Severity is nigh
Tis neare me Lord Yet I have found.
Th'effectes of mercy to abound
Those now I supplicate may attend
To the last periode of my end./

[94ᵛ] We must not run into weeke Conditions and consent to a dishonourable Mar- 131
riage: and then lay it vpon the appointment of Heaven. I thinke noe such thing
ought to be imputed. Not but that their may be singular virtue in a person of a
low Fortune. There may be also the same in one of a Considerable: And I thinke
itis a great folly of which ones ^my^ self is the onely accessary by impairing
the prosperity God hath given use.[447] To cast my self and a future issue[xli] into
meannes. When I may arrise to better. When fond affection and deluded Iudgement is thus insnared into Errour the vnhappiness. (we)^I^ must own as the
Contriver and Carver off: And not lay it on Distiny: (For we must know if we
will consent to vnhappy choices Distiny will not contradict it.) and we must sit
downe vnder the burden of that griviance our own weeke choice makes.
And ^Yet^ if we are in the care of God, with our endeavours will prevent our
vnhappines.
The best way is not to stay by the temptation, which may insinuate into a weekenes
of consent. and bring an vndervalueing alteration of life.

[95ʳ] Now if itis vrged There is extrordinary virtues. and endowments. does contract 132
affection. Without relation to Fortune. and tis not so meane a thing as that, dus
make to be beloved. Tis Answered. If there is such a thing as Virtue to be loved
for it self. Let my Amoret[448] entertaine me as his Friend, and not victiate[449] a

---

[446] This is a large and florid signature, resembling in size and style the inscription of her name and motto on fol. 2ʳ. See Introduction, p. 36.

[447] i.e., us

[448] sweetheart

[449] vitiate: to impair or corrupt

[xli] jssue

Noble frindship with interist, or any other respect but pure amity.[450] Yet certainly because itis rare and scarce such a thing, as virtue to be ~~loved~~ esteemed for it self, (especially in single men and single women). I doe rather hold the converse of such is not without great caution to be: neither of married persons. lest a vicious end ensues. since men adoar their company for aduantage to themselues.

Nor can I beleeve when they say. That men had rather be in the Socciety of Women. And women loves better that of men.

Noe, I doe discover by a comparison. not to give credid to wordes. The King courts the city and loves it because itis rich. And then it will be safe to the King. As a Rich Wise Woman is loved And if she does not love againe. it is noe matter if she is not Wise and Rich.

For my part I doe noe Injury to none by not Loveing. But if I doe I may doe real [95ᵛ] Injuries. | where I am already engaidged. To my Deceased Friends posterity.[451]   133
As for my body it can be enjoyed but by one. And I hope itis the worst part of me. and that w*h*ich every servant, made[452] and Country Wench may excel mine, and can give the same satisfaction as mine. But that w*h*ich my desier is should far excel my body is my soule, and the virtues & quallities of that. And this I thinke may be vseful to more then one. and not confined to a single person. and if any thing in me is to be loved I hope tis my mind. And that I deny not a Frindly correspondanc to you, nor any beside. Thus all my Friends may pertake of me and enjoy me. and be married in the Dearenesses and vsefulnes and benefits of Frindship. And more then one can be satisfied with those lawful intimacies of Frindship. and correspondancies of lawful publicke safe conferrencies. which is the better part of me. and w*h*ich true virtue should most affect. And thus I may be pertakers of the noblenes of yo*u*r parts. by an open and free amity.[453]

& Thus that person w*h*ich pretends soe great affection to me may be satisfied with ~~the~~ an honest conversation. and such Lawful allowed conferrencies.

[96ʳ] I was in discourse with a Gentleman.[454] He had many arguments to prove. The   134
Papists had not Idolatry by their pictures. This he sed Monsier Amaruth.[455] did prove in a book he set out.[456] Wherein he shewes. The Idolatry of several Nations.

---

[450] friendly relations. KA's use of "pure amity" clearly implies an absence of amorous feeling.

[451] KA's deceased husband, Thomas Austen

[452] i.e., maid

[453] See note 450, above.

[454] KA's suitor. Todd, "'I do no injury'," 210, names him as Alexander Callendar, a Scottish physician, although no source is given.

[455] Probably Moise Amyraut (1596–1664), a French theologian.

[456] Amyraut published prolifically in French, and KA describes her suitor as having lived in France for 18 years (fols. 97ʳ⁻ᵛ); Amyraut's *A Treatise Concerning Religions, In*

as the Ancient Egiptianes. to be perfect Idolatry. but of the papists not ^to^ be such. I Answered divers thinges to it And tho at last I did not disaprove according as it might be :The haveing ^a^ picture of christ or of Saints. Yet let M*onsie[u]*r Amaruth say w*h*at he pleased. I must condemn the Romanists of Superstitious and Idolatrous adoaring theires.

He then sed to me. and protested if I was a very begger women if I wud have him he wud have me, and he wud discourse with me all day. For he never taulket with me but learned Something of me. I told him. he was mistaken and if I was soe endead he wud not.

For my part I declined all things might give him a vaine encouradgement. and told him I was like pennelope, alwayes employed.[457] I ses he her lovers could not abide her for it.

[96ᵛ] When I was returning home from Mrs Al: he sed. You would not take pity if one should grow distracted for you. There is noe fear of *th*at sed I: Then ^as^ he took me by the hand. he sed. what a hand was there to be adoard: I answered him. looking Vpon a tuft of gras w*h*ich had growing init a Yallow flower: That that spier of gras was fitter to be adoared then my hand: I allas ses he we are all but gras. but shadowes. And when ever we see the gras we are to adoar the Creator in it./ 135

I thinke at that time he was not very well: for afterwards he sed that on that evening he first began to fel his head acke. which grew for 4 daies very paineful. So that eleven dayes after he ended his life on the 7th of ~~August~~^ouctober^ 1665 at Tillingham in Essex:

He was one that much observed Dreames. Yet he had seldome any that boded any good to him. but foretold him of Disasters. w*h*ich I tooke notice of: The night before he died. He told a very long Dreame of many Circumstances in it. How that he was in a great. place. like a Church. and saw many friends and Mr Iohn Austen.[458] and he was in a habit all in white & over that Long white gar-
[97ʳ] ment a short. | blacke Coat. and his haire short and a litle hat. And people sed he was in Orders. Noe but I am not sed I: Then I kneeled on a Stone. and prayed a great while. Then he sed he meet me walkeing with a gentlewoman. and I told him I had a minde to goe to such a Ladys house if I could git in. He sed he wud goe and help me to accomodation there. & soe I did. And it was a very curious house. where the Lady did governe and order every thing in ~~with~~ ^a^ most ex- 136

Refutation of the Opinion which accounts all Indifferent was published in English translation in 1660.

[457] Penelope, the true-hearted wife of Odysseus, who whiled away his absence through weaving.

[458] KA's brother-in-law John Austen, who died in 1659. See Introduction, pp. 11–13.

act order and prudence. And then I waket being caled by an other Name. caled: Kingsman:[459]

I then asked him after he had repeated this Dream what he thought of it. Nothing atall. Yet at first sed it was a very strange Dreame. & he had had many strange ones of late. Then I sed. I ame to goe to the King at Oxford about my busines and you wil be well and goe with me. Ses he I had rather goe to the King of Heaven. and I hope he is. who departed the next day.

His eminence in learning and in all the accomplishments of a gentleman for his prudence and parts might well make him arrive at high places and to aime at promotions in England was the occasion he left France a place where he had dwelt 18 yeares. and found much Contentment. a place which when he found by changing from it could not meet with preferment in England. (much obstructed by the Cloud and disrellish of his Country) (Being a Scot) This made him often as he sed sigh: that he was parted from his beloved Country France. And this among other Frownes of Fortune did give depression to his spirit. That at^on^ the last night he had in this world. did expresse how he had pased through many Checkes of Fortune. Itis supposed made some impressiones on his minde. Together with late apprehensions at the place where he went with me to be freed from the danger of the Pest.[460] and there he took notice of Night Birds of Screetch Owles.[461] as he concluded one of the house wud dye. Nay when his Sickenes did. increase My own Feares suggested his end was nigh. and revoulued to me a Dreame. in its full meaning.

Book: K: pag. 213:[462]

And in that place and Roome where I was. then at Mr Woods: was the very same fashione & situation as I saw in my Dreame. The grave stone I bought. in such a corner was represented. as Tillingham Church stands; and that place where he was buried. And surely his worth and merit deserves to have a memorial of a stone infixed over his grave. he lyeing buried in such a remote place from his Friends

He found his death in that Country. And I was nigh meeting with mine there also. at that time he had layen about 5 dayes ill.

How shall I be able to recite. this act of Commemoration by the escapeing emmediate Death on a surprice. I being the moment before in perfect health. a Fall off a Tree where I was siting in contentment. That had seates on the Tree. easy

---

[459] KA differentiates the name "Kingsman" here by using a slightly larger font.
[460] i.e., pestilence
[461] See note 468, below.
[462] *Book K* is another of KA's manuscripts, in which her dream of the restoration was also recorded (see fol. 73ʳ); see Textual Introduction, p. 43.

to goe up in. Yet in returne I fell from a hight about 3 4[463] yards to *th*e ground. which bruised my face of the left side. And my Right Thumbe put out of joynt. So that I lay dead at present and had not the least sence of my faling.

Yet it pleased my God to send two women who saw me fall. w*hi*ch if they had not seen me fall. The Hedges and bushes wud have made me vndiscovered to any and I doe not know but I might have layen more then a day in that very lonely place. These women had then come a mile from their dweling (and) One of them was vnwilling to come because that tree had frighted many a person that it was ha[u]nted with sprites. and the fearful woman took me to be one. Yet by the confidence of the other they came and found me without any sence They took me up and I fel downe agen being all in blood by my fal at the nose. at length I began |

[98ᵛ] to speak Yet could not in a good while recover to know how I came by that hurt. 139 and much amased to see my self in that disorder. They brought me to the house where I lodged two Feeldes from *th*e place I fell: There by Gods blesing I recovered my great illnes by Cordiales. w*hi*ch the Sickenes of vomiting up blood divers times by the way. had weekened my spirits. My Temples had laied upon it 4 Leeches. Yet my Face and head was in a numed[464] maner for a Fortnight.

Thus it pleased my God to be my delieverer. Then when I had a sensible impresion I was but a wind a puffe.[465] and if the Almighty had not sent & helpet me I had bin blowne out. and should noe more returned till the great Day:[466] /on *th*e 2d of Octo*ber* 1665 my fall/[467]

On my Fall off the Tree.

18 It might have bin a fatal Tree,
And my last acts catastrophe.
Yet all wayes from that remote part,
My Genius ever did divert.
An vncuth way as if dark owles
And dismal night Burds made ^had:^ controules[468]
At last was thwarted[xlii] by my Fate
Ta'pproach that most vnhappy bate.

---

[463] The numerals 3 and 4 are written one over the other, so it cannot be discerned which is the error and which is the correction.

[464] i.e., numbed

[465] Allusion to Job 7:7

[466] i.e., the Day of Judgement

[467] This date has been inserted in a different ink into a blank half-line; the poem which begins below continues in this different ink.

[468] KA also refers to "Night Birds" and "Screetch Owles" in her suitor's dream of this period; see fol. 97ᵛ. The imagery recalls Isaiah 34:14.

[xlii] I have silently corrected KA's inverted "wh" here.

Book M   *151*

    Laid to intrap: If Fame say right
    A recepticle 'twas did Fright.
[99^r] Revoulted spirits that place did haunt[469]   140
    Yet some are of opinnion can't.
    What were those foes? for what conspire?
    I have not Logicke to enquier.
    I cant detirminate that thing
    Onely a supposition bring
    Admit the crew of Belsebub.
    Waighted my rival with their Club.
    And that the regiment of Hell
    Had there conventred[470] out a spell.
    (To make my Traverse more repleate.)
    (And more then earthly foes to meete)[xliii]
    The plot was broake, and Heavens bright eye
    Dissolued their blacke Confederacy.
    Then came the help of my great guide
    Who took notice I did slide
    And the blessed spirites attended.
    Then was seene how they befriended.
    Then from the brinke of death did save
    Another life at instance gave
    The same life Lord let me for ever lay
    And hence forth dedicate both night and day
    Texalt thy praises which soe much abound.
    In all my preseruations doe resound./
        His High favours was thus showne
        Vnto me, who deseru'ed none.   pag 148[471]

[99^v] Meditations on the Sickenes and of Highbury.   141
    Through six afflictions God has promised to cary his children. and in the seaventh they shal be delievered.[472] Six I have pased. six yeares of Divers mixtures

---

    [469] See fol. 98^r for the tree's reputation.
    [470] KA appears to have coined a verb here from "conventicle," the term for a clandestine meeting, associated with Nonconformist sects and with witchcraft.
    [471] See KA's p. 148 (fol. 103^r).
    [472] Job 5:19

    [xliii] Single large parentheses encompass this couplet.

full of accidents and encounters extrordinary for a single woman to pas.[473] And let me repeat the divers emergincies I have bin put to for the supplying great vndertakeings. and how I have pased through not withstanding my preventions. Since Aug*ust* 1664: to Mich*ael*mas 1665:
My expentiones in my building.
Every Termes bils of expence.
Williames buriall[474]
Mr Cruse Cheate
A Tennants' cheate

The vexatious Shuite[475] of Symons	40 – 0 – 0
The renewing the Lease of Deane Hardy	80 – 0 – 0
The expence at Parliment	
The Looseing by a pecke pocket	14 – 0 – 0
The Lending money to Cosen Wil*liame* in neccesity) onely for 2 months and vnpaid yet)[476]	336 – 0 – 0
Expence to maintaine my son at Oxford.[477]	
My help to Cosen Varney in his vrgent need	40 – 0 – 0
giveing Cosen AR:	5 – 0 – 0

[100ʳ]

£   142

My helpeing S*i*r T: with	200 – 0 – 0
then when I was to git & did git for them ^builders^	300 – 0 – 0

All these sumes I raised w*hi*ch found some w*ha*t difficult by reason of hinderances. viz.

	£
The not receiveing at Mid: 1665 of the King	700
Not rec*eiveing* Cosen williames money in may[478]	250:
Rent of arreare expected in Essex[479]	150
Of Cosen Parnam	50
Of Fines of houses	200
And the abateing of *th*e rent of a house I had let	£20 p*er* an*num*
And the Looseing for *th*e time of building the swan.[480]	£100 p*er annum*

---

[473] For further meditations on a six-year period and its significance, see fol. 76ᵛ and note 341, above; also see Introduction, pp. 15–16.

[474] The burial of KA's servant, William Chandeler. See fols. 2ʳ, 38ᵛ, 54ʳ.

[475] i.e., suit (lawsuit)

[476] A single parenthesis encompasses the two lines of this entry. See fols. 100ʳ, 109ᵛ.

[477] See fols. 43ʳ–44ᵛ, 82ᵛ, 114ᵛ.

[478] See fols. 99ᵛ, 109ᵛ.

[479] See also fol. 109ᵛ.

[480] For "the Swan my buildings," see fol. 90ʳ and Introduction, p. 18. For further references to many of these expenses, see fol. 109ᵛ.

Book M   *153*

At this time is arrived that most bountious blessing of Highbury. which I hope will well wade me through. the residue of my expencive buildings. and disappointment of rents: from a genneral. cause:^stroak.^

[100ᵛ] Far be it from me to imagine I have had those helps and delieverances from my difficultes by the Conduct of my own Vnderstanding. Not possible to bin defended with out a greater help. And I have found by reliance on my good God, an enterist in those promises. That all things worke for the best.[481] And I have found the assistance and Ministry of Angels.[482] I have bin comforted by the Spirit of Divine Comfort and mercy. to whom be ascribed the full glory of every delieverance and blesing, that helps one through intricacies by a miracle. and when he sends me Losses dus also send me helps to a wonder. O that I may be fit for such aids and mercies. and that my children may grow up to honour the God of their Fathers.

By the delieverances I have received from my most gracious God. My Faith. My hope, does promise his Future Mercy for my eternal good. And my God is able to delieuer me in this dreadful seauenth year a yeare where the Angel of his displeasure convayes darts of speedy death.[483] Yet I trust (to those who are smiten) tis onely a temporary anger. That anger which will end in everlasting favour. Now [101ʳ] from this temporary Momentary Stroake. God Almighty | if he pleases can free me his most vnworthy servant and my children, and Relations.

Surely this seaventh yeare wherein I am involued in a^this^ genneral Callamity,[484] may well reckown compleates out seavene affli[c]tiones.[485]

O Heaven if thy gracious Will, manifests thy praise and good pleasure by delieverance from this seaventh, this Lamentable Callamity. that strickes so terrible in all places. And give a rescue and freedome from our threatning Aduarsaries, and a stop to their vnjust[xliv] trouble. How shal I endeavour to live a new life. O if Heaven will give to me the greatest provedential perfection of mine to me, in the dispencing his stroakes, and send delieverance to me. As now I am sure will be, either in this life or a better. What a heart ought I to have. to be disposed and devoted to his glory.

---

[481] Echoes Romans 8:28
[482] See fols. 6ʳ–9ʳ.
[483] i.e., the plague
[484] i.e., the plague
[485] This is a further reference to Job 5:19; see note 341, above.

[xliv] I have silently lowered a capital "J", as this word is hyphenated across a line ending as "vn-Just".

19.[xlv] Some worke of piety goe then and shew.
    A life of purity I ever owe.
    All humble thankes, a life of ful addres
    Vnto thy Alter pay, from me thats les
    Then the least mit[486] of what thy goodnes throwes.
    Stil Streames of boverty,[487] sure a Mountaine owes.
[101ᵛ] I never can dischardge so great a sume   145
    Lord teach me w*ha*t to doe. Thou bidst me come
    Come to that Ocean, where I stil have found
    Exalted mercies In its triumph Crown'd.
    With rais'd Devotion, and with ardent zeal,
    Declare me what to doe, Something reveale
    Since grace and glory all high things wilt give
    Teach me with curcumspection how to live
    From Speciall favours[488] begs enlardged desier
    My soule in all its motions may move higher
    That Heaven and earth, to all I may display
    The Love of Iesu, and his soveraigne stay.
    And by an outward, and an inward Story,
    Render my praises to that immense glory./

Let me ever give. praise to thy name. for thy mercies, and receiveing the satisfaction of my hopes from thy plentousnes and Loveing kindnes. Let me never ascribe to my self any honour, or the Glory or thankes of any good action, or prosperous succes. But to thee who art the authour of & giver of all good things. And preserue me from worshiping or Loving any vaine imagination & making any thing be my Confidence besides thee

[102ʳ] 20 This is endead a Copious Theame   146
    I have not words enough can speake
    These actes of Conduct and of grace./
    To Cellebrate my great preservers praise

---

    [486] i.e., mite

    [487] i.e., poverty

    [488] See Introduction, pp. 27–28, and Alexandra Walsham, *Providence in Early Modern England* (Oxford: Oxford University Press, 1999), 12, for discussion of "special" or "particular" providences.

    [xlv] KA numbers this poem in the right-hand margin, probably because there is an inkblot in the left hand margin. I have regularized the number's placement.

Some Angel write that never hath decaies
My imperfectiones dus admit noe skill
Theres soe much vannity and soe much ill
Most glorious Lord, send out thy brightsome Ray
Then my stupidity shall shine like day
And be vnvailed from its gloomy Night
And thy vnparral'd favours shall indite
Me a weake woman in my dangers strong
Conducted by thy blesing all along.
In all my straightes. when dangers sunk me downe
God was my Castle and my high renowne.
I am allas. I am so weak a thing.
Neither assistance or can merit bring
Thy supreame mercies. mercies. doe vnfold
Can never with the tongue of men be told
O Fountaine of immesurable Love.
What vast degrees transcendent goodnes move.[xlvi]

[102ᵛ] Heaven Earth and Hell, all speak w*ha*t thou hast done.   147
Earth thy full blesings, From th'Abise[489] thy son
Ransom'd from terrour and at last provide
A Hill of glory never to divide
Ravisant[490] happines at glories throne
There know thy praises without Learning one./

21 Has Conduct carried me through seaven great yeares
   Great in perplexities, and great in feares.
   Great Griefes with Iob: could hardly be exprest
   Neither by sighings, or by teares redrest
   Six folded trials. and a seaventh as great.
   By a perticular and genneral waight.[491]
   Hard knot negotiates by oppresion knit
   A Dread consumeing sickenes came, And yet

---

[489] i.e., the abyss

[490] i.e., ravissant: ravishing, delightful (*OEDO* 2)

[491] This poem, and in particular these first six lines, are KA's most explicit reference to Job 5:19, which encapsulates her belief that six trials will be followed by deliverance in a seventh. See also fol. 76ᵛ and note 341, above; also see Introduction, pp. 15–16.

[xlvi] Catchword: Heaven

Mercy out shined all those dark eyed Clouds
Design'd to me, in Seaven yeares ruged folds
The Wise Egiptianes deemed six compleate
The Divine Scriptures dus the same repeate.
Six hardest trials, and to give renowne
There comes a seaventh. this is afflictions Crowne

[103ʳ] My Gracious Lord, wilt thou'admit to me   148
Thy Dearest) Favours. soe much glory see.
        Speciall)[492]
O that vpon thy Alter I may lay.
A Contrite heart. and perfectly obay.
That every day and minute be confind,
Thy bright Memorials to bear in minde
And to the future gennerations tell.
How high, how excellent, thy glories swell.[493]

O God that art worthy to be praised with

A weeke before I had my fall. I hered of a boy in that hundred[494] that was a plowing. and when his fellow plowman went in for some occastion in to the house. He went up a paire Tree. and presently fell downe and broak his necke. & never stured[495] more. It might have bin the same to me./.[496]

[103ᵛ]   On that day Highbury came out of Lease.   149
    Mic*h*aelmas 1665.[497]

Am I the person am to reap the first fruites of that long expectation, and enter into those pleasant feeldes of a faire inheritance. And that it should be appointed for my Children. Tis a blesing I know not how to receive. Yet let me and mine ever remember, That we receive our prosperity, and enter into a Lardge revennue through the Iawes of death, and by the heapes of Mortality. That we may

---

[492] KA's amendment here emphasizes the idea of special or particular providences. See note 488, above.

[493] This poem articulates KA's revised sense of purpose following her dream of monition. See fol. 21ʳ and note 79, above.

[494] a subdivision of a county or shire, having its own court

[495] i.e., stirred

[496] These lines relate to KA's reference on fol. 99ʳ. She has added the lines here to spare space at the bottom of the page.

[497] See fols. 48ʳ–49ʳ and note 173, above, for the thirty-six-year lease period on Highbury; and see Introduction, p. 11.

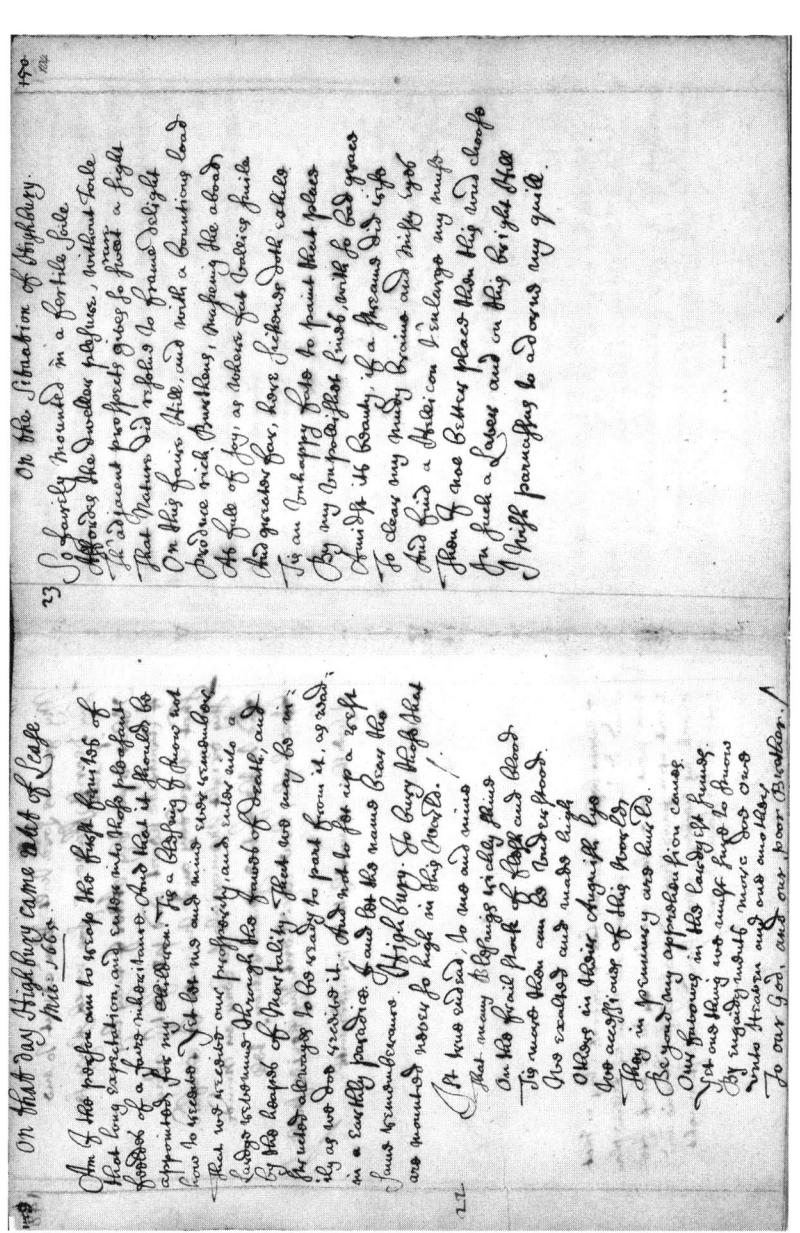

Figure 9. *Book M*, fols. 103ᵛ–104ʳ. See Introduction, p. 34.
©The British Library Board, Additional Manuscript 4454.

be instructed allwayes to be ready to part from it, as readily as we doe receive it. And not to set up a rest in a Earthly Paradice. I and let the name bear the same rememberance. Highbury:[498] To bury those that are mounted never so high in this World./.

22   Ist true endead, to me and mine
      That many Blesings richly shine
      On the frail stock of flesh and blood
      Tis more then can be vnderstood.
      We exalted and made high
      Others in their Anguish lye
      We accessiones of this world
      They in pennury are hurld.
      Beyond my apprehension comes.
      Our favours in the lardgest sumes.
      Yet one thing we must sure to know
      By engaidgments more doe owe
      Vnto Heaven and one another
      To our God, and our poor Brother./

[104ʳ]   On the Situation of Highbury.[499]   150

23 So fairely mounted in a fertile Soile[500]
   Affordes the dweller plesure, without Toile
   Th'adjacent prospects gives so sweet^rare^ a sight
   That Nature did resolue to frame delight
   On this faire Hill, and with a bountious load
   Produce rich Burthens, makeing the aboad
   As full of joy, as where fat vallies smile
   And greater far, here Sickenes doth exhile.
   Tis an vnhappy fate to paint that place

---

[498] KA differentiates "Highbury" from the surrounding text by using a slightly larger font.

[499] This poem is anthologized by Stevenson and Davidson, *Early Modern Women Poets*, 315–16. For critical discussions, see also Pamela Hammons, "Katherine Austen's Country-House Innovations," *Studies in English Literature* 40 (2000): 123–37; and Sarah Ross, "'And trophes of his praises make': Providence and Poetry in Katherine Austen's Book M, 1664–1668," in *Early Modern Women's Writing: Selected Papers from the Trinity/Trent Colloquium*, ed. Victoria E. Burke and Jonathan Gibson (Aldershot: Ashgate, 2004), 181–204. See also Introduction, pp. 33–34.

[500] See KA's earlier reference to Highbury's "Fertile Soile" (fol. 79ᵛ).

By my vnpollishet Lines, with so bad grace
Amidst its beauty, if a streame did rise
To clear my mudy braine and misty eyes
And find a Hellicon[501] t'enlarge my muse
Then I noe better place then this wud choose
In such a Laver[502] and on this bright Hill
I wish parnassus to adorne my quill.

[105ʳ] When I deduct the Legacy my D*ear*e mother left me (at her Decease.)[503] and se‑ 152
vere it from my Husbands estate: I have added to our estate by Gods great bles‑
ing. vpon me these seaven yeares of my widdowhood. such another estate as was
left to me and my children.[504]
And if we inherit Highbury. is as much as any one of those two parts.
I doe reckowne our estate in 3 parts.
First what my Husband left.
2d w*h*at by Gods extrordinary blesing aded
3d that Long expectation. the discourse of many. the interruption of more.
And that soe much should come in my possesion o my God w*h*at am I to receive
soe much. And that by such plentiful acquisitions. Our God should please to free
me and mine from agreat many of those huge miseries of want. w*h*ich doe af‑
flict the most of mankind. Yet our God pleases to mingle some bitternesses in my
Comforts. Grant Lord they may be aduantagies to me of wisedome and piety. to
draw me from the love and desier of this world to the pursuit of the Divine and
Spiritual Felicities will last for ever.

[105ᵛ] O that Heaven wud direct me what I should doe whether I shal glorify his name 153
by a contemplative private life. or by an active publike life.[505] Direct thy Servant
in w*h*at may be conduceing[506] to thy prais. and not to me o lord but to thy name
be the glory of my whole life.[507]
Tis the infinitie desier of my soule to glorify thy name. that I may become an In‑
strument to serue my God Take not thy assistance away from me. give thy bles‑

---

[501] Helicon: the mountain favored by the Greek muses.
[502] A vessel for washing and/or any spiritually cleansing agency (*OEDO*, n. 2). KA is referring back to the hypothetical stream which will rise from the "Helicon" of Highbury to clear her muddy brain. (Helicon was also the source of an inspiring stream.)
[503] KA's mother left her £2000 at her death; see Introduction, pp. 8, 13.
[504] This second estate seems to be "the Swan my buildings"; see fols. 79ᵛ and note 360, above.
[505] See Introduction, pp. 35–39, for KA's intended audience.
[506] i.e., conducive
[507] Echoes Psalm 115:1

ing to my endeavours & give me vnderstanding w*h*at to doe. and wisdome to act thy blesed commands. and continually guided to dischardg those things put in my hand to act.

O God that art worthy to be praised with all pure and holy praise. Therefore thy Saintes prais thee. with all thy Creatures. Thou art to be praised for thou hast made me Joyful.

We are not to disclose the secrets of a King
But itis honourable to reveale the workes of God.[508]

[106ʳ]   Meditation: 154

Bles thy servant with wisdome and industry to the performance of my Duty in this world. that the genneration to come may find my help & assistance as I have found and bin greately blessed by the endustry and imployment of my predecessors./.

[106ᵛ]   Feb*ru*ary 1665/.[509]   155

Surely I ought to sit downe and call my own wayes to rememberance. Nay and let me call the workes of my God into memory with me whose favours and the outgoeings of my God hath so ^many^ eminent wayes appeard to me. never to be forgotten one moment of my life

O God Allmighty be with me stil in the many Tryals that attend my life. Thy Grace was sufficient for St Paul.[510] I know thou wilt afford it soe for me.

And now I am detained with suspention between hope and feare w*h*at my Aduarsaries will doe shortly. I can have that retreate to Davieds confident Argument That had over Come the Lion and the bear: might also vanquish Stout Golliah.[511]

~~24~~ O spare me that I may recover
Strength to pas my Troubles over
Then in thy aid and not to me
I may exalt thy Majesty.
Thou'rt greater then my potent foes.
When they invent me many woes.
O thou art higher to subdue
((All)^~~tho~~^ Tho they band)^convent^ with all their Crue[512]

---

[508] Apocrypha, Tobit 12:7
[509] i.e., February 1665/6
[510] 2 Corinthians 12:9
[511] 1 Samuel 17: 34–37, 48–51
[512] KA has changed "All tho they band with all their Crue" to "Tho they convent with all their Crue." Convent: to gather illicitly.

Book M 161

    In my Destitute Condition
    Thou'rt my Soveraigne I pettition
    Tis thou who dost Low orphantes right
    And to depressed Widdowes Fight
[107ʳ] Mercy that has bin often found   156
    Thy mercy that is often Crown'd
    Vpon my weeakenes let me find
    When mens Justice may be blind
    Vnvaile o God their dire desceate.[513]
    Noe more their Furrowes may repeate
    Vpon our shoulders,[514] nor their Rod
    Stil interrupt our peacefull boade.[515]
    Give us quiet and then wee
    Will give our selues up unto thee.
    Or if a mighty Knot Conspire
    Our ouerthrow. then be thou nigher
    I know canst make a gaine to lose
    And sublinaries[516] be noe Crose.
    To thy great pleasure lowly yeeld
    Or loose, or win In thee Ile build./.

King David was the great example of trouble and confidence in that trouble to his meditations I resort to, and he that was his retreate shal be mine.
As now I can say ^<.>[517] him^ many are the troubles of *t*he rightous.[518]
I trust that second part shal also declare.
The Lord delieueres them out of all./.[519]

[107ᵛ] This conflict and stratagem of my Enemies deuices against us, by the former gra- 157
cious ~~encouradgements~~ ^experien<ces>^ of my Heavenly Fathers delieuerances to me. Giues me encouradgement I shal be victorious ouer them. My God if that blesing I obtaine in behalfe for a helples Family I am guardia<n>[520] And if the

---

    [513] i.e., deceit
    [514] Allusion to Psalm 129:3.
    [515] Probably a shortened form of "abode," with the sense of "A temporary remaining [on earth]; a stay" (*OEDO*, n¹ 2)
    [516] i.e., sublunaries: inferiors, earthly beings
    [517] There may be a shorthand symbol here, probably meaning "with."
    [518] Psalm 34:19
    [519] Psalm 34:19 (the "second part" of the verse).
    [520] The end of this word is lost in the manuscript's binding.

winges of prosperity and peace pitch[521] vpon our dweling, Make me o God to be as humble as I now am often dejected, often disturbed, Yet how soe euer thy disposal shall command. I trust shal be fited by those suffering graces to attend thy will, Because I know my enemies can goe noe further, Nor doe noe more then by thy permistion./.

My Nansy[522] is busie and inquisitive in to all things of Husfry.[523] to be informed, and to learne, and euery country affaire delightes in, which I am very well pleased to see, And if it be the Will of God may she neuer come to such a taske as I haue. Yet why should I say soe, Is not that all sufficient Father of mercies[524] able to help her as to me. That she as well as I may see euery day assisted, relieved through w*h*at heape of troubles God shal cast. ~~upon~~:

[108ʳ] On Feb*ruary* 12: 1665:[525] on Sister Austens renewing agen her pretention for 158 the Red Lion.[526]

What will envy hatred and Couetiousnes doe. Noe boundes these enormities hath. It canceles all obligations. respects, and gratitude. And comes now to Triumph and to perfect the ruine to an Orphant. by its endeauour.

All allong I haue bin persequted for Highbury. I must haue an addition from them. Tis not sufficient to enjoy £350 for life.[527] He will deny her *th*e blesing of her posterity to keep away and beguile as much more. This is not all insatiable thurst drives at. Will compase vnjustly the rest for euer.

Lord Let these draging away of our estate from men by the Cords of Couetiousnes and opprestion be soe many chaines, soe many Lynes. to pul us vnto that place of the Blessed where noe enemy[xlvii] can assault us./

---

[521] to land, to light

[522] Nansy: KA's daughter, Anne (a common diminutive, perhaps used to differentiate from Anne's grandmother, Anne Austen [see fol. 93ᵛ]).

[523] i.e., housewifery (hussifry)

[524] 2 Corinthians 1:3

[525] i.e., 12 February 1665/6

[526] For KA's dispute with Susanna Austen over the Red Lion, see note 373, above, and Introduction, pp. 11–13.

[527] KA's husband, Thomas, had left £350 to his brother John (Thomas Austen's will, National Archives, PROB 11/285).

[xlvii] I have silently corrected "ememy".

Book M   163

[108ᵛ] On Voll*antin*es day: this 14 Feb*ruary* 1665 / my Iewel.)[528]   159

25 Wellcome thou best of Vollantines
   Firmer to me then Louer's twines[529]
   Allas they vanish but this lye
   A pledge, a suertie Annually.
   Grand Omen of a bles't presaige
   To Wade me through a stormy age.
   Throughout my desert sollitude
   A reflex[530] brings beyond my food.
   When I am poor by vast expence
   Supplied haue bin beyond my sence
   In this scarce year, Dire want was seene
   To many thousands in extreeme,
   In my obliedged enterprise.
   Where many Fallauces did rise
   Successive burdens came a pace
   And poissed euen in that chace
   My Deare propitious Vollantine
   Seauen Annual curquites[531] didst confine.
   (This day assau<.>tments makes me sad)
   (This day reboundments makes me glad.)[532] [xlviii]

[109ʳ] Why shud I speake thus to a stone?   160
   Vnto a thing, that life has none?
   We know that heretofore was told
   By outward thinges did secreets hold
   Why may not I this Iewel prise
   Wherein Misterious reccord lies[533]

---

[528] i.e., 14 February 1665/6. For KA's "providential jewel," see note 327, above.

[529] i.e., entwinements

[530] reflection of light (*OED*, n. 1a), perhaps literal (light reflecting in the jewel) as well as figurative (the light of hope, sustenance beyond food).

[531] seven yearly circuits of the earth around the sun (i.e., seven years)

[532] Single large parentheses encompass this couplet.

[533] In the four preceding lines, KA constructs her jewel as providential, as she has done elsewhere in *Book M* (see note 327, above). She is, however, careful in the following eight lines to deny that she is placing too great a belief in its significance, insisting instead that "Heauen is my great resorting Rocke."

[xlviii] Catchword: Why

Nor is it That I doe adoar
As its a Key, or is the door
Similitude of Prouidence
Declaring Stories out from thence
Heauen is my great resorting Rocke
There am I Harbour'd in my shocke[534]
From thence his Hand will place a Crowne
Of ample joyes. Sinke sorrowes downe.

most Welcom day, wherein I found a Ray,
For 15 yeares has been a Chanting Lay.

[109ᵛ] March 20: 1665:[535]   161

Our estate is sunke now almost to halfe it was: w*h*ich seemes to be a paradox. At this time that it appeares to *th*e eye of the world, to be quit[e] as much againe. if not twice more. Now let me doe as the Merchant to save his Credid and to promote his aduenture. Let me borrow too and keep up my repute. and freely pay the encombents[536] and taxes & debtes I am engaidged. And there may come a prize in the bennefit of Highburys Farmery. and my buildings[537] Fines may wade me ouer these present blocks. & failances[538] w*h*ich are not a few.

The rents of Essex. for about a year and half is oweing.[539] £70 more a year and quarters rent. nigh me.

£200 p*er* an*num* is in my hands *tha*t was rented of houses & Land: My Building continnues a dead Druge.[540] £700 I received enterist for is at an end. £200 Cosen W:[541] can receive none of this year and quarter. Highbury is a hazard in too respects in the opposition. and in the ill management. And stil I am attended with Law shuites.[542] Sister Austen[543] agen and another Troublesome man. sues in forme of paupery. These make up to me a Triple Tax: Now that *th*e Taxes by appointment are doubled: by mollestations are Trepbled too. How I shall come

---

[534] See note 402, above.

[535] i.e., 20 March 1665/6

[536] i.e., encumbrance: a burden on property, such as a liaibility or a mortgage (*OEDO*, n 4).

[537] KA's building at the Swan; see note 426, above, and Introduction, p. 13.

[538] i.e., failings

[539] See also fol. 100ʳ.

[540] See fols. 90ʳ, 100ʳ and 112ᵛ for KA's building at the Swan, and delays to the project.

[541] Cousin William; see fols. 99ᵛ–100ʳ.

[542] i.e., suits

[543] Susanna Austen: see note 373, above, and Introduction, pp. 11–13.

Book M 165

off of all: Time must tel *th*e Narration whether good or bad: : (And now doe borrow good sums.)[544]

And now must I reckown up my errour that I haue bin mistaken in my account, and Calculated wrong by measuring that Highbury and the swan wud arrive both together in their profits at Mic*hae*lmas last.[545] Tis true then my build‑ [110ʳ] ings were | most of them finishet. & the other out of Lease. Yet accidents and 162 Genneral troubles, and the vnsseasonable former year of drouth and mortality hath gaue an interruption. So that at this time in stead of profit. They are a Hydrea, a Cormorant of a double Head. deuowres[546] all I can procure, (and makes me fil the Chardg of Oxford and neccesary things more pinching.) £40 ^in a <. . ..>^ is p<..> Taxes for Highbury. £33: Fee farme: & to fit it up: by gates and fences &c. / There is nothing but has interruptions. and these litle things may blow away./

O my God thou hast helpet thy seruant through infinite many plunges, and obstacles formerly. and stil there dus grow more. and more will arrise while this world is stroud[547] with Thornes. and Thistles with rugednes & trouble. Lord let me never detirmine when my Tumults. when my Crosses, when my disappointments shal cease: But informe my self to waight thy leisure. to learne w*ha*t my duty is, My part of the Couenant that is the Condition for me to performe. of resignation and Obediance: Not to place my expectation on the promised part. For I know not thy pleasure whether the ful performance of it may not be respited, til that time when I may be sure by the Merits of my sauiour. noe interruption shal euer come. Noe Inherritance in danger of wresting away, Noe impositions there, w*hi*ch sin and (the) misery to distroy Mankind enforces by the Law of that deplorable Neccessity./

[110ᵛ]   One perswading me to pul downe that old building on   [*unp*]
            the east side of our house.   to build it new:

I dont loue to blot out orriginals. Noe that was their old grandfathers habitation. Richard Austens.[548] It shul remayne as ancient Euidences to obliedg our thankfulnes to God Allmighties goodnes. And that low vnvniforme building we wil leaue it for Fansy to model And itis supposed if she well contrive it may make a many faire roomes. And tho the Front ^it^ is plaine the adjacent dimensions and Galleries it convayes you to, may not make you vnwilling to salute *th*e Threshold. Yet I doe not by this discourse. put a barr. but that other reasons. may take place.

---

[544] This parenthetical insertion is in a smaller font, to squeeze it into available space at the line ending.

[545] See fol. 79ᵛ for this calculation.

[546] i.e., devours

[547] i.e., strewed

[548] KA's husband's grandfather? (Her children's grandfather was Thomas Austen.)

Aduising to Marry: and to keep w*h*at I could. (If I doe:) [549]
It shal never be sed I lived a widow (now almost 8 years) vnder the vaile of Hipocrisy, pretending to Honour the memory of my deceased Friend. And make it the foundation of my perticular Fortune, and raise a second bed. Tis true I will allow a proportion to my self and my two younger children shal haue there part. to doe them good in the World as well as my selfe. For my eldest I never intended him but with a proviso. which I hope by God Allmightes blesing he will not need our three enteristes./

[111ʳ]   1666   163

Tho I may be mistaken in many conceits of things Yet let me endeauour to trace the loue and fauour of God. to me in his many kind dispensations to me, tho they appear at first sight displeasant./[550]

The accidents and Crosses and vnkindneses we meet with in this world is like a paire of Staires one part of which goes down into a deep dungion. The uper part convayes you to lardg and beautiful roomes. For when we murmur and repine our discontents are apt to end in a cloudy Mallancholy or produce passionate designs of revenge and retributions towards our enemies

But when we improue our afflictiones and turne & look upon the right side of them. When we cast away the malice of men, when we wil not look on enterists and fortunes are supplanted of. When we are patient at our chardge, to defend our Title another reapes the benefit of. ^by^ All this is to Look upon him that sees it best to be soe. that intends my future happines by a medicinal draught. Let them proue supplanters and lesen my own estate, and giue me expences. Yet this wil be for good. And tis not from my enemies tis appointed from my best Friend to doe me good by them. Therefore wil I look stil upwards w*h*at the meaning of my God is. who can best dispose of accidents. And how shud I see the Grace of my God. ^then^ ~~Surely~~ through these dark shadowes I may behold his bright protection to me & mine / To him I repose and fly to.

[111ᵛ] My God I doe acknowledg thy prouidence in prefering me and bringing me in to this 164 Condition, and giueing me just confidence and hope of prosperous expectation.

O God preserue me in it, and suffer not these hopes *th*at haue honest grounds of establishment. Let not the envy & Injusti[c]es of men curcumvent me of. And for as much my oppositions are powerful, my enterprise hard, and how can I goe in and out before so many Contests and burdens as lye before me.

---

[549] This is the only point in *Book M* at which KA allows any possibility that she might remarry. See Introduction, p. 14.

[550] i.e., unpleasant

O God doe I not read Dauids story how weeke he was. brought up to tend on ewes. and Cattel. Not to gouerne men and Territories.[551] Thou didst give to him a Generous Noble, Wise, Spirit to quallify him before he was possesour of what was promised him, O God endue thy seruant with fitnes for my Condition; giue me a supply of prudence, of Iudgement of Consideration and activenes. to performe w*h*at I am steward of to thy Glory. and not vnto my own

But if our God deny us the accessions of this world w*h*ich is our right from the Law of men, and cast upon this family all the intendments of our aduarsaries: Depriue us of that Louely sete of Highbury. If we loose Fleetstreet Estate. And tho we neuer shal posses that Gift of Durhams.[552] If 15 hundred pound a year is gone. (w*h*ich now appears upon the sale and flight from^to^ my Son) and not one remayning to him. The pag behind tels me If Heauen permits it. Heauen will dispose it for the best[553]

And now I haue propounded the preparations of hope and fear, of Gain and lose. before me. And in the way of my life find disgusts and vnpleassantneses. In soe much |

[112ʳ] 1666. 165

as these litle occurrences makes me long for rest and peace and freedome, for Sollomons dessemation[554] of Mediocrity, for one handful of quiet rather then too handfuls with Trouble.[555]

I shal conclud my Meditations with my Sauiours resignation (when the sin of all mankind depresed him) And tho I dare not make a parralel between momentary earthly troubles. And my sauioures for worlds of sinneres: Yet I am incited from him our Captaine. And in my soule shal say his words. of releasement, w*h*ich refreshes me. For there o my sauiour in thy bitter agony, tho it was not long ere ^it^ was ouer Yet thou wast strengthened by an Angel[556] to sustaine that stroak of wrath. Thou art the Angel of the Couenant[557] I appeal and shelter my self. til all these Callamities are ouer in thy time.

[112ᵛ] I see seldome any thing must happen to me but must look big: not one Law suit 166
but diveres together.

Now not one house or ground to let. but almost all.

---

[551] David, author of the Psalms. 1 Samuel 16–17.

[552] i.e., the Red Lion and Durhams; see note 373, above, and Introduction, pp. 11–13.

[553] KA has written on her previous page that "God . . . can best dispose of accidents" (fol. 111ʳ).

[554] promulgation (*OEDO*)

[555] Ecclesiastes 4:6. See KA's earlier discussion of mediocrity, fols. 49ᵛ–50ʳ.

[556] Luke 22:43

[557] Malachi 3:1

<::> Accidents by sickenes. brought some in to my hand: But too great estates to us lie in my hand, my Buildings & Highbury.[558]

S*ir* Ieffery Pamers teling me. our busines was ordered to be brought before the privy Counsel.[559]
Did I think I was come to the Haven and am I siting still in the storme?[560] Have I entertained my selfe with pleasing expectation that if I lived to this day, my molestations and rencounteres with my aduarsaries should be ended.
Stil I am attacket, am pursued by them.
When I view over the assurances and hopes I have had in this book of my meditations As sometimes I am puting on wreathes of victory, I have overcome my enemies and my feares But such is the vnsurenes of every ground in this world to Anchor on. as I soone come to wade in deep places againe.[561]
The moone hath not more variations then the affaires of this life. Then the ebes and flowes of Fortune.
Allas with how many various accidents are we assaulted in this life, as sometimes am in hope sometimes in fear. sometime haue the apprehention of peace and delieuerance and freedome from environements
My errour hath bin I haue anticipated these desieres too soone. haue created ~~Halcione~~ imaginary[xlix] Halcione dayes.[562]   Well tho I am assaulted [113ʳ] stil by[l] | Aduarsaries and cannot tell when a dismition[563] will come. Yet if I consider in all that hath befallen me to this day, I haue found a supportation, a shelter, a hope And surely this is delieuerance to me all along. Neither have I beene really molested this last year and ½: never since February 1664:[564] by Law or Parliment Yet on euery occasion of the Parl*iment* siting, puts me to be on my watch: As when it was in Apriel 65: then in Oct*ober* 65: at Oxford: Then agen at Westminster. All w*h*ich times noe oppertunity was gaue to molest me. Now tis

---

[558] i.e., two estates: KA's buildings at the Swan, and Highbury. See note 426, above, and Introduction, pp. 8–11, 13.

[559] A petition to Whitehall on 10 April 1666 again called for Highbury to be recovered by the Crown (*CSPD, 1665–1666*, 344–45). See Introduction, p. 11.

[560] See note 402, above.

[561] See fol. 38ʳ.

[562] Calm days on which kingfishers were said to float on the water.

[563] dismission (i.e., dismissal; *OEDO*)

[564] i.e., February 1664/5, when KA attended the Committee of Parliament at Westminster. See fol. 59ᵛ and following; also see Introduction, pp. 10–11.

[xlix] jmaginary
[l] Catchword: ad-

Book M   *169*

in Sep*tember* 66: And it[li] may please God to prevent their doeing us danger. as his preventive favour in our Aid hath either to[565] disappointed them.†

These two whole yeares haue bin genneral greuiances to be afflicted with.[566]

    Feb*ruary* 65:[567] a Law suite did begin againe that was ended. not as yet ^grown^ to a Disturbing proceed

†I And now hath disapointed them also: And soe far is the ground of our hope, as there is. litle fear.

[113ᵛ] 26 Great God thy mercies how can I vnfold.   168
    They are so numerous not to be told.
    Deepe are th'imprestions of th'Almighties love,
    To wonder and astonishment doe move.
    Impossible to thinke, to speake, to write.
    And whats immesurable ^innumerable^ to indite.
    Lord in the masse, and ~~by~~ of their vollumes I
    Can onely speake, and they transcend the Sky.
    But the perticulars that my God hath wrought
    For soule and body, is beyond all thought.
    My wonder rises stil to such a hight
    Can onely gaze vpon that mountaines sight
    Tis my high Ioy. when in Heavens orb refine'd
    Shal vnderstand that love with a new minde
    With new Capacities, and with a beame
    Drawne from his glory Clarrify my Dime[568]
    My purblind soule. fit me for that aboade.
    To enter in the Temple of my God.
    Cellestial Solloquies inspired shal learne
    And to etternity singe notes serene.

---

    [565] *sic* (i.e., hitherto)

    [566] KA seems to be referring to the two years covered in the main chronology of *Book M*, 1664–1666.

    [567] i.e., February 1665/6. See note 373, above, and fol. 108ʳ for "Sister Austens renewing agen her pretention for the Red Lion."

    [568] KA here writes the "i" over another letter, no longer legible. Her meaning is unknown.

    [li] jt

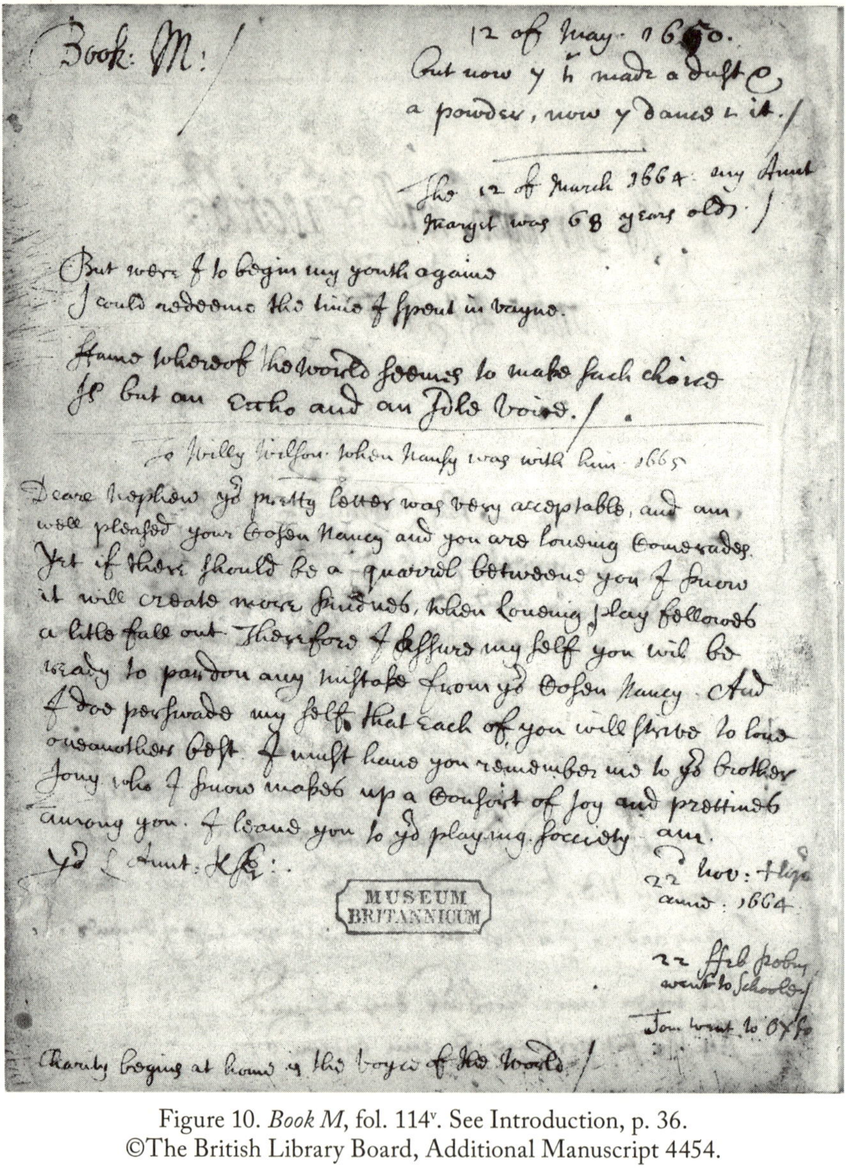

Figure 10. *Book M*, fol. 114ᵛ. See Introduction, p. 36.
©The British Library Board, Additional Manuscript 4454.

[114ʳ] <div style="text-align:center">My strength will I ascribe
vnto my God⁵⁶⁹</div> [unp]

D*eare* Sis*ter*: I hope now this Callamity⁵⁷⁰ is allmost gone. to haue an opportunity to see you. The absence of Friendes in a time of so many feares was with more impatience then when safety and health gave more confidence of the well fair one of another.

By my danger I pased: I see itis not the goeing away from (danger) can free one from peril. But it pleased God when soe great a Callamity was in the Kingdome to give me a perticular hazard. tho not in the same (degree. &) maner.

Stil when more troubles doe abound
By thy supportance. I am crown'd./

[114ᵛ]⁵⁷¹ **Book: M:/**   12 of May. 1650.   [unp]
but now <.> <.> made a dust &
a powder, now <.> dance <.> it./⁵⁷²

The 12 of March 1664: my Aunt
Marget was 68 years old. /.

But were I to begin my youth againe
I could redeeme the time I spent in vayne.

Fame whereof the world seemes to make such choice
Is but an Eccho and an Idle voice./⁵⁷³

To Willy Wilson. when Nansy⁵⁷⁴ was with him. 1665
Deare nephew y*our* pretty letter was very acceptable, and am well pleased your Cosen Nancy and you are loueing Comerades. Yet if there should be a quarrel

---

⁵⁶⁹ This inscription is in a large, florid script, like that of the title pages. The phrase echoes Psalm 68:34; see also fol. 55ʳ.

⁵⁷⁰ i.e., the plague

⁵⁷¹ For the layout of fol. 114ᵛ, see Introduction, p. 36, and Fig. 10, p. 170.

⁵⁷² KA uses shorthand symbols which I have been unable to decipher.

⁵⁷³ These two couplets are taken from Samuel Daniel's "The Complaint of Rosamond," *Delia. Contayning certayne Sonnets: with the complaint of Rosamond* (first published in 1592), lines 251–52 and 258–59; they are the concluding couplets of two adjacent seven-line stanzas.

⁵⁷⁴ KA's daughter Anne; see fol. 107ᵛ.

betweene you I know it will create more kindnes, when Loueing play fellowes a litle fall out. Therefore I assure my self you wil be ready to pardon any mistake from yo*ur* Cosen Nancy. And I doe perswade my self that each of you will strive to loue oneanother best. I must haue you remember me to yo*ur* brother Iony. who I know makes up a Consort of Ioy and prettines among you. I leaue you to yo*ur* playing. socciety am
Yo*ur* L*oveing* Aunt: K*atherine*

22d Nov*ember*: <. . .>
anne: 1664:

22 Feb*ruary* Robin
went to Schoole

Tom went to Oxford[575]

Charity begins at home is the voyce of the world./[576]

---

[575] See fols. 43ʳ–44ᵛ, 82ᵛ, 114ᵛ.

[576] This aphorism is taken from Sir Thomas Browne, *Religio Medici* (1642), 126.

Appendix

The following selections reprint source-texts for six sets of folios from *Book M*, enabling readers to observe how Katherine Austen engages with other works. I hope that readers will find it useful and interesting to be able to compare these source-texts with Austen's own writings.

It is impossible, however, to illustrate fully the scope and nature of Austen's borrowings in *Book M*, particularly when she jumps freely and flexibly between sources—for example, on fols. 13ʳ-16ʳ, when she moves between sermons by Gauden, Taylor and Donne. For most passages in *Book M*, it is only possible in this edition to alert readers, via the footnotes to the transcription, to the texts of which Austen makes use. Readers will be able to locate these other sources on the EEBO website should they wish to investigate further.

The following representative samples are listed according to the folio numbers in *Book M* to which each source-text relates.

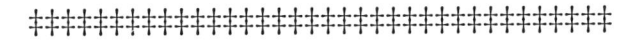

‡‡‡‡‡‡‡‡‡‡‡‡‡‡‡‡‡‡‡‡‡‡‡‡‡‡‡‡‡‡‡‡‡‡‡‡‡

1. See fols. 19ʳ–20ʳ:

Daniel Featley, "Whom have I in Heaven but thee," *Clavis Mystica* (1636), 546–50.

fixe our thoughts, or afford us any solid comfort or contentment? Who can aime steadily at a moving mark? or build firmly upon sinking sand? or hold fast a vanishing shadow? or rest himself upon the wings of the wind? as impossible is it to lay any sure ground of contentment, or foundation of happinesse in the unstable vanities and uncertaine comforts of this life. How can they fulfill our desires, or satisfie our appetites, which are not only empty, but emptinesse it selfe? How can they establish our hearts, sith they are altogether unstable themselves? How can they yeeld us any true delight or contentment, which have no verity in them, but are shadowes and painted shewes, like the carved dishes *Caligula* set before his flatterers; or the grapes drawn by *Zeuxis*, wherewith he deceived the birds? The best of them are no better than the apples of Sodome, of which *Pliny* and *Solinus* write, that they are apples whilest you behold them, but ashes when you touch them: or like the herb Sardoa in Sardinia, upon which if a man feed, it so worketh upon his spleen, that he never leaveth laughing, till he dyeth through immoderate mirth. Honours, riches, pleasures are but glorious titles written in golden characters; under them we find nothing but vanity: under the title of nobility nothing but a brag of our parents vertue, and that is vanity; under honour nothing but the opinion of other men, and this can be but vanity; under glory but breath and wind, and this is certainly vanity; under pleasure but [b] repentance & folly, and is not this vanity? under sumptuous buildings, rich hangings, & gorgeous apparell, but ostentation of wealth and outward pomp, & this is vanity of vanity. Nobility in the originall of it is but the infamy of *Adam*: (for it knew not *Hevah* till after his fall & grievous prevarication) beauty the daughter of corruption, apparell the cover of shame, gold & silver the dregs of the earth, oyles & costly ointments the sweat of trees, silkes & velvets the excrements of wormes; and shall our immortall spirit, nobly descended from the sacred Trinity, match so low with this neather world, and take these toyes and trifles for a competent dowry?

And let this suffice to be spoken to the words for their full explication; let us now heare what they speake to us for our further use and instruction.

{ 1. They speake to our faith, that it be resolved upon God only.
{ 2. To our devotion, that it be directed to God only.
{ 3. To our love, that it be entirely fixed on God only.

{ 1. True faith saith, *whom have I in heaven but thee* to relye upon?
{ 2. True religion saith, *whom have I but thee* to call upon?
{ 3. True love saith, *whom have I but thee* to settle upon?

No Papist can beare a part with *David* in this song, saying, *whom have I in heaven but thee, O Lord?* for they have many in heaven, to whom they addresse their prayers in generall, & often solicite them upon speciall occasions: as for raine, for faire weather, in a common plague, in danger of childbirth, in perills by sea, in perills by land, for their owne health and recovery, and for the safety of their beasts & cattell; as appeares by the formes of prayers yet extant in their Liturgies, Offices, Manuels, & Service books. Doubtlesse these *monopolies* were not granted to Saints in *Davids* time; for he had recourse every-where to God immediately for any thing he stood in need of:

[b] *Eras. Apoph. Demos.* Non emam tanti pœnitere.

The devout soules Motto.

of: neither had the ancient Fathers any knowledge of so many new *masters of requests* in heaven, to preferre their petitions to God: for they addressed themselves all to one Mediatour betwixt God and man, the man Christ Jesus, who sitteth at the right hand of his Father, to take all our petitions, & to recommend them unto him. I can make no other construction of the words of [c] *Origen, Wee must religiously worship or invocate none but God and his only begotten Son. We must call upon none but God*, saith [d] *Jerome*. [e] *Tertullian* goeth farther on our way, *We can pray to none other but God: whatsoever is to be wished for Cæsar, as he is a man or a Prince, I cannot begge it of any other than of him from whom I know I shall receive what I aske, because he alone can performe it, and I his servant depend upon none but him*. But what stand I upon the testimonies of two or three Fathers? the whole Synod of Laodicea condemneth the superstitious errour of some, who *taught, that we ought to use Angels as mediatours between God and us*, and to *pray unto them*. And for Saints, who have no more commission to solicit our busines in heaven than Angels, howsoever it pleased the ancient Church to make honourable mention of them in their publike Service, as we doe of the blessed Virgin, the Archangel, the Apostles & Evangelists; yet S.[g] *Austin* cleareth the Christians of those times from any kind of invocation: *The Martyrs*, saith he, *in their place and ranke are named, yet not called upon by the Priest, who offereth the sacrifice*. Invocation is the highest branch of divine worship, and they who bow downe to, and call upon Saints, consequently put Saints in Gods room; & beleeve in them: *Quomodo enim invocabunt, in quos non credunt? How*[h] *shall they call on them, on whom they have not beleeved?* They who call upon Saints deceased, & hope for any benefit by such prayers, must be perswaded that the Saints are present in all places, to heare their prayers, and receive their petitions, and that they understand particularly all their affaires, and are privie to the very secrets of their hearts; and is not this to make gods of Saints?

[i] *Qui fingit sacros auro vel marmore vultus,*
non facit ille deos: qui rogat ille facit.

Yea, but say our Romish adversaries, had you a suit to the King, you would *make a friend at Court*, & employ some in favour with his Majesty to solicit your affaires; why take ye not the like course in your businesse of greater importance in the Court of Heaven? We answer:

First, because God himselfe checketh such carnall imaginations, and overthroweth the ground of all such arguments by his holy Prophet, saying, [k] *My thoughts are not your thoughts, neither are your waies my waies*. Therefore we are brought to the presence of kings (saith S.[l] *Ambrose*) *by lords & officers, because the king is a man;* & all cannot have immediate accesse unto him, neither will he take it well, that all sorts of people at all times should presse upon him: but it is not so with God: he calleth all [m] unto him, calls upon all to [n] call upon him, & promiseth help & [o] salvation to all that shall so do: *neither need we any spokes man* (saith he) *to him, save a devout and religious mind*.

Secondly, admit the proportion to hold between the King of Heaven and

---

c Lib.8.cont. Cel. Μόνῳ προσκυνητέον τῷ ἐπὶ πᾶσι Θεῷ καὶ μονογενεῖ.
d Hieron. in Prov.l.1.c 2.
Neminem invocare nisi Deum debemus.
e Tertul.apol. c.30. Quæcunque hominis & Cæsaris vota sunt, hæc ab alio orare non possum, quàm à quo scio me consecuturum, quoniam & ipse est qui solus præstat, & ego familus ejus qui eum solum invoco.
f Theod.com. in 2.ad Colos. Synodus Laodicea lege prohibuit, ne præcarentur Angelos, ubi agit de oratoriis Michaelis, & eos perstringit qui dicebant oportere per Angelos divinam sibi benevolentiam conciliare.
g Aug.l.22. de civit.Dei c.10. Martyres suo loco & ordine nominantur, non tamen à Sacerdote qui sacrificat, invocantur.
h Rom.10.14.
i Mart.epigr.
k Esay 55.8.
l Amb. in ep. ad Rom.1.1. Itur ad reges per tribunos,

& comites, quia homo utique rex est, ad Deum quem nihil latet promerendum suffragatore non est op[us], sed mente devotâ. m Mat.11.28. Come unto mee all that labour, &c. n Psal.50.15. Call upon mee in the day of trouble, and I will heare, &c. o Joel 2.32. Whosoever shall call upon the Name, &c.

earthly

earthly Princes, yet the reason holdeth not: for if the King appoint a certain officer to take all supplications, and exhibit all petitions unto him, hee will not take it well, if we use any other; but so it is in our present case, God hath appointed us a [p] Mediator not only of redemption, but also of [q] intercession, who is not only [r] able, but most willing to preferre all our suits, & procure a gracious answer for us: *for we have not an high Priest, which cannot be touched with the feeling of our infirmities, but was in all points tempted like as we are, yet without sin: let us therfore come boldly unto the throne of grace, that we may obtain mercy, and find grace to help in time of need.* Wee know not whether Saints heare us, or rather we know they heare us not: *Esay* 63.16. Abraham *is ignorant of us, and Israel acknowledgeth us not.* If they heare us, we know not whether God will heare them for us; but wee know that our Saviour heareth us, and that God alwaies heareth him when he prayeth for us: *John* 11.42. *I know that thou hearest mee alwaies.*

Yet our Saint-invocators have one refuge to flye unto, and they hold it a very safe one: We call upon the living, say they, to pray for us; why may we not be so far indebted to the Saints departed, who the further they are from us, the neerer they are to God? If it be no wrong to Christs intercession to desire the prayers of our friends in this life, neither can it be any derogation to his Mediatourship to call upon Saints deceased. Of this argument [s] *Bellarmine* as much braggeth, as *Peleus* of his sword, *Profectò istud argumentum hæretici nunquam solvere potuerunt*, the hereticks, saith he, were never able to untie this argument. I beleeve him, because there is no knot at all in it. For,

First, we do not properly invocate any man living, ἐπικαλούμεθα ὡς ὁμοδούλους we call to them to assist us with their prayers, we call not upon them, as putting any confidence in them. When at parting we usually commend our selves to our friends, and desire them to commend us to God in their prayers, we require of them a duty of Christian charity; we do them therein no honour, much lesse performe any religious service to them, as the Church of Rome doth to Saints deceased.

Secondly, when wee pray them to pray for us, wee make this request to them, as co-adjutors, to joyn with us in the duty of praier, not as mediators, to use their favour with God, or plead their merits, as Papists do in their Letanies, *adjuring* God (as it were) by the faith of Confessors, & constancy of Martyrs, & chastity of virgins, & abstinence of monks, & merits of all Saints.

Thirdly, God commandeth the living to have a fellow-feeling of one anothers miseries, and to [t] pray one for another; but he no where layeth such an injunction upon the dead to pray for us, or upon us to pray to them:

Fourthly, we have many presidents in Scripture of the faithfull, who have earnestly besought their brethren to remember them in their [u] prayers; but among all the songs of *Moses*, psalmes of *David*, complaints of *Jeremy*, and prayers of Prophets and Apostles, you shall not find any one directed to any Saint departed; from the first of *Genesis* to the last Verse of the *Apocalypse*, there is no precept for the invocation of Saints, no example of it, no promise unto it.

Fifthly & lastly, we entreat not any man living to pray for us, but either by word of mouth when he is present with us, or by some friend, who wee know will acquaint him with our desire, or by letters, when we have sure

meanes

The devout soules Motto. 549

meanes to conveigh them to him, whereby hee may understand how the case standeth with us, & what that is in particular for which we desire his prayers. All which reasons faile in the invocation of Saints deceased: for wee have no messengers to send to them, nor means to conveigh letters to the place where they are, neither are they within hearing, neither can we be any way assured that they either know our necessities, or are privie to the secrets of our heart. For the Mathematicall glasse, w[ch] some of the Schoolmen have set in heaven, wherein (they say) the Saints in heaven see all things done upon earth, to wit, in God, who seeth all things; it hath bin long since beat into pieces: for I demand, Is this essence of God a necessary glasse, or a voluntary? that is, Do they see all things in it, or such things only as it pleaseth him to present to their view? if they see all things, their knowledge must needs be infinite as Gods is, they must needs comprehend in it all things past, present & future; yea, the thoughts of the heart, w[ch] God peculiarly [x]assumeth to himself: yea, the day of Judgment, which our Saviour assureth us *no man knoweth, not the*[y] *Angels in heaven, nor the son of* [z] *man, as man*. If they see only such things as God is pleased to reveale unto them, how may he that prayeth unto them be assured, that God wil reveale unto them either his wants in particular, or his prayers? how can he pray unto them in faith, who hath no word of faith, whereby hee may be assured either that God revealeth his prayers to them, or that God will accept their prayers for him? Certainly, there was no such chrystal instrument as Papists dream of, to discover unto Saints departed the whole earth, & all things that are in it in the time of *Abraham, Isaac,* or *Josiah*: for St. *Austin* in his book *de* [a] *curâ pro mortuis,* out of the second book of *Kings,* & the 63. of *Esay* concludeth, that sith *kings see not the evils which befal their people after their death; & sith parents are ignorant of their children, without doubt the Saints departed have no intelligence how things pass after their death here upon earth.* So far is it fr[=o] being a branch of their happines, to know the passages of human affaires here, that S.[b] *Jerom* maketh it a part of their happines, that they are altogether ignorant of them: *happy Nepotian, who neither heareth nor seeth any of those things,* w[ch] would vexe his righteous soule, & do cause us who see & hear them, often to water our plants.

By this which hath bin said, any whose judgements are not fore-stalled, may perceive the impiety of that part of Romish piety which concerneth invocation of Saints; it is not only needless & fruitless, but also superstitious, & most sacrilegious: for it robbeth God of a speciall part of his honour, and wrongeth Christ in his office of mediatour. When he holdeth out his golden sceptre unto us, & calleth to us, saying, *Come unto me, come by me, I am the way,* shal we run to any other to bring us to him? shall we seek a way to the way? shall we use mediatours to our mediatour? this were to lay a like imputation upon our Redeemer, to that which S.[c] *Austin* casteth upon the heathen *Apollo, the interpreter of the gods needeth an interpreter, & we are to cast lots upon the lot it selfe*. Let it not seem burthensome unto you, my deare brethren, that I speak much in behalf of him, who alone speaketh in behalf of us all: we cannot do our Redeemer a worser affront, we cannot offer our mediatour a greater wrong, than to goe from him whom God hath appointed our perpetuall advocate & intercessor, & imploy Saints in our suites to God, as if they were in greater grace with the Father, or they were better affected to us than he. Have we the like experience of their love as we have of his? did they pawn their lives for us? have they ransomed

---

x *Apoc.*2.23. *I am he that searcheth the heart and reines.*

y *Mat.*24.36 z *Mar.*13.32 *But of that day and houre knowth no man, no not the Angels that are in heaven neither the son, but the Father.*

a *Cap.*13. Si parentes non intersunt, qui sunt alii mortuorum, qui noverunt quid agamus, quid ve patiamur, & ibi sunt spiritus defunctorum ubi non vident quæcunque aguntur, ne even, une in istâ vitâ hominibus.

b *Jerom. in epitaph. Nepot* Fœlix Nepotianus qui hæc non audit, non videt.

c *De civit. Dei l.*1. Interpres deorum egetinterprete, & sors ipsa referenda est ad sortes.

550   *The devout soules Motto.*

med us with their bloud? will he refuse us, who gave us himselfe? will he not powre out hearty prayers for us, who powred out his heart bloud for us? will he spare breath in our cause, who breathed out his soule for us? shall we forsake the *fountain of living water*, and *draw out of broken cisternes that can hold no water*? shall we run from the source to the conduit for the water of life? from the sun to the beam for light of knowledge? from the head to the members for the life of grace? from the king to the vassall for a crowne of glory?

But I made choice of this Scripture rather to stirre up your devotion, than to beat down Popish superstition; therfore I leave arguments of confutation, & set to motives of perswasion. Look how the Opal presenteth to the eye the beautifull colours of almost all precious stones; so the graces, vertues, & perfections of all natures shine in the face of God to draw our love to him: among which, two most kindle our affection, vertue and beauty; nothing so lovely as vertue, which is the beauty of the mind: & beauty, which is the chief grace and vertue of the body. To give vertue her due, wch is the first place, we speak not so properly, when we say that God hath any vertue, as when we attribute to him all vertue in the abstract, all wisdom, all justice, all holines, all goodnes. Goodnes is the rule of our will, but Gods will is the rule of goodnes it selfe: we are to doe things because they are just & good; but contrariwise things are just & good because God doth them; therfore if vertue be the *load-stone* of our love, it wil first draw it to God, whose nature is the perfection of all vertue. As for beauty, what is it but proportion & colour? the beauty of colour it self is light, & light is but a shadow or obscure delineation of God, whose face darkneth the sun, & dazleth the eies of the Cherubins, who to save them, hold their wings before them like a plume of feathers. A glympse wherof when the Prophet *David* saw, he was so ravished with it, that as if there were nothing else worthy the seeing, & it were impossible to have enough of so admirable an object, he crieth out, ^d*seek his face evermore*; not so much for the delight he took in beholding it, as for the light he received from it. For beholding the glory of God *as in a mirrour with open face, we are changed into his image*, & after a sort made partakers of the *divine nature*. O my soul, saith a Saint of God, mark what thou lovest; for thou becommest like to that wch thou likest, *Si coelum diligis, coelum es, si terram diligis, terra es, audeo dicere, si Deum diligis, Deus es*: if thou sincerely & perfectly lovest heavenly objects, thou becomest heavenly, if carnall, thou becomest sensuall, if spirituall, thou becomest ghostly, if God, thou becomest divine. Let us stay a while, & consider what a wonderful change is wrought in the soule of man by the power of divine love; surely though a deformed Black-a-moor look his eies out upon the fairest beauty the world can present, hee getteth no beauty by it, but seems the more ougly by standing in sight of so beautiful a creature: the sun burns them black, & darkeneth their sight, who long gaze upon his beams; but contrarily, the Sun of righteousnes the more we looke upon him, the more he enlighteneth the eies, & maketh them fair, & their faces shine who behold him, as *Moses* his did, after he came down from the Mount where he had parley with God. O then let us love to behold him, the sight of whose countenance will make us fair & lovely to behold: let us conform our selvs to him, who wil transform us into himself: let us reflect the beams of our affection upon the *father of lights*: let us knit our hearts to him, whom *freely* to love is our *bounden duty*, to embrace is *chastity*, to marry is *virginity*, to serve is *liberty*, to desire is *contentment*, to imitate is *perfection*, to enjoy is everlasting happines. To whom, &c.

d *Psa.* 105. 4.

Pou'in. in o. we. li hun amemus quem amare debuum, quem amplecti chastitas, cui nubere virginitas, &c.

2. See fols. 25ʳ–27ʳ:

Jeremy Taylor, Sermon IX, "Of Godly Fear," (*Eniautos*, 1653), Part III, 114–24.

SERMON, IX.
Part III.

I Am now to give account concerning the excesse of fear, not *directly* and *abstractedly* as it is a *passion*, but as it is subjected in *Religion*, and degenerates into *superstition*: For so among the Greeks, *fear* is the ingredient and half of the constitution of that folly; Δεισιδαιμονία φοβόθεια said *Hesychius*, it is a fear of God, Δεισιδαίμων ϕιλὸς that's more; it is a timorousnesse: the *superstitious* man is afraid of the gods (said the Etymologist) δειλὸς τὰς θεοὺς ὅπερ τὰς τυράννας, fearing of God as if he were a tyrant, and an unreasonable exacter of duty upon unequall terms, and disproportionable, impossible degrees, and unreasonable, and great and little instances.

1. But this fear some of the old Philosophers thought unreasonable in all cases, even towards God himself; and it was a branch of the Epicurean Doctrine, that God medled not any thing below, and was to be loved and admired, but not feared at all; and therefore they taught men neither to fear death, nor to fear punishment after death, nor any displeasure of God: *His terroribus ab Epicuro soluti non metuimus Deos*, said *Cicero*; and thence came this acceptation of the word, that *superstition* should signifie an unreasonab'e fear of God: It is true, he and all his scholars extended the case beyond the measure, and made all fear unreasonable; but then, if we upon grounds of reason and divine revelation shall better discern the measure, of the fear of God; whatsoever fear we find to be unreasonable, we may by the same reason call it *superstition*, and reckon it criminall, as they did all fear; that it may be call'd *superstition*, their authority is sufficient warrant for the grammar of the appellative; and that it is *criminall*, we shall derive from better principles.

But besides this, there was another part of its definition, Δεισιδαίμων, ὁ τὰ εἴδωλα σέβων εἰδωλολάτρης, the superstitious man is also an Idolater, δειλὸς ἐργ' θεοῖς, one that is afraid of something besides God. The *Latines* according to their custome, imitating the *Greeks* in all their learned notices of things, had also the same conception of this, and by their word [*Superstitio*] understood the worship of *Dæmons* or separate spirits; by which they meant, either their *minores Deos*, or else

Of godly Fear.

A | else their ἥρωας ἀποθεωθέντας their braver personages whose souls were supposed to live after death; the fault of this was the object of their Religion; they gave a *worship* or a *fear* to whom it was not due; for when ever they worship'd the great God of heaven and earth, they never cal'd that *superstition* in an evill sense, except the Ἄθεοι, they that beleeved there was no God at all. Hence came the etymology of superstition: it was a worshipping or fearing the spirits of their dead *Heroes, quos superstites credebant,* whom they thought to be alive after their ἀποθέωσις or Deification; or, *quos superstantes credebant,* standing in places and thrones above us; and it

B | alludes to that admirable description of old age which *Solomon* made beyond all the Rhetorick of the *Greeks* and *Romans* [*Also they shall be afraid of that which is high, and fears shall be in the way*] intimating the weaknesse of old persons, who if ever they have been religious, are apt to be abused into superstition; They are *afraid of that which is high,* that is, of spirits and separate souls, of those excellent beings which dwell in the regions above; meaning, that then they are superstitious. However, fear is most commonly its principle, alwaies its ingredient. For if it enter first by credulity and a weak perswasion, yet it becomes incorporated into the spirit of the

C | man, and thought necessary, and the action it perswades to dares not be omitted, for fear of an evill themselves dream of: upon this account the sin is reducible to two heads: the 1. is, Superstition of an undue object. 2. Superstition of an undue expression to a right object.

1. Superstition of an undue object, is that which the Etymologist cals τῶν εἰδώλων σέβασμα the worshipping of idols; the Scripture addes θύειν δαιμονίοις a *sacrificing to Dæmons* * in St. *Paul* and in * *Baruch*; where although we usually read it *sacrificing to Devils,* yet it was

D | but accidentall that they were such; for those indeed were evill spirits who had seduced them, and tempted them to such ungodly rites; (and yet they who were of the *Pythagorean* sect, pretended a more holy worship, and did their devotion to Angels:) But whosoever shall worship Angels do the same thing; they worship them because they are good and powerfull, as the Gentiles did the Devils whom they thought so; and the error which the Apostle reproves, was not in matter of Judgement, in mistaking bad angels for good, but in matter of manners and choice; they mistook the creature for the Creator; and therefore it is more fully expressed by St. *Paul* in a generall signification, *they worshipped the creature,* παρὰ τὸν κτίσαντα *be-*

E | *sides the Creator,* so it should be read; if we worship any creature *besides God,* worshipping so as the worship of him becomes a part of Religion, it is also a direct *superstition*; but concerning this part of superstition, I shall not trouble this discourse, because I know no Christians blamable in this particular but the Church of *Rome,* and they that communicate with her in the worshipping of Images, of Angels,

Serm. IX.

Eccles. 12. 5.

* 1 Cor. 10. 20.
* 4. 7.

Rom. 1. 25.

Of godly Fear.

gels, and Saints, burning lights and perfumes to them, making offerings, confidences, advocations and vowes to them, and direct and solemn divine worshipping the Symbols of bread and wine, when they are consecrated in the holy Sacrament. These are direct superstition, as the word is used by all Authors profane and sacred, and are of such evill report, that where ever the word Superstition does signifie any thing criminall, these instances must come under the definition of it. They are λατρεία ἢ κτίσεως; a λατρεία παρὰ ἢ κτίσαντα, a *cultus superstitum*, a *cultus Daemonum*, and therefore besides that they have ἴδιον ἔλεγχον, a proper reproof in Christian Religion, are condemned by all wise men, which call *superstition* criminall.

But as it is superstition to worship any thing παρὰ ἢ κτίσαντα *besides the Creator*, so it is superstition to worship God παρὰ τὸ ἐυγνωμον, παρὰ τὸ πρέπον, παρ' ὃ δεῖ, otherwise then is decent, proportionable or described. Every inordination of Religion that is not in defect, is properly called superstition: ὁ μὲν εὐσεβὴς φίλος Θεῷ, ὁ δὲ δεισιδαίμων κόλαξ Θεῷ, said *Maximus Tyrius*, The true worshipper is a lover of God, the superstitious man loves him not, but flatters: To which if we adde, that fear, unreasonable fear is also superstition, and an ingredient in its definition; we are taught by this word to signifie all irregularity and inordination in actions of Religion. The summe is this; the *Atheist* cal'd *all worship of God superstition*, the *Epicurean* cal'd *all fear of God superstition*, but did not condemn his *worship*; the other part of wise men cal'd *all unreasonable fear*, and inordinate worship superstition, but did not condemn *all fear*: But *the Christian*, besides this, cals *every error* in worship in the *manner*, or *excesse*, by this name, and condemns it.

Now because the three great actions of Religion are, *to worship God, to fear God, and to trust in him*, by the inordination of these three actions, we may reckon three sorts of this crime; *the excesse of fear*, and *the obliquity in trust*, and *the errors in worship*, are the three sorts of *superstition* : the first of which is only pertinent to our present consideration.

1. Fear is the duty we owe to God as being the God of power and Justice, the great Judge of heaven and earth, the avenger of the cause of Widows, the Patron of the poor, and the Advocate of the oppressed, a mighty God and terrible, and so essentiall an enemy to sin, that he spared not his own Son, but gave him over to death, and to become a sacrifice, when he took upon him our Nature, and became a person obliged for our guilt. *Fear* is the great bridle of intemperance, the modesty of the spirit, and the restraint of gaieties and dissolutions; it is the *girdle* to the soul, and the handmaid to repentance, the arrest of sin, and the cure or antidote to the spirit of reprobation; it preserves our apprehensions of the divine Majesty, and hinders our single actions from combining to sinfull habits; it is the mother of consideration, and the nurse of sober counsels, and

it

Of godly Fear.

it puts the soul to fermentation and activity, making it to passe from trembling to caution, from caution to carefulnesse, from carefulnesse to watchfulnesse, from thence to prudence, and by the gates and progresses of repentance, it leads the soul on to love, and to felicity, and to joyes in God that shall never cease again. Fear is the guard of a man in the dayes of prosperity, and it stands upon the watch-towers and spies the approaching danger, and gives warning to them that laugh loud, and feast in the chambers of rejoycing, where a man cannot consider by reason of the noises of wine, and jest, and musick: and if prudence takes it by the hand, and leads it on to duty, it is a state of grace, and an universall instrument to infant Religion, and the only security of the lesse perfect persons; and in all senses is that homage we owe to God who sends often to demand it, even then when he speaks in thunder, or smites by a plague, or awakens us by threatning, or discomposes our easinesse by sad thoughts, and tender eyes, and fearfull hearts, and trembling considerations.

But this so excellent grace is soon abused in the best and most tender spirits; in those who are softned by Nature and by Religion, by infelicities or cares, by sudden accidents or a sad soul; and the Devill observing, that fear like spare diet starves the fevers of lust, and quenches the flames of hell, endevours to highten this abstinence so much as to starve the man, and break the spirit into timorousnesse and scruple, sadnesse and unreasonable tremblings, credulity and trifling observation, suspicion and false accusations of God; and then vice being turned out at the gate, returns in at the postern, and does the work of hell and death by running too inconsiderately in the paths which seem to lead to heaven. But so have I seen a harmlesse dove made dark with an artificiall night, and her eyes ceel'd and lock'd up with a little quill, soaring upward and flying with amazement, fear and an undiscerning wing, she made toward heaven, but knew not that she was made a train and an instrument, to teach her enemy to prevail upon her and all her defencelesse kindred: so is a superstitious man, zealous and blinde, forward and mistaken, he runs towards heaven as he thinks, but he chooses foolish paths; and out of fear takes any thing that he is told or fancies; and guesses concerning God by measures taken from his own diseases and imperfections. But fear when it is inordinate, is never a good counsellor, nor makes a good friend; and he that fears God as his enemy is the most compleatly miserable person in the world. For if he with reason beleeves God to be his enemy, then the man needs no other argument to prove that he is undone then this, that the fountain of blessing (in this state in which the man is) will never issue any thing upon him but cursings. But if he fears this without reason, he makes his fears true by the very suspicion of God, doing him dishonour, and then do-

L ing

118   *Of godly Fear.*

SERM. IX.

ing those fond and trifling acts of jealousie which will make God to be what the man feared he already was; We do not know God, if we can think any hard thing concerning him. If God be mercifull, let us only fear to offend him; but then let us never be fearfull, that he will destroy us when we are carefull not to displease him. There are some persons so miserable and scrupulous, such perpetuall tormentors of themselves with unnecessary fears, that their meat and drink is a snare to their consciences; if they eat, they fear they are gluttons, if they fast, they fear they are hypocrites, and if they would watch, they complain of sleep as of a deadly sin; and every temptation though resisted, makes them cry for pardon; and every return of such an accident, makes them think God is angry; and every anger of God will break them in pieces.

These persons do not beleeve noble things concerning God, they do not think that he is as ready to pardon them, as they are to pardon a sinning servant; they do not beleeve how much God delights in mercy, nor how wise he is to consider and to make abatement for our unavoidable infirmities; they make judgement of themselves by the measures of an Angell, and take the accounts of God by the proportions of a Tyrant. The best that can be said concerning such persons is, that they are hugely tempted, or hugely ignorant. For although *ignorance* is by some persons named *the mother of devotion*; yet if it fals in a hard ground, it is *the mother of Atheisme*, if in a soft ground, it is *the parent of superstition*: but if it proceeds from evill or mean opinions of God, (as such scruples and unreasonable fears do many times) it is an evill of a great impiety, and in some sense, and if it were in equall degrees, is as bad as Atheisme; for he that sayes there was no such man as *Julius Cæsar*, does him lesse displeasure, then he that sayes there was, but that he was a Tyrant, and a bloudy parricide. And the *Cimmerians* were not esteemed impious for saying that there was no sun in the heavens; But *Anaxagoras* was esteemed irreligious for saying the sun was a very stone: And though to deny there is a God is a high impiety and intolerable, yet he sayes worse, who beleeving there is a God sayes, he delights in humane sacrifices, in miseries and death, in tormenting his servants, and punishing their very infelicities and unavoidable mischances. To be God, and to be essentially and infinitely good, is the same thing, and therefore to deny either is to be reckoned among the greatest crimes in the world.

Adde to this, that he that is afraid of God, cannot in that disposition love him at all; for what delight is there in that religion which drawes me to the Altar as if I were going to be sacrificed, or to the Temples as to the Dens of Bears? *Oderunt quos metuunt, sed colunt tamen*: whom men fear they hate certainly, and flatter readily, and worship timorously; and he that saw *Hermolaus* converse with *Alexander*; and *Pausanias* follow *Philip* the *Macedonian*; or *Chæreas*

kissing

Of godly Fear.

A kissing the feet of *Cajus Caligula* would have observed how sordid men are made with fear, and how unhappy and how hated Tyrants are in the midst of those acclamations, which are loud, and forc'd, and unnaturall, and without love or fair opinion. And therefore although the *Atheist* sayes there is no God, the *scrupulous, fearfull,* and *superstitious man* does heartily wish what the other does beleeve.

B But that the evill may be proportionable to the folly, and the punishment to the crime, there is no man more miserable in the world, then the man who fears God as his enemy, and Religion as a snare, and duty as intolerable, and the Commandements as impossible, and his Judge as implacable, and his anger as certain, unsufferable, and unavoidable: whither shall this man goe? where shall he lay his burden? where shall he take sanctuary? for he fears the Altars as the places where his soul bleeds and dies; and God who is his Saviour he looks upon as his enemy; and because he is Lord of all, the miserable man cannot change his service unlesse it be apparently for a worse. And therefore of all the evils of the minde, *fear* is certainly the worst and the most intolerable;

C *levity* and *rashnesse* have in it some spritefulnesse, and greatnesse of action; *anger* is valiant; *desire* is busie and apt to hope; *credulity* is oftentimes entertain'd and pleased with images and appearances: But *fear* is dull, and sluggish, and treacherous, and flattering, and dissembling, and miserable, and foolish. Every false opinion concerning God is pernicious and dangerous; but if it be joyned with trouble of spirit, as fear, scruple or superstition are, it is like a wound with an inflamation, or a strain of a sinew with a contusion, or contrition of the part, painfull and unsafe; it puts on to actions when it self is driven; it urges reason, and circumscribes it, and makes it pityable, and ridiculous in its consequent follies; which if we

D consider it, will sufficiently reprove the folly, and declare the danger.

Almost all ages of the world have observed many instances of fond perswasions and foolish practises proceeding from violent fears and scruples in matter of Religion. *Diomedon* and many other Captains were condemned to dye, because after a great *Naval victory* they pursued the flying enemies, and did not first bury their dead. But *Chabrias* in the same case first buryed the dead, and by that time the enemy rallyed, and returned and beat his Navy, and made his masters pay the price of their importune superstition; they fear'd

E where they should not, and where they did not, they should. From hence proceeds observation of signs, and unlucky dayes; and the people did so when the *Gregorian* account began, continuing to call those unlucky dayes which were so signed in their tradition or *Erra pater*, although the day upon this account fell 10 dayes sooner; and men were transported with many other trifling contingen-

Of godly Fear.

gencies and little accidents; which when they are one entertain'd by weaknesse, prevail upon their own strength, and in sad natures and weak spirits have produced effects of great danger and sorrow. *Aristodemus* King of the *Messenians* in his warre against the *Spartans*, prevented the sword of the enemies by a violence done upon himself, only because his dogs howl'd like wolves, and the Soothsayers were afraid because the *Briony* grew up by the wals of his Fathers house: and *Nicias* Generall of the *Athenian* forces sate with his armes in his bosome, and suffered himself and 40000 men tamely to fall by the insolent enemy, only because he was afraid of the labouring and eclipsed Moon. When the Marble statues in *Rome* did sweat (as naturally they did against all rainy weather) the *Augures* gave an alarum to the City; but if lightning struck the spire of the Capitoll, they thought *the summe of affairs*, and the Commonwealth it self was indanger'd. And this *Heathen folly* hath stuck so close to the *Christian*, that all the Sermons of the Church for 1600 years have not cured them all: But the practises of weaker people and the artifice of ruling Priests have superinduced many new ones. When Pope *Eugenius* sang Masse at *Rhemes*, and some few drops from the Chalice were spilt upon the pavement, it was thought to foretell mischief, warres, and bloud, to all Christendome, though it was nothing but carelesnesse and mischance of the Priest: and because *Thomas Becket* Archbishop of *Canterbury* sang the Masse of *Requiem* upon the day he was reconcil'd to his Prince, it was thought to foretell his own death by that religious office: and if men can listen to such whispers, and have not reason and observation enough to confute such trifles, they shall still be afrighted with the noise of birds, and every night-raven shall foretell evill as *Micaiah* to the King of Israel, and every old woman shall be a Prophetesse, and the events of humane affairs which should be managed by the conduct of counsell, of reason, and religion, shall succeed by chance, by the flight of birds, and the meeting with an evill eye, by the falling of the salt, or the decay of reason, of wisdome, and the just religion of a man.

To this may be reduc'd the observation of dreams, and fears commenced from the fancies of the night. For the superstitious man does not rest, even when he sleeps, neither is he safe because dreams usually are false, but he is afflicted for fear they should tell true. Living and waking men have one world in common, they use the same air and fire, and discourse by the same principles of Logick and reason; but men that are asleep have every one a world to himself, and strange perceptions; and the superstitious hath none at all; his reason sleeps, and his fears are waking, and all his rest, and his very securities to the fearfull man turn into afrights and insecure expectation of evils, that never shall happen; they make their rest uneasie and chargeable, and they still vex their weary soul,

Of godly Fear.

A soul, not considering there is no other sleep, for sleep to rest in: and therefore if the sleep be troublesome, the mans cares be without remedy till they be quite destroyed. Dreams follow the temper of the body, and commonly proceed from trouble or disease, businesse or care, an active head and a restlesse minde, from fear or hope, from wine or passion, from fulnesse or emptinesse, from phantastick remembrances or from som *Dæmon* good or bad: they are without rule and without reason, they are as contingent as if a man should study to make a Prophesie, and by saying 10000 things may hit upon one true, which was therefore not foreknown though it was forespoken: and they have no certainty becaufe they have no naturall causality nor proportion to those effects which many times they are said to foresignifie. The dream of the yolk of an egge importeth gold (faith *Artemidorus*) and they that use to remember such phantastick idols are afraid to lose a friend when they dream their teeth shake, when naturally it will rather signifie *a scurvy*; for a naturall indisposition and an imperfect sense of the beginning of a disease, may vex the fancy into a symbolicall representation; for so he man that dreamt he swam against a stream of bloud, had a Plurisie beginning in his side: and he that dreamt he dipt his foot in water, and that it was turn'd to a Marble, was intic'd into the fancie by a beginning dropsie: and if the events do answer in one instance, we become credulous in twenty; for want of reason we discourse our selves into folly and weak observation, and give the Devill power over us in those circumstances in which we can least resist him. Ἐν ὥραν δεμνίης μεγαθενει̃, *A theef is confident in the twilight*; if you suffer impressions to be made upon you by dreams, the Devill hath the reins in his own hands, and can tempt you by that which will abuse you when you can make no resistance. *Dominica* the wife of *Valens* the Emperor dreamt that God threatned to take away her only son for her despitefull usage of St. *Basil*: the fear proceeding from this instance was safe and fortunate; but if she had dreamt in the behalf of a Heretick, she might have been cousened into a false proposition upon a ground weaker then the discourse of a waking childe. Let the grounds of our actions be noble, beginning upon reason, proceeding with prudence, measured by the common lines of men, and confident upon the expectation of an usuall providence. Let us proceed from causes to effects, from naturall means to ordinary events, and believe *felicity* not to be a *chance* but a *choice*, and *evill* to be the daughter of *sin* and the *Divine anger*, not of *fortune* and *fancy*; let us fear God when we have made him angry; and not be afraid of him when we heartily and laboriously do our duty; our fears are to be measured by open revelation and certain experience, by the threatnings of God and the sayings of wise men, and their *limit* is *reverence*, and *godlinesse* is their *end*; and then fear shall be a duty, and a rare instrument of many:

Serm. IX.

Eurip.

Of godly Fear.

Serm. IX.

many: in all other cases it is superstition or folly, it is sin or punishment, the Ivy of Religion, and the misery of an honest and a weak heart, and is to be cured only by reason and good company, a wise guide and a plain rule, a cheerfull spirit and a contented minde, by joy in God according to the commandements, that is, *a rejoycing evermore.*

2. But besides this superstitious fear, there is another fear directly criminall, and it is cald, *worldly fear*, of which the Spirit of God hath said, *But the fearfull and incredulous shall have their part in the lake that burneth with fire and brimstone, which is the second death*; that is, such fears which make men to fall in the time of persecution, those that dare not own their faith in the face of a Tyrant, or in despite of an accursed Law. For though it be lawfull to be afraid in a storm, yet it is not lawfull to leap into the sea; though we may be more carefull for our fears, yet we must be faithfull too; and we may flie from the persecution till it overtakes us, but when it does, we must not change our Religion for our safety, or leave the robe of Baptisme in the hand of the tempter, and run away *by all means.* St. *Athanasius* for 46 years did run and fight, he disputed with the *Arrians* and fled from their Officers; and that flies, may be a man worth preserving, if he bears his faith along with him, and leaves nothing of his duty behinde; but when duty and life cannot stand together, he that then flies a persecution by delivering up his soul, is one that hath no charity, no love to God, no trust in promises, no just estimation of the rewards of a noble contention. *Perfect love casts out fear* (saith the Apostle) that is, he that loves God will not fear to dye for him, or for his sake to be poor. In this sense no man can fear man and love God at the same time; and when St. *Laurence* triumph'd over *Valerianus*, St. *Sebastian* over *Diocletian*, St. *Vincentius* over *Dacianus*, and the armies of Martyrs over the *Proconsuls*, accusers, and executioners, they shew'd their love to God by triumphing over fear, and *leading captivity captive* by the strength of their Captain, whose *garments were red from Bozrah.*

3. But this fear is also tremulous and criminall, if it be a trouble from the apprehension of the mountains and difficulties of duty, and is called *pusillanimity.* For some see themselves encompassed with temptations, they observe their frequent fals, their perpetuall returns from good purposes to weak performances, the daily mortifications that are necessary, the resisting naturall appetites, and the laying violent hands upon the desires of flesh and bloud, the uneasinesse of their spirits, and their hard labours, and therefore this makes them afraid; and because they despair to run through the whole duty in all its parts and periods, they think as good not begin at all, as after labour and expence to lose the Jewell and the charges of their venture. St. *Austin* compares such men to children and phantastick

Revel. 21. 8.

Of godly Fear.

sick persons affrighted with phantasmes and specters; *Terribiles visu formæ*, the sight seems full of horror, but touch them and they are very nothing, the meer daughters of a sick brain, and a weak heart, an infant experience and a trifling judgement: so are the illusions of a weak piety, or an unskilfull unconfident soul; they fancy to see mountains of difficulty, but touch them and they seem like clouds riding upon the wings of the winde, and put on shapes as we please to dream. He that denies to give almes for fear of being poor, or to entertain a Disciple for fear of being suspected of the party, or to own a duty for fear of being put to venture for a crown, he that takes part of the intemperance because he dares not displease the company, or in any sense fears the fears of the world, and not the fear of God, this man enters into his portion of fear betimes, but it will not be finished to eternall ages. To fear the censures of men when God is your Judge, to fear their evill when God is your defence, to fear death when he is the entrance to life and felicity, is unreasonable and pernicious; but if you will turn your passion into duty, and joy, and security, fear to offend God, to enter voluntarily into temptation, fear the alluring face of lust, and the smooth entertainments of intemperance, fear the anger of God when you have deserved it, and when you have recover'd from the snare, then infinitely fear to return into that condition, in which whosoever dwels is the heir of fear and eternall sorrow.

Thus farre I have discoursed concerning good fear and bad, that is, *filiall* and *servile*: they are both good, if by *servile* we intend *initiall* or the new beginning fear of penitents; a fear to offend God upon lesse perfect considerations: But *servile* fear is vitious when it still retains the affection of slaves, and when its effects are hatred, wearinesse, displeasure, and want of charity: and of the same cogitations are those fears which are superstitious, and worldly.

But to the former sort of vertuous fear, some also adde another which they call *Angelicall*, that is, such a fear as the blessed Angels have, who before God hide their faces, and tremble at his presence, and *fall down before his footstool*, and are ministers of his anger and messengers of his mercy, and night and day worship him with the profoundest adoration. This is the same that is spoken of in the Text: *Let us serve God with reverence and godly fear*; all holy fear partakes of the nature of this which Divines call *Angelicall*, and it is expressed in acts of adoration, of vowes, and holy prayers, in hymnes, and psalmes, in the eucharist and reverentiall addresses; and while it proceeds in the usuall measures of common duty, it is but *humane*; but as it arises to great degrees, and to perfection, it is *Angelicall* and *Divine*; and then it appertains to *mystick Theologie*, and therefore is to be considered in another place; but for the present, that which will regularly concern all our duty, is this, that when the fear of God is the instrument of our duty,

or

Serm. IX. or Gods worship, the greater it is, it is so much the better. It was an old proverbiall saying among the *Romans*, *Religentem esse oportet, religiosum, nefas*; *Every excesse in the actions of religion is criminall*; they supposing that in the services of their gods, there might be too much. True it is, there may be too much of their undecent expressions, and in things indifferent, the very multitude is too much, and becomes an undecency: and if it be in its own nature undecent or disproportionable to the end, or the rules, or the analogy of the Religion, it will not stay for numbers to make it intolerable; but in the direct actions of glorifying God, in doing any thing of his Commandements, or any thing which he commands, or counsels, or promises to reward, there can never be excesse or superfluity: and therefore in these cases, *do as much as you can*; take care that your expressions be prudent, and safe, consisting with thy other duties; and for the passions or vertues themselves, let them passe from beginning to great progresses, from man to Angel, from the imperfection of man to the perfections of the sons of God; and when ever we go beyond the bounds of Nature, and grow up with all the extention, and in the very commensuration of a full grace, we shall never go beyond the excellencies of God: For ornament may be too much, and turn to curiosity; cleanlinesse may be changed into nicenesse; and civill compliance may become flattery; and mobility of tongue may rise into garrulity; and fame and honour may be great unto envie; and health it self, if it be athletick, may by its very excesse become dangerous: but wisdome, and duty, and comelinesse, and discipline, a good minde, and eloquence, and the fear of God, and doing honour to his holy Name, can never exceed: but if they swell to great proportions, they passe through the measures of grace, and are united to felicity in the comprehensions of God, in the joyes of an eternall glory.

Serm.

3. See fols. 29ʳ–30ʳ:

Jeremy Taylor, Sermon XIII, "Of Lukewarmnesse and Zeal...," (*Eniautos*, 1653), Part III, 176.

176   *Of Lukewarmneſſe and Zeal.*

S<small>ER</small>.XIII. sold to redeem Captives when there is a great calamity imminent, and prepared for reliefe and no other way to ſuccour it.

But in the whole, the duty of zeale requires that we neglect an ordinary viſit rather then an ordinary prayer, and a great profit rather then omit a required duty. No excuſe can legitimate a ſin; and he that goes about to diſtinguiſh between his duty and his profit, and if he cannot reconcile them, will yet tie them together like a Hyæna and a Dog, this man pretends to Religion, but ſecures the world, and is indifferent and lukewarme towards that, ſo he may be warme and ſafe in the poſſeſſion of this.

2. To that fervour and zeal that is neceſſary and a duty, *it is required that we be conſtant and perſevering. Eſto fidelis ad mortem,* ſaid the Spirit of God to the Angel of the Church of *Smyrna*, *Be faithfull unto death, and I will give thee a crown of life*: For he that is warm to day, and cold to morrow, zealous in his resolution and weary in his practiſes, fierce in the beginning, and ſlack and eaſie in his progreſſe, hath not yet well choſen what ſide he will be of; he ſees not reaſon enough for Religion, and he hath not confidence enough for its contrary; and therefore he is *duplicis animi*, as St. *James* calls him, *of a doubtfull mind*. For Religion is worth as much to day as it was yeſterday, and that cannot change though we doe; and if we doe, we have left God, and whither he can goe that goes from God, his owne ſorrowes will ſoon enough inſtruct him. This fire muſt never goe out, but it muſt be like the fire of heaven, it muſt ſhine like the ſtarres, though ſometimes cover'd with a cloud, or obſcur'd by a greater light; yet they dwell for ever in their orbs, and walk in their circles, and obſerve their circumſtances, but goe not out by day nor night, and ſet not when Kings die, nor are extinguiſh'd when Nations change their Government: So muſt the zeal of a Chriſtian be, a conſtant incentive of his duty, and though ſometimes his hand is drawne back by violence or need, and his prayers ſhortned by the importunity of buſineſſe, and ſome parts omitted by neceſſities, and juſt complyances, yet ſtill the fire is kept alive, it burns within when the light breaks not forth, and is eternall as the orb of fire, or the embers of the Altar of Incenſe.

3. No man is zealous as he ought, but *he that delights in the ſervice of God*: without this no man can perſevere, but muſt faint under the continuall preſſure of an uneaſie load. If a man goes to his prayers as children goe to ſchoole, or give alms as thoſe that pay contribution, and meditate with the ſame willingneſſe with which young men die, this man does *perſonam ſuſtinere*, he acts a part which he cannot long perſonate, but will find ſo many excuſes and ſilly devices to omit his duty, ſuch tricks to run from

4. See fols. 36ʳ–38ʳ: Jeremy Taylor, *The Rule and Exercises of Holy Living* (1650), 153–55.

Chap. 2.   *Of Contentedeſſe.*   Sect. 6. 153

and the ſoul make up the whole man: and when the daughter of *Stilpo* proved a wanton, he ſaid it was none of his ſin, and therefore there was no reaſon it ſhould be his miſery: And if an enemy hath taken all that from a Prince whereby he was a King; he may refreſh himſelf by conſidering all that is left him, whereby he is a man.

<small>Si natus es Trophime ſolus omnium hac lege Ut ſem creant tibi res arbitrio tuo Felicitatem hanc ſi quis promiſit Deum Iraſcereris jure, non malâ is fide Et improbe egiſſet. Menan.</small>

4. Conſider that ſad accidents and a ſtate of affliction is a School of vertue: it reduces our ſpirits to ſoberneſſe, and our counſels to moderation; it corrects levity, and interrupts the confidence of ſinning. *It is good for me (ſaid David) that I have been afflicted, for thereby I have learned thy Law. And I know (O Lord) that thou of very faithfulneſſe haſt cauſed me to be troubled.* For God, who in mercy and wiſdom governs the world, would never have ſuffered ſo many ſadneſſes, and have ſent them eſpecially to the moſt vertuous and the wiſeſt men, but that he intends they ſhould be the ſeminary of comfort, the nurſery of vertue, the exerciſe of wiſdom, the tryal of patience, the venturing for a crown, and the gate of glory.

<small>119. Pſalm. 10. part. v. 3.</small>

5. Conſider that afflictions are oftentimes the occaſions of great temporal advantages: and we muſt not look upon them as they ſit down heavily upon us, but as they ſerve ſome of Gods ends, and the purpoſes of univerſal Providence: And when a Prince fights juſtly, and yet unproſperouſly, if he could ſee all thoſe reaſons for which God hath ſo ordered it, he would think it the moſt reaſonable thing in the world, and that it would be very ill to have it otherwiſe. If a man could

G 5   have

154 Chap. 2. *Of Contentednesse.* Sect. 4.

have opened one of the pages of the Divine counsel, and could have seen the event of *Josephs* being sold to the Merchants of Amalek, he might with much reason have dried up the young mans tears: and when Gods purposes are opened in the events of things, as it was in the case of *Joseph*, when he sustained his Fathers family and became Lord of Egypt, then we see what ill judgement we made of things, and that we were passionate as children, and transported with sence and mistaken interest. The case of *Themistocles* was almost like that of *Joseph*, for being banished into Egypt, he also grew in favour with the King, and told his wife, *He had been undone, unlesse he had been undone.* For God esteems it one of his glories that he brings good out of evil, and therfore it were but reason we should trust God to govern his own world as he pleases: and that we should patiently *wait till the change cometh, or the reason be discovered.*

And this consideration is also of great use to them who envy at the prosperity of the wicked, and the successe of Persecutors, and the baits of fishes, and the bread of dogs. God fails not to sow blessings in the long furrows which the plowers plow upon the back of the Church: and this successe which troubles us will be a great glory to God, and a great benefit to his Saints and servants, and a great ruine to the Persecutors, who shall have but the fortune of *Theramenes* one of the thirty Tyrants of Athens, who scap'd when his house fell upon him, and was shortly after put to death with torments by his Collegues in the Tyranny.

To which also may be added that the great evils wch happen to the best and wisest men are

one

Chap. 2.   *Of Contentednesse.*   Sect. 4.   155

one of the great arguments, upon the strength of which we can expect felicity to our souls, and the joyes of another world. And certainly they are then very tolerable and eligible, when with so great advantages they minister to the faith and hope of a Christian. But if we consider what unspeakable tortures are provided for the wicked to all eternity, we should not be troubled to see them prosperous here, but rather wonder that their portion in this life is not bigger, and that ever they should be sick, or crossed, or affronted, or troubled with the contradiction and disease of their own vices, since if they were fortunate beyond their own ambition it could not make them recompence for one houres torment in Hell, which yet they shall have for their eternall portion.

After all these considerations deriving from sence and experience, grace and reason, there are two remedies still remaining, and they are *Necessity* and *Time*.

6. For it is but reasonable to bear that accident patiently which God sends, since impatience does but intangle us like the fluttering of a bird in a net, but cannot at all ease our trouble, or prevent the accident: it must be run thorough, and therefore it were better we compose our selves to a patient, then to a troubled and miserable suffering. *Nemo recusat ferre quod necesse est pati.*

7. But however, if you will not otherwise be cured, time at last will do it alone; and then consider, do you mean to mourne *alwayes*, or but *for a time*? If alwayes; you are miserable and foolish. If for a time; then why will you not apply those reasons to your grief at first, with which you will cure it at last

5. See fols. 36ʳ–38ʳ

Jeremy Taylor, Sermon XXV, "The Miracles of Divine Mercy," (*Eniautos*, 1653) Part I, 325–26.

The Miracles of the divine Mercy.

the secret worm that lay at the root of the plant, shall be drawn forth and quite extinguished. For so have I known a luxuriant Vine swell into irregular twigs, and bold excrescencies, and spend it self in leaves and little rings, and affoord but trifling clusters to the wine-presse, and a faint return to his heart which longed to be refreshed with a full vintage: But when the Lord of the vine had caused the dressers to cut the wilder plant and made it bleed, it grew temperate in its vain expense of uselesse leaves, and knotted into fair and juicy bunches, and made accounts of that losse of blood by the return of fruit: So is an afflicted Province, cured of its surfets, and punished for its sins, and bleeds for its long riot, and is left ungoverned for its disobedience, and chastised for its wantonnesse, and when the sword hath let forth the corrupted blood, and the fire hath purged the rest, then it enters into the double joyes of restitution, and gives God thanks for his rod, and confesses the mercies of the Lord in making the smoke be changed into fire, and the cloud into a perfume, the sword into a staffe, and his anger into mercy....

Had not David suffered more if he had suffered lesse, and had he not been miserable unlesse he had been afflicted? he understood it well when he said, *It is good for me that I have been afflicted.* He that was rival to *Crassus*, when he stood candidate to command the Legions in the *Parthians* warre was much troubled that he missed the dignity, but he saw himself blessed that he scaped the death, and the dishonour of the overthrow, by that time the sad news arrived at Rome. The Gentleman at *Marseilles* cursed his starres that he was absent when the ship set sail to sea, having long waited for a winde, and missed it; but he gave thanks to the providence that blest him with the crosse, when he knew that the ship perished in the voyage, and all the men were drowned: And even those virgins and barren women in Jerusalem, that longed to become glad mothers, and for want of children would not be comforted, yet when Titus sacked the City, found the words of Jesus true *Blessed is the womb that never bare, and the paps that never gave suck.* And the world being governed with a rare variety, and changes of accidents, and providence; that which is a misfortune in the particular, in the whole order of things becomes a blessing bigger then we hoped for, then when we were angry with God for hindring us, to perish in pleasant waves, or when he was contriving to pour upon thy head a mighty blessing. Do not think the Judge condemns you when he chides you, nor think to read thy own finall sentence by the first half of his words; *stand still* and see how it will be in the whole event of things; let God speak his minde out; for it may be, this sad beginning is but an art to bring in, or to make thee to esteem, and entertain, and understand the blessing.

SERMON XXV.

E e   They

326   *The miracles of the divine* Mercy.

SERMON XXV.

They that love to talk of the mercies of the Lord, and to recount his good things, cannot but have observed that God delights to be called by such Appellatives which relate to miserable and afflicted persons : *He is the Father of the fatherlesse*, and an *avenger of the widowes cause, he standeth at the right hand of the poor to save his soul from unrighteous Judges*, and *he is with us in tribulation*: And upon this ground, let us account whether *mercy* be not the greater ingredient in that death and deprivation, when I lose a man and get God to be my Father; and when my weak arm of flesh is cut from my shoulder, and God makes me to lean upon him, and becomes my Patron and my Guide, my Advocate and Defender: and if in our greatest misery Gods mercy is so conspicuous, what can we suppose him to be in the endearment of his loving Kindnesse? If his vail be so transparent, well may we know that upon his face dwels glory, and from his eyes light, and perpetuall comforts run in channels, larger then the returns of the Sea, when it is driven and forced faster into its naturall course, by the violence of a tempest from the North. The summe is this, God intends every accident should minister to vertue, and every vertue is the mother and the nurse of joy, and both of them daughters of the Divine goodnesse, and therefore, if our sorrows do not passe into comforts, it is besides Gods intention; it is because we will not comply with the act of that mercy which would save us by all means, and all varieties, by health and by sicknesse, by the life and by the death of our dearest friends, by what we choose and by what we fear; that as Gods providence rules over all chances of things, and all designes of men, so his mercy may rule over all his providence.

Ser-

6. See fol. 91ᵛ:

John Donne, "Preached at the funerals of
Sir William Cokayne, Knight, Alderman of London,
December 12. 1626"
Sermon LXXX, (*LXXX Sermons*, 1640), 824–26.

| 824 | *Preached at S. Pauls.* | SERM. LXXX. |

Gods recapitulation of all that he had said before, in his *Fiat lux*, and *Fiat firmamentum*, and in all the rest, said or done, in all the six dayes. Propose this body to thy consideration in the highest exaltation thereof; as it is the *Temple of the Holy Ghost*: Nay, not in a Metaphor, or comparison of a Temple, or any other similitudinary thing, but as it was really and truly the very body of God, in the person of Christ, and yet this body must wither, must decay, must languish, must perish. When *Goliah* had armed and fortified this body, And *Iezabel* had painted and perfumed this body, And *Dives* had pampered and larded this body, As God said to *Ezekiel*, when he brought him to the *dry bones, Fili hominis, Sonne of Man, doest thou thinke these bones can live?* They said in their hearts to all the world, Can these bodies die? And they are dead. *Iezabels* dust is not Ambar, nor *Goliahs* dust *Terra sigillata*, Medicinall; nor does the Serpent, whose meat they are both, finde any better rellish in *Dives* dust, then in *Lazarus*. But as in our former part, where our foundation was, That in nothing, no spirituall thing, there was any perfectnesse, which we illustrated in the weaknesses of Knowledge, and Faith, and Hope, and Charity, yet we concluded, that for all those defects, God accepted those their religious services; So in this part, where our foundation is, That nothing in temporall things is permanent, as we have illustrated that, by the decay of that which is Gods noblest piece in Nature, The body of man; so we shall also conclude that, with this goodnesse of God, that for all this dissolution, and putrefaction, he affords this Body a Resurrection.

Resurrectio.

The Gentils, and their Poets, describe the sad state of Death so, *Nox una obeunda*, That it is one everlasting Night; To them, a Night; But to a Christian, it is *Dies Mortis*, and *Dies Resurrectionis*, The day of Death, and The day of Resurrection; We die in the light, in the sight of Gods presence, and we rise in the light, in the sight of his very Essence. Nay, Gods corrections, and judgements upon us in this life, are still expressed so, *Dies visitationis*, still it is a Day, though a *Day of visitation*; and still we may discerne God to be in the action. The *Lord of Life* was the first that named *Death*; *Morte*

Gen. 2.

morieris, sayes God, Thou shalt die the Death. I doe the lesse feare, or abhorre Death, because I finde it in his mouth; Even a malediction hath a sweetnesse in his mouth; for there is a blessing wrapped up in it; a mercy in every correction, a Resurrection upon every Death. When *Iezabels* beauty, exalted to that height which it had by art, or higher then that, to that height which it had in her own opinion, shall be infinitely multiplied upon every Body; And as God shall know no man from his own Sonne, so as not to see the very righteousnesse of his own Sonne upon that man; So the Angels shall know no man from Christ, so as not to desire to looke upon that mans face, because the most deformed wretch that is there, shall have the very beauty of Christ himselfe; So shall *Goliahs* armour, and *Dives* fulnesse, be doubled, and redoubled upon us, And every thing that we can call good, shall first be infinitely exalted in the goodnesse, and then infinitely multiplied in the proportion, and againe infinitely extended in the duration. And since we are in an action of preparing this dead Brother of ours to that state, (for the Funerall is the Easter-eve, The Buriall is the depositing of that man for the Resurrection) As we have held you, with Doctrine of Mortification, by extending the Text, from *Martha* to this occasion; so shall we dismisse you with Consolation, by a like occasionall inverting the Text, from passion in *Martha's* mouth, *Lord, if thou hadst been here, my Brother had not dyed*, to joy in ours, *Lord, because thou wast here, our Brother is not dead.*

In vita.

The Lord was with him in all these steps; with him in his life; with him in his death; He is with him in his funerals, and he shall be with him in his Resurrection; and therefore, because the Lord was with him, our Brother is not dead. He was with him in the beginning of his life, in this manifestation, That though he were of Parents of a good, of a great Estate, yet his possibility and his expectation from them, did not slacken his own industry; which is a Canker that eats into, nay that hath eat up many a family in this City, that relying wholly upon what the Father hath done, the Sonne does nothing for himselfe. And truly, it falls out too often, that he that labours not for more, does not keepe his own. God imprinted in him an industrious disposition, though such hopes from such parents might have excused some slacknesse, and God prospered his industry so, as that when his Fathers estate came to a distribution by death, he needed it not. God

Psal. 81. 11.

was with him, as with *David* in a Dilatation, and then in a Repletion; God enlarged him, and then he filled him; He gave him a large and a comprehensive understanding, and with it, A publique heart; And such as perchance in his way of education, and in our

narrow

Appendices 203

Serm. LXXX. *Preached at S. Pauls.* 825

A narrow and contracted times, in which every man determines himselfe in himselfe, and scarce looks farther, it would be hard to finde many Examples of such largenesse. You have, I thinke, a phrase of Driving a Trade; And you have, I know, a practise of Driving away Trade, by other use of money; And you have lost a man, that drove a great Trade, the right way in making the best use of our home-commodity. To fetch in Wine, and Spice, and Silke, is but a drawing of Trade; The right driving of trade, is, to vent our owne outward; And yet, for the drawing in of that, which might justly seeme most behoofefull, that is, of Arts, and Manufactures, to be imployed upon our owne Commodity within the Kingdome, he did his part, diligently, at least, if not vehemently, if not passionately. This City is a great Theater, and he Acted great and various parts in it; And all well; And when he went higher, (as he was often heard in Parliaments, at Councell tables, and in more private accesses to the late King of ever blessed memory) as, for

B that comprehension of those businesses, which he pretended to understand, no man doubts, for no man lacks arguments and evidences of his ability therein, So for his manner of expressing his intentions, and digesting and uttering his purposes, I have sometimes heard the greatest Master of Language and Judgement, which these times, or any other did, or doe, or shall give, (that good and great King of ours) say of him, That he never heard any man of his breeding, handle businesses more rationally, more pertinently, more elegantly, more perswasively; And when his purpose was, to do a grace to a Preacher, of very good abilities, and good note in his owne Chappell, I have heard him say, that his language, and accent, and manner of delivering himselfe, was like this man. This man hath God accompanied all his life; and by performance thereof seemes to have made that Covenant with him, which he made to *Abraham*, *Multiplicabo te vehementer, I will multiply thee exceedingly.* He multiplied his estate so, as was fit to endow | Gen. 17. 2.

C many and great Children; and he multiplied his Children so, both in their number, and in their quality, as they were fit to receive a great Estate. God was with him all the way, In *a Pillar of Fire*, in the brightnesse of prosperity, and in the *Pillar of Clouds* too, in many darke, and sad, and heavy crosses: So great a Ship, required a great Ballast, So many blessings, many crosses; And he had them, and sailed on his course the steadier for them; The *Cloud* as well as the *Fire*, was a *Pillar* to him; His crosses, as well as his blessings established his assurance in God; And so, in all the course of his life, *The Lord was here*, and therefore *our Brother is not dead*; not dead in the evidences and testimonies of life; for he, whom the world hath just cause to celebrate, for things done, when he was alive, is alive still in their celebration.

The Lord was here, that is, with him at his death too. He was served with the Processe | *In morte.* here in the City, but his cause was heard in the Country; Here he sickned, There he lan-

D guished, and dyed there. In his sicknesse there, those that assisted him, are witnesses, of his many expressings, of a religious & a constant heart towards God, and of his pious joyning with them, even in the holy declaration of kneeling, then, when they, in favour of his weakenesse, would disswade him from kneeling. I must not defraud him of this testimony frō my selfe, that into this place where we are now met, I have observed him to enter with much reverence, & compose himselfe in this place with much declaration of devotion. And truly it is that reverence, which those persons who are of the same ranke that he was in the City, that reverence that they use in this place, when they come hither, is that that makes us, who have now the administration of this Quire, glad, that our Predecessors, but a very few yeares before our time, (and not before all our times neither) admitted these Honourable and worshipfull Persons of this City, to sit in this Quire, so, as they do upon Sundayes: The Church receives an honour in it; But the honour is more in their

E reverence, then in their presence; though in that too: And they receive an honour, and an ease in it; and therefore they do piously towards God, and prudently for themselves, and gratefully towards us, in giving us, by their reverent comportment here, so just occasion of continuing that honour, and that ease to them here, which to lesse reverend, and unrespective persons, we should be lesse willing to doe. To returne to him in his sicknesse; He had but one dayes labour, and all the rest were Sabbaths, one day in his sicknesse he converted to businesse; Thus; He called his family, and friends together; Thankfully he acknowledged Gods manifold blessings, and his owne sins as penitently: And then, to those who were to have the disposing of his estate, joyntly with his Children, he recommended his servants, and the poore, and the Hospitals, and the Prisons, which, according

| 826 | *Preached at S. Pauls.* | SERM. LXXX. |

cording to his purpose, have beene all taken into confideration; And after this (which was his Valediction to the world) he seemed alwaies loath to returne to any worldly bufineffe, His laft Commandement to Wife and Children was Chrifts laft commandement to his Spoufe the Church, in the Apoftles, *To love one another.* He bleft them, and the Eftate devolved upon them, unto them: And by Gods grace fhall prove as true a Prophet to them in that bleffing, as he was to himfelfe, when in entring his laft bed, two dayes before his Death, he faid, *Help me off with my earthly habit, & let me go to my laft bed.* Where, in the fecond night after, he faid, *Little know ye what paine I feele this night, yet I know, I fhall have joy in the morning*; And in that morning he dyed. The forme in which he implored his Saviour, was evermore, towards his end, this, *Chrift Iefus, which dyed on the Croffe, forgive me my fins; He have mercy upon me:* And his laft and dying words were the repetition of the name of Jefus; And when he had not ftrength to utter that name diftinctly and perfectly, they might heare it from within him, as from a man a far off; even then, when his hollow and remote naming of Jefus, was rather a certifying of them, that he was with his Jefus, then a prayer that he might come to him. And fo *The Lord was here*, here with him in his Death; and becaufe *the Lord was here, our Brother is not dead*; not dead in the eyes and eares of God; for as the blood of *Abel* fpeaks yet, fo doth the zeale of Gods Saints; and their laft prayers (though we heare them not) God continues ftill; and they pray in Heaven, as the Martyrs under the Altar, even till the Refurrection.

In funere.

He is with him now too; Here in his Funerals. Buriall, and Chriftian Buriall, and Solemne Buriall are all evidences, and teftimonies of Gods prefence. God forbid we fhould conclude, or argue an abfence of God, from the want of Solemne Buriall, or Chriftian Buriall, or any Buriall; But neither muft we deny it, to be an evidence of his favour and prefence, where he is pleafed to afford thefe. So God makes that the feale of all his bleffings to *Abraham, That he fhould be buried in a good age*; God eftablifhed *Iacob* with that promife, *That his Son Iofeph fhould have care of his Funerals:* And *Iofeph* does caufe his fervants, *The Phyfitians, to embalme him, when he was dead.* Of Chrift it was Prophecied; *That he fhould have a glorious Buriall*; And therefore Chrift interprets well that profufe, and prodigall piety of the Woman that poured out the Oyntment upon him, *That fhe did it to Bury him;* And fo fhall *Iofeph* of Arimathea be ever celebrated, for his care in celebrating Chrifts Funerals. If we were to fend a Son, or a friend, to take poffeffion of any place in Court, or forraine parts, we would fend him out in the beft equipage: Let us not grudge to fet downe our friends, in the Anti-chamber of Heaven, the Grave, in as good manner, as without vaine-glorioufneffe, and waftfulneffe we may; And, in inclining them, to whom that care belongs, to expreffe that care as they doe this day, *The Lord is with him*, even in this Funerall; And becaufe *The Lord is here, our brother is not dead*; Not dead in the memories and eftimation of men.

Gen. 15.
Gen. 46.
Gen. 50.
Efay 11.10.
Matt. 26.

In refurrectione.
G:n.46.4.

And laftly, that we may have God prefent in all his Manifeftations, *Hee that was, and is, and is to come*, was with him, in his life and death, and is with him in this holy Solemnity, and fhall bee with him againe in the Refurrection. God fayes to *Iacob, I will goe downe with thee into Egypt, and I will alfo furely bring thee up againe.* God goes downe with a good man into the Grave, and will furely bring him up againe. When? The Angel promifed to returne to *Abraham* and *Sarah*, for the affurance of the birth of *Ifaac, according to the time of life*; that is, in fuch time, as by nature a woman may have a childe. God will returne to us in the Grave, *according to the time of life*; that is, in fuch time, as he, by his gracious Decree, hath fixed for the Refurrection. And in the meane time, no more then the God-head departed from the dead body of our Saviour, in the grave, doth his power, and his prefence depart from our dead bodies in that darkneffe; But that which *Mofes* faid to the whole Congregation, I fay to you all, both to you that heare me, and to him that does not, *All ye that did cleave unto the Lord your God, are alive, every one of you, this day*; Even hee, whom wee call dead, is alive this day. In the prefence of God, we lay him downe; In the power of God, he fhall rife; In the perfon of Chrift, he is rifen already. And fo into the fame hands that have received his foule, we commend his body; befeeching his bleffed Spirit, that as our charity enclines us to hope confidently of his good eftate, our faith may affure us of the fame happineffe, in our owne behalfe; And that for all our fakes, but efpecially for his own glory, he will be pleafed to haften the confummation of all, in that kingdome which that Son of God hath purchafed for us, with the ineftimable price of his incorruptible blood. *Amen.*

Gen. 18. 10.

Deut. 4. 4.

FINIS.

Bibliography

1. Manuscripts

i) British Library, London:

Additional MS. 4454, Katherine Austen's *Book M*
Harleian MS. 2311, Anna Cromwell Williams's book of devotions

ii) Corporation of London Record Office, Guildhall, London:

Orphans Finding Book, 1643–1661
Orphans Ledger, 1627–1648
Orphans Recognizances, 1639–1644

iii) London Metropolitan Archives, Islington, London:

Courts Leet and Baron ACC/2844/012, 1653–1657
G.L.R.O. map, 3274 JI, 1854
HB/C/027, Indenture of Bargain and Sale, Red Lion
SC/PHL/02/1190–143, Austen memorial, St Leonard's Shoreditch (photograph)

iv) National Archives, Kew, London:

C5/41/3, f. 2, Thomas Austen's reply to Sir Allen Apsley (1662)
C10/78/1, Susanna Austen v. Katherine Austen and Thomas Austen (1662)
C10/96/1, Thomas Austen v. Susanna Austen, William Spire and Francis Stephens (1665 [actually 1666])
C10/98/1, Thomas Austen v. Susanna Austen (1666)
C10/109/4, Thomas Austen v. William Spire and Francis Stephens (1666)
C10/109/5, Susanna Austen v. Thomas Austen (1666)

E214/215, Charles I, Thomas Austen, and John Apsley (1639)

PROB 11/182, the will of Robert Wilson
PROB 11/187, the will of John Highlord
PROB 11/205, the will of Katherine Rudd / Wilson / Highlord
PROB 11/285, the will of Thomas Austen, Katherine Austen's husband
PROB 11/296, the will of John Austen
PROB 11/375, the will of Katherine Austen

v) Yale University Library, New Haven, Connecticut:
Microfilm MISC 326, Alice Thornton's book of remembrances

2. Pre-1700 printed works

The date given is the date of the first edition of each work, unless otherwise stated, and the place of publication is London, unless otherwise stated.

Amyraut, Moise. *A Treatise Concerning Religions, In Refutation of the Opinion which accounts all Indifferent*. 1660.
Bacon, Francis. *The Historie of the Raigne of King Henry the Seuenth*. 1622.
Beadle, John. *Journal of a Thankful Christian*. 1656.
Brome, Richard. *A Jovial Crew; or, The Merry Beggars*. 1652.
Browne, Thomas. *Religio Medici*. 1642.
Camden, William. *Remaines Concerning Britain*. 6th impression. 1657.
Corbett, Richard. *Certain Elegant Poems*. 1647.
———. *Poëtica Stromata, or A Collection*. 1648.
Daniel, Samuel. *Delia. Contayning certayne Sonnets: with the complaint of Rosamond*. 1592.
Donne, John. *LXXX Sermons*. 1640.
Featley, Daniel. *Clavis Mystica; A Key Opening Divers Texts of Scripture*. 1636.
Fell, John. *The Life of The most Learned, Reverend and Pious D^r. H. Hammond*. 1661.
Fuller, Thomas. *The Holy State and The Profane State*. 4th ed. 1663 (1st ed., 1642).
Gauden, John. *A sermon preached in the Temple-chappel, at the funeral of the Right Reverend ... Dr. Brounrig*. 1660.
———. *A discourse of artificial beauty, in point of conscience between two ladies*. 1656.
Goodwin, Philip. *The Mystery of Dreams, Historically Discoursed*. 1658.
Hall, Joseph. *The Arte of Divine Meditation*. 2nd ed. 1607 (1st ed., 1606).
———. *Holy Obseruations. Also Some fewe of Davids Psalmes Metaphrased*. 1607.
———. *Occasional Meditations*. 2nd ed. 1631 (1st ed., 1630).
Herbert, Edward, Lord of Cherbury. *The life and raigne of King Henry the Eighth*. 1649.
King, Henry. *Poems, Elegies, Paradoxes, and Sonnets*. 1657. 2nd ed., 1664.

Plato his Apology of Socrates, and Phaedo. 1675.
Taylor, Jeremy. *Eniautos: A course of sermons for all the Sundaies of the year.* 1653.
———. *The Rule and Exercises of Holy Living.* 1650.
Walton, Izaak. *The Lives of Dr John Donne, Sir Henry Wotton, Mr Richard Hooker, Mr George Herbert.* 4th ed. 1675 (1st ed., 1640).
Wotton, Sir Henry. *Reliquæ Wottonianæ.* 1651.

3. Post-1700 printed works:

Anselment, Raymond A. "Katherine Austen and the Widow's Might." *Journal for Early Modern Cultural Studies* 5 (2005): 5–25.
———. "'My first Booke of my Life': The Apology of a Seventeenth-Century Gentry Woman." *Prose Studies* 24 (2001): 1–14.
———. "Seventeenth-Century Manuscript Sources of Alice Thornton's Life." *Studies in English Literature* 45 (2005): 135–55.
———. ed. *The Occasional Meditations of Mary Rich, Countess of Warwick.* MRTS 363. Tempe: ACMRS, 2009.
Beal, Peter. *Index of English Literary Manuscripts*, vol. 1, *1450–1625*. London: Mansell, 1980; vol. 2, *1625–1700*. London: Mansell, 1987–1993.
Beavan, A. B. *The Aldermen of the City of London.* 2 vols. London: The Corporation of the City of London, 1908.
Bennett, J. A. W. and H. R. Trevor-Roper, eds. *The Poems of Richard Corbett.* Oxford: Clarendon Press, 1955.
Blain, Virginia, Patricia Clements, and Isobel Grundy, eds. *The Feminist Companion to Literature in English.* London: B. T. Batsford, 1990.
Botonaki, Effie. "Seventeenth-Century Englishwomen's Spiritual Diaries: Self-Examination, Covenanting, and Account Keeping." *Sixteenth Century Journal* 30 (1999): 3–21.
Brenner, Robert. *Merchants and Revolution: Commercial Change, Political Conflict, and London's Overseas Traders, 1550–1653.* Cambridge: Cambridge University Press, 1993.
Brown, Sylvia. *Women's Writing in Stuart England: The Mothers' Legacies of Dorothy Leigh, Elizabeth Joscelin, and Elizabeth Richardson.* Thrupp, Gloucestershire: Sutton Publishing, 1999.
Burke, John. *A Genealogical and Heraldic History of the Commoners of Great Britain and Ireland.* 4 vols. London: Henry Colburn, 1838.
———and John Bernard Burke. *A Genealogical and Heraldic History of the Extinct and Dormant Baronetcies of England, Ireland, and Scotland.* 2nd ed. London: John Russell Smith, 1844.
Burke, Victoria. "Let's Get Physical: Bibliography, Codicology, and Seventeenth-Century Women's Manuscripts." *Literature Compass* 4/6 (2007): 1667–82.

———. "Women and Early Seventeenth-Century Manuscript Culture: Four Miscellanies." *The Seventeenth Century* 12 (1997): 135–50.

——— and Sarah C. E. Ross. "Elizabeth Middleton, John Bourchier, and the Compilation of Seventeenth-Century Religious Manuscripts." *The Library*, 7th ser., 2 (2001): 131–60.

Campbell, Mary Baine. "Dreaming, Motion, Meaning: Oneiric Transport in Seventeenth-Century Europe." In *Reading the Early Modern Dream: The Terrors of the Night*, ed. Katharine Hodgkin, Michelle O'Callaghan, and S. J. Wiseman. New York: Routledge, 2008. 15–30.

Carlton, Charles. "The Dream Life of Archbishop Laud." *History Today* 36 (1986): 9–15.

Chambers, Robert. *The Book of Days: A Miscellany of Popular Antiquities*. 2 vols. London: W. & R. Chambers, 1832.

Charlton, Kenneth. *Women, Religion, and Education in Early Modern England*. London and New York: Routledge, 1999.

Clarke, Elizabeth. "Herbert's House of Pleasure? Ejaculations Sacred and Profane." *George Herbert Journal* 19 (1996): 55–71.

Colclough, David. Review of *Early Modern Women's Manuscript Writing: Selected Papers of the Trinity-Trent Colloquium*. *Early Modern Literary Studies* 11 (2005): 8.1–3.

Coolahan, Marie-Louise. "Redeeming Parcels of Time: Aesthetics and Practice of Occasional Meditation." *The Seventeenth Century* 22 (2007): 124–43.

Crawford, Patricia, "Women's Dreams in Early Modern England." In *Dreams and History: The Interpretation of Dreams from Ancient Greece to Modern Psychoanalysis*, ed. Daniel Pick and Lyndal Roper. London and New York: Brunner-Routledge, 2004. 91–103.

——— and Laura Gowing, eds. *Women's Worlds in Seventeenth-Century England: A Sourcebook*. London and New York: Routledge, 2000.

Dale, T. C. *The Inhabitants of London in 1638*. 2 vols. London: The Society of Genealogists, 1931.

Dowd, Michelle M., and Julie A. Eckerle, eds. *Genre and Women's Life Writing in Early Modern England*. Aldershot: Ashgate, 2007.

Duncan-Jones, Katherine, and Jan van Dorsten, eds. *Miscellaneous Prose of Sir Philip Sidney*. Oxford: Clarendon Press, 1973.

Erickson, Amy Louise. *Women and Property in Early Modern England*. London: Routledge, 1993.

Eulogium (Historiarum sive temporis), vol. 1. London: Longman, Brown, Green, Longmans, and Roberts, 1858.

Ezell, Margaret. "Domestic Papers: Manuscript Culture and Early Modern Women's Life Writing." In *Genre and Women's Life Writing in Early Modern England*, ed. Dowd and Eckerle, 33–48.

———. "Elizabeth Delaval's Spiritual Heroine: Thoughts on Redefining Manuscript Texts by Early Women Writers." *English Manuscript Studies* 3 (1992): 216–37.

Fisken, Beth Wynne. "Mary Sidney's Psalmes: Education and Wisdom." In *Silent But for the Word: Tudor Women as Patrons, Translators, and Writers of Religious Works*, ed. Margaret P. Hannay. Kent, OH: Kent State University Press, 1985. 166–83.

Foster, Joseph. *Alumni Oxonienses: The Members of the University of Oxford, 1500–1714*. 4 vols. Oxford: Parker, 1891.

George, Margaret. *Women in the First Capitalist Society: Experiences in Seventeenth-Century England*. Brighton: Harvester Press, 1988.

Graham, Elspeth. "Women's Writing and the Self." In *Women and Literature in Britain, 1500–1700*, ed. Helen Wilcox. Cambridge: Cambridge University Press, 1996. 209–33.

———, Hilary Hinds, Elaine Hobby, and Helen Wilcox, eds. *Her Own Life: Autobiographical Writings by Seventeenth-Century Englishwomen*. London: Routledge, 1989.

———, Hilary Hinds, Elaine Hobby, and Helen Wilcox. "'Pondering All These Things in Her Heart': Aspects of Secrecy in the Autobiographical Writings of Seventeenth-Century Englishwomen." In *Women's Lives / Women's Times: New Essays on Auto/Biography*, ed. Trev Lynn Broughton and Linda Anderson. Albany, NY: State University of New York Press, 1997. 51–71.

Greene, Roland. "Sir Philip Sidney's Psalms, the Sixteenth-Century Psalter, and the Nature of the Lyric." *Studies in English Literature* 30 (1990): 19–40.

Hamlin, Hannibal. *Psalm Culture and Early Modern English Literature*. Cambridge: Cambridge University Press, 2004.

Hammons, Pamela. "Despised Creatures: The Illusion of Maternal Self-Effacement in Seventeenth-Century Child Loss Poetry." *English Literary History* 66 (1999): 25–49.

———. "Katherine Austen's Country-House Innovations." *Studies in English Literature* 40 (2000): 123–37.

———. *Poetic Resistance: English Women Writers and the Early Modern Lyric*. Aldershot: Ashgate, 2002.

———. "Rethinking Women and Property in Sixteenth- and Seventeenth-Century England." *Literature Compass* 3/6 (2006): 1386–1407.

———. "Widow, Prophet, and Poet: Lyrical Self-Figurations in Katherine Austen's 'Book M' (1664)." In *Write or Be Written: Early Modern Women Poets and Cultural Constraints*, ed. Barbara Smith and Ursula Appelt. Aldershot: Ashgate, 2001. 3–27.

Hannay, Margaret P. "Joining the Conversation: David, Astrophil, and the Countess of Pembroke." In *Textual Conversations in the Renaissance: Ethics, Authors, Technologies*, ed. Zachary Lesser and Benedict S. Robinson. Aldershot: Ashgate, 2006. 113–27.

———. "'So May I with the *Psalmist* Truly Say': Early Modern Englishwomen's Psalm Discourse." In *Write or be Written: Early Modern Women Poets and Cultural Constraints*, ed. Smith and Appelt. 105–34.

———, Noel J. Kinnamon, and Michael G. Brennan, eds. *The Collected Works of Mary Sidney Herbert, Countess of Pembroke*. 2 vols. Oxford: Clarendon Press, 1998.

Historical Manuscripts Commission, 8th Report, part 1, section 1. Darlington: H.M.S.O., 1881.

Hobbs, Mary, ed. *The Stoughton Manuscript: A Manuscript Miscellany of Poems by Henry King and his Circle, circa 1636*. Aldershot: Scolar Press, 1990.

Hodgkin, Katharine, Michelle O'Callaghan, and S. J. Wiseman, eds. *Reading the Early Modern Dream: The Terrors of the Night*. New York and London: Routledge, 2008.

Holland, Peter. "'The Interpretation of Dreams' in the Renaissance." In *Reading Dreams: The Interpretation of Dreams from Chaucer to Shakespeare*, ed. Peter Brown. Oxford: Oxford University Press, 1999. 125–46.

Houlbrooke, Ralph, ed. *English Family Life, 1576–1716: An Anthology from Diaries*. Oxford: Basil Blackwell, 1988.

Howard, Joseph Jackson and Joseph Lemuel Chester, eds. *The Visitation of London, Anno Domini 1633, 1634, and 1635*. 2 vols. London: The Harleian Society, 1880.

Hunter, Michael. "How to Edit a Seventeenth-Century Manuscript: Principles and Practice." *The Seventeenth Century* 10 (1995): 277–310.

Huntley, Frank Livingstone. *Bishop Joseph Hall and Protestant Meditation in Seventeenth-Century England*. MRTS 1. Binghamton, NY: Medieval & Renaissance Texts & Studies, 1981.

Jackson, Charles, ed. *The Autobiography of Mrs. Alice Thornton, of East Newton. Co. York*. Surtees Society 62. London: The Surtees Society, 1875.

James, Bruno Scott. *The Letters of St. Bernard of Clairvaux*. London: Burns Oates, 1953.

Johnson, A. H. *The History of the Worshipful Company of the Drapers of London*. 5 vols. Vol. 3, *From the Accession of James I, 1603–1920*. Oxford: Clarendon Press, 1914–1922.

Journals of the House of Commons, vol. 3 (25 April 1660 – 29 July 1667).

Journals of the House of Lords, vol. 12 (1666–1675).

Keynes, Geoffrey, ed. *The Works of Sir Thomas Browne*. 6 vols. London: Faber and Faber, 1931.

Klene, Jean, ed. *The Southwell-Sibthorpe Commonplace Book: Folger MS V.b.198*. Renaissance English Text Society, 7th ser., 20. Tempe: Medieval & Renaissance Texts & Studies, 1997.

Kugler, Anne. *Errant Plagiary: The Life and Writing of Lady Sarah Cowper, 1644–1720*. Stanford: Stanford University Press, 2002.

Lamb, Mary Ellen. "The Sociality of Margaret Hoby's Reading Practices and the Representation of Reformation Interiority." *Critical Survey* 12 (2000): 17–32.

Lewalski, Barbara. *Protestant Poetics and the Seventeenth-Century Religious Lyric.* Princeton: Princeton University Press, 1979.

Liu, Tai. *Puritan London: A Study of Religion and Society in the City Parishes.* London: Associated University Press, 1986.

Marcus, Leah S., Janel Mueller, and Mary Beth Rose, eds. *Elizabeth I: Collected Works.* Chicago and London: University of Chicago Press, 2000.

McDonald, James H. and Nancy Pollard Brown, eds. *The Poems of Robert Southwell, S. J.* Oxford: Clarendon Press, 1967.

MacFarlane, Alan, ed. *The Diary of Ralph Josselin, 1616–1683.* Records of Social and Economic History, n.s. 3. London: Oxford University Press for The British Academy, 1976.

McLuskie, Kathleen. "The 'Candy-Coloured Clown': Reading Early Modern Dreams." In *Reading Dreams: The Interpretation of Dreams from Chaucer to Shakespeare*, ed. Brown. 147–67.

Marotti, Arthur F. *Manuscript, Print, and the English Renaissance Lyric.* Ithaca: Cornell University Press, 1995.

Marshall, Peter and Alexandra Walsham, eds. *Angels in the Early Modern World.* Cambridge: Cambridge University Press, 2006.

Mendelson, Sara Heller. "Stuart Women's Diaries and Occasional Memoirs." In *Women in English Society, 1500–1800*, ed. Mary Prior. London: Methuen, 1985. 181–210.

——— and Patricia Crawford. *Women in Early Modern England, 1550–1720.* Oxford: Clarendon Press, 1998.

Nares, Robert, James Orchard Halliwell-Phillipps, and Thomas Wright. *A Glossary: Or, Collection of Words, Phrases, Names, and Allusions to Customs, Proverbs, Etc., which Have Been Thought to Require Illustration, in the Words of English Authors, Particularly Shakespeare, and His Contemporaries.* London: J. R. Smith, 1859.

Nelson, John. *The History and Antiquities of the Parish of Islington, in the County of Middlesex.* 2nd ed. London: for the author, 1823.

Pearl, Valerie. *London and the Outbreak of the Puritan Revolution: City Government and National Politics, 1625–43.* Oxford: Oxford University Press, 1964.

Poole, Kristen. "'The Fittest Closet for All Goodness': Authorial Strategies of Jacobean Mothers' Manuals." *Studies in English Literature* 1 (1995): 69–88.

Rathmell, J. C. A., ed. *The Psalms of Sir Philip Sidney and the Countess of Pembroke.* New York: New York University Press, 1963.

The Records of the Honourable Society of Lincoln's Inn. 2 vols. Vol. 1, *Admissions 1420–1799.* [London]: Lincoln's Inn, 1896.

Roberts, Sasha. "Reading in Early Modern England: Contexts and Problems." *Critical Survey* 12 (2000): 1–16.

Ross, Sarah. "'And Trophes of his praises make': Providence and Poetry in Katherine Austen's *Book M*, 1664–1668." In *Early Modern Women's Writing: Selected Papers from the Trinity/Trent Colloquium*, ed. Victoria E. Burke and Jonathan Gibson. Aldershot: Ashgate, 2004. 181–204.

Smith, Logan Pearsall, ed. *The Life and Letters of Sir Henry Wotton*. 2 vols. Oxford: Clarendon Press, 1907.

Smith, Nigel. *Literature and Revolution in England, 1640–1660*. New Haven and London: Yale University Press, 1994.

———. *Perfection Proclaimed: Language and Literature in English Radical Religion, 1640–1660*. Oxford: Clarendon Press, 1989.

Snook, Edith. *Women, Reading, and the Cultural Politics of Early Modern England*. Aldershot: Ashgate, 2005.

Steen, Sara Jayne. "Behind the Arras: Editing Renaissance Women's Letters." In *New Ways of Looking at Old Texts: Papers of the Renaissance English Text Society, 1985–1991*, ed. W. Speed Hill. Binghamton, NY: Medieval & Renaissance Text & Studies in conjunction with Renaissance English Text Society, 1993. 229–38.

Stevenson, Jane and Peter Davidson, eds. *Early Modern Women Poets (1520–1700): An Anthology*. Oxford: Oxford University Press, 2001.

Stretton, Tim. *Women Waging Law in Elizabethan England*. New York: Cambridge University Press, 1998.

Taft, Robert F. "Christian Liturgical Psalmody: Origins, Development, Decomposition, Collapse." In *Psalms in Community: Jewish and Christian Textual, Liturgical, and Artistic Traditions*, ed. Harold W. Attridge and Margot E. Fassler. Atlanta: Society of Biblical Literature, 2004. 7–32.

Targoff, Ramie. *Common Prayer: The Language of Public Devotion in Early Modern England*. Chicago: University of Chicago Press, 2001.

Thomas, Keith. *Religion and the Decline of Magic*. London: Weidenfeld and Nicolson, 1971.

Todd, Barbara. "'I do no injury by not loving': Katherine Austen, a Young Widow of London." In *Women and History: Voices of Early Modern England*, ed. Valerie Frith. Toronto: Coach House Press, 1995. 202–37.

———. "The Remarrying Widow: A Stereotype Reconsidered." In *Women in English Society 1500–1800*, ed. Prior. 54–92.

———. "The Virtuous Widow in Protestant England." In *Widowhood in Medieval and Early Modern Europe*, ed. Sandra Cavallo and Lyndan Warner. Harlow, Essex: Pearson Education, 1999. 66–83.

Trill, Suzanne. *Lady Anne Halkett: Selected Self-Writings*. Aldershot: Ashgate, 2007.

———. "'Speaking to God in His Phrase and Word': Women's Use of the Psalms in Early Modern England." In *The Nature of Religious Language: A Colloquium*, ed. Stanley E. Porter. Sheffield: Sheffield Academic Press, 1996. 269–83.

The Victoria County History of Middlesex, ed. T. F. T. Baker. Vols. 5–11. Oxford: Oxford University Press for the Institute of Historical Research, 1985–1998.

Walsham, Alexandra. *Providence in Early Modern England.* Oxford: Oxford University Press, 1999.

——— and Peter Marshall, eds. *Angels in the Early Modern World.* Cambridge: Cambridge University Press, 2006.

Weber, Max. *The Protestant Ethic and the Spirit of Capitalism.* London: Allen & Unwin, 1976.

Weidhorn, Manfred. *Dreams in Seventeenth-Century English Literature.* The Hague: Mouton, 1970.

Zim, Rivkah. *English Metrical Psalms: Poetry as Praise and Prayer, 1535–1601.* Cambridge: Cambridge University Press, 1987.

Topical Guide

A guide to some major topics and categories of meditation in *Book M* (by folio)

Accounts, financial and spiritual: 39^r, 52^r, 63^r, 79^v, 99^v–100^r, 105^r, 108^r, 109^v–110^r

Adversity and prosperity: 3^{r-v}, 36^v, 42^r, 45^r, 65^r, 71^r, 73^v, 76^r, 80^r, 90^v, 91^v, 92^v, 94^v, 103^v, 107^v

Angels: 3^r, 6^r–9^r, 11^r, 13^r, 16^r, 18^r, 22^r, 40^r, 61^v, 63^r, 87^r, 88^v, 89^v, 61^v, 100^v, 102^r, 112^r

Audience: 4^v, 42^r–44^v, 48^r, 51^v, 82^v, 92^r–94^v; 99^v, 100^v, 103^v, 105^v, 106^v, 107^v, 114^v

Austen, Thomas, (KA's deceased husband): 1^r, 15^r, 23^r, 42^r, 60^v–61^r, 64^{r-v}, 68^v, 71^v, 75^v, 95^v, 105^r, 110^v

Backfilled meditations (clear examples): 10^v, 12^v, 22^v, 36^v, 49^v, 55^v, 73^v, 78^r, 112^v, 114^v

Birthdays: 1^r, 2^r, 3^v, 40^r, 51^v, 53^v, 54^r, 72^r, 77^r–79^r, 114^v

Children, about: 23^r, 42^r, 46^{r-v}, 56^r, 61^v, 67^v, 69^v, 72^r, 75^r, 76^v, 81^v, 82^v, 86^v, 100^v, 101^r, 103^v, 105^r, 110^v, 111^v, 114^v

———, to: 3^{r-v}, 42^r–44^v, 51^v, 82^v, 92^r–94^v; 99^v, 100^v, 107^v, 114^v

Deaths, dates of, and other memorials: 1^r–2^r, 3^{r-v}, 10^v, 40^r, 38^v, 46^{r-v}, 53^v–54^r, 72^r, 96^v

Dreams, visions and prophecies: 3^{r-v}, 7^r–8^r, 10^r–17^r, 21^r–22^r, 24^r–26^r, 31^r–33^r, 38^v, 54^r, 60^v–61^r, 63^v–65^v, 73^v, 74^v–75^v, 88^r, 96^v–99^v, 103^r

Durhames: 51^v, 111^v

Highbury: 3^r, 4^r, 48^r–49^r, 56^v–57^r, 59^v, 60^v–61^r, 62^v, 64^r–65^r, 67^v, 70^v, 72^v, 76^v, 79^v, 84^v, 90^r, 92^v, 99^v, 100^r, 103^v–104^r, 105^r, 108^r, 109^v–110^r, 111^v, 112^v–113^r

Honour: 3^v, 22^v, 24^r, 28^v, 40^r, 42^r, 49^r–50^r, 57^v, 68^v, 78^r, 79^v, 90^v, 91^v, 92^v–94^v, 94^v, 101^v, 105^v, 110^v

Industry and spending time: 16^r, 51^v, 56^r, 67^v, 68^v, 72^v, 73^v, 75^v, 91^v, 92^v–94^v, 96^r, 106^r, 114^v

Newington Barrow: see Highbury

Plague (see also Sickness): 3^v, 79^r, 86^r–89^v, 94^r, 97^v, 99^v, 100^v–101^r, 102^v, 114^r

Poetry: 3^v, 4^v–5^r, 35^v, 40^v–41^v, 46^r–47^r, 53^v, 57^v–60^r, 61^v–62^r, 62^v–64^r, 65^v–67^r, 69^r, 71^v, 84^v–85^r, 86^r, 89^r, 94^r, 98^v–99^r, 101^r–103^r, 103^v–104^r, 106^v–107^r, 108^v–109^r, 113^v, 114^r, 114^v

Providences, special or peculiar: 7^r, 13^r, 21^{r-v}, 62^{r-v}, 64^r, 65^v–66^r, 76^v, 79^r, 80^r, 89^v, 91^r, 98^v, 101^v, 103^r, 106^v, 111^v

Providential jewel: 3^v, 12^r, 74^v, 76^r, 92^r, 108^v–109^r

Psalms: 20^r, 21^r, 22^r, 35^v, 38^r, 39^v, 40^r, 55^r, 56^v–58^r, 61^r–63^r, 65^r, 70^v, 72^r–73^r, 74^r–75^v, 77^r–78^r, 80^v–82^r, 86^r, 88^v–89^v, 105^v, 107^r, 109^r, 111^v, 112^v, 114^r

Red Lion (and Susanna Austen): 3^{r-v}, 45^r, 64^v, 81^r–83^v, 108^r, 109^v, 111^v, 113^r

Sermon paraphrases: 3^r, 6^r–9^r; 13^r–20^r; 25^r–31^r, 35^v

Sickness (see also Plague): 3^v, 12^r, 46^{r-v}, 54^r, 61^r–62^v, 72^r, 74^r

Six/seven years (see also Troubles, Widowhood and Remarriage): 12^r, 40^r, 56^v, 60^r, 62^r, 65^v, 68^r–69^r, 75^v, 76^v, 99^v, 102^v–103^r, 108^v

Swan: 79^v, 90^r, 100^r, 105^r, 109^v, 112^v

Tom at Oxford: 3^r, 43^r–44^v, 82^v, 99^v, 114^v

Troubles (see also Widowhood and Remarriage): 35^v–41^r and 56^v–71^r (KA's own designation; see n. p. 119); see also 3^r–4^r, 7^r, 27^r, 52^r, 55^v, 72^r, 76^{r-v}, 80^v, 81^r, 84^v, 86^r, 91^v, 99^r–100^r, 101^r, 102^v–103^r, 106^v, 107^r, 107^v, 110^r, 112^v, 114^r

Widows and orphans: 35^v, 57^r, 58^r, 60^r, 62^v, 65^r, 67^v, 68^r, 69^r, 71^v, 75^r, 80^{r-v}, 81^v, 82^v, 106^v, 108^r,

Widowhood and remarriage (see also Six/seven years): 40^r, 49^r, 50^r, 67^v–70^r, 71^v, 76^r, 78^r, 90^v–91^r, 94^v–98^r, 105^r, 110^v

Concordance of Biblical References

Acts	Page(s)
16:9–10	55
26:16–19	55
27:14–44	82

1 Chronicles
| 21:10–14 | 139 |
| 21:12 | 137 |

2 Chronicles
| 18:26 | 55 |

1 Corinthians
| 2:9 | 140 |

2 Corinthians
| 12:9 | 160 |
| 1:3 | 162 |

Deuteronomy
| 31:6 | 82 |

Ecclesiastes
3:1–8	85, 105
4:6	19n, 167
6:28	83
8:1	92

Exodus
3:8, 17	126
12:41	138
13:5	126
13:21–2	55

Ezekiel
| 1 | 55 |
| 10 | 55 |

Galatians
| 5:22 | 99 |

Genesis
1:16	142
15:1	55
15:13	138
21:17–18	55
22:1–13	124
22:11–12	55
22:15–18	55
41:32	60
50:15–21	70

Hebrews
1:1	25, 64
1:2	64
13:5	82

Isaiah
10:1–2	16–17, 133
30:20	55
34:14	150
40:31	83
59:1	138

Job
5:6	131
5:19	16, 126n, 151, 153, 155
7:7	150

John
| 17:17 | 65 |
| 14:27 | 98 |

Joshua
| 10:13 | 55 |

Judges
| 6 | 55 |
| 7:13–15 | 64 |

1 Kings
| 22:27 | 55 |
| 8:39, 43 | 115 |

2 Kings
2:9	64
2:12	62n
19:35	108
20	37
20:1–6	68n, 125

Luke
| 6:28 | 101 |
| 22:43 | 167 |

Malachi
  3:1   167
Mark
  2:3–12   56
Matthew
  5:44   101
  6:13   99
Numbers
  14:14   55
Philippians
  4:7   118
Psalms
  3:1   122
  9:9   68, 122
  14:32   140
  16:5   130
  16:11   67
  17:7   108
  17:14   101
  18:28   108
  27   31, 103, 122
  28:1   107
  31:15   128
  31:16   100
  34:19   161
  36:9   67
  37:39   68
  43:3   119
  51:8   100
  51:15   37, 125
  62:2, 6–8   97–98
  66:13–14   124
  68   30
  68:28   97
  68:34   36, 41, 97, 171
  69:2   109
  73:25   54, 65
  76   140
  78:46   130
  81:7   55
  84:11   109
  91   31, 138–39
  103:15–16   121
  107   124
  107:23–30   136
  112–118   124
  115:1   159
  118:17   4, 16, 26, 29, 35, 37, 67, 109, 125
  119:14   30
  120:1   131–32
  120:2   132
  121   29–30, 132–33
  125:3   138
  129:3   161
  132:1   99
  136   113
  137:5, 7   138
  138:7–8   131
  139:18   84
  143:2   84
  145–50   127
  146:9–10   101
  147   29–30
  149   127–28
Proverbs
  16:9   125
Revelation
  3:10   140
  4   55
  15:7   114
Romans
  8:28   153
  11:36   67
1 Samuel
  3:4–14   55
  16–17   167
  17:34–37
  48–51   160
Tobit (Apocrypha)
  12:7   160

General Index

Abraham, 20, 55, 125, 136, 138
Alcock, Stephen, 9
Álvarez de Toledo y Pimentel, Don Fernando, third Duke of Alba, 123
Amyraut, Moise, 147–48
Anderson, Linda, 5n
Andronicus, 25
Angels, 2, 21, 23, 41, 52, 54–59, 62, 64, 66, 68, 84, 108, 110, 137, 139, 140, 153, 155, 167
Anglo-Dutch war, 52, 122–23
Anselment, Raymond, 2n, 4n, 14n, 38, 103n, 140
Appelt, Ursula, 2n
Apsley, Allen (1566/7–1636), 9, 9n, 10–11, 90n, 91n, 100n
Apsley, Allen (1616–1683), 10
Apsley, Lucy. *See* Hutchinson, Lucy
Ashe, Grace, 27, 31, 39, 96
Ashe, Joseph, 79n, 96n
Ashe [née Wilson], Mary, 79n, 96n
Attridge, Harold W., 124n
Austen, Anne (KA's daughter), 10, 14–15, 20n, 36, 69, 86, 94, 118, 121, 124, 137, 144, 153, 156, 159, 162, 166, 171–72
Austen, Anne (KA's mother-in-law), 15, 69n, 95, 144, 162n
Austen, John (KA's brother-in-law), 9, 11–13, 21n, 25, 57n, 88, 95, 97, 111–12, 131, 134, 148, 162n
Austen, Sir John, M. P. (KA's grandson), 11, 13, 15
Austen, Katherine (KA's niece, daughter of John and Susanna Austen), 11–12, 95n, 134
Austen, Richard (KA's husband's grandfather?), 165

Austen, Robert (KA's son), 7, 10, 14, 20n, 27, 36, 52, 86, 89–90, 94, 118, 121, 124, 137, 143–44, 153, 156, 159, 166, 172
Austen [née Winstanley], Susanna, 11–13, 29–30, 52, 53, 88, 112, 131–34, 162, 164, 169n
Austen, Thomas (KA's husband), 6, 8–10, 10n, 11–13, 15, 18, 20n, 21, 25, 27, 33, 51, 57n, 64, 67n, 69, 84n, 86, 96n, 106–7, 110n, 111–12, 116, 120, 125, 132n, 143–44, 147, 159, 162n
Austen, Thomas (KA's father-in-law), 8–10, 10n, 12n, 16, 25, 111–12, 116, 143, 165n
Austen, Thomas (KA's son), 1, 10–14, 18–19, 20n, 36, 52, 86–87, 90n, 94, 107, 115–16, 118, 121, 124, 126, 132–34, 137, 142–44, 153, 156, 159, 162, 166–67, 172
Bacon, Francis, 21, 43, 77
Baker, T. F. T., 8n, 13n, 15n
Beadle, John, 22, 28
Beal, Peter, 33n
Beard, Thomas, 22
Beaufort, Lady Margaret, 21, 77
Beavan, A.B., 7
Bellarmine, Robert [Roberto Bellarmino], Cardinal, 66
Bible, 3
Bides, Sir Thomas, 121
Bingen, Hildegard von, 21
Birch, Thomas, 41
Birkenhead, Cousin, 121
Birkenhead, Sir John, 25, 107, 121n
Blain, Virginia, 15n
Book of Common Prayer, 28, 30, 97, 99, 139

Botonaki, Effie, 28n
Boyle, Robert, 3
Brennan, Michael G., 31n
Brenner, Robert, 7n
Broke, Doctor, 97
Brome, Richard, 32, 77
Broughton, Trev Lynn, 5n
Brown, Nancy Pollard, 30n
Brown, Peter, 24n
Brown, Sylvia, 35n
Browne, Sir Thomas, 24, 172
Brownrig, Ralph, bishop of Exeter, 21, 23, 62–4
Burke, John, 7, 12n, 15n, 79n, 96n, 121n
Burke, John Bernard, 12n, 15n, 79n, 96n
Burke, Victoria E., 2n, 3n, 6, 43n, 158n
Burton, Lady Frances, 21, 42, 43, 57

Callendar, Alexander (? KA's suitor), 5, 14, 20, 26, 43, 146–49, 147n
Calvin, John, 28–29
Cambridge, 57
Camden, William, 21, 43, 77n
Campbell, Mary Baine, 2n, 60n
Carlton, Charles, 24n, 61n
Cavallo, Sandra, 2n
Chambers, Robert, 76n
Chandeler, William (KA's servant), 4n, 51–52, 82, 97, 152
Chaney, Mr., 78
Charlton, Kenneth, 20
Chatham, 78
Chester, Joseph Lemuel, 6n
Chillingworth, Mr., 97
Clarke, Elizabeth, 32n
Clements, Patricia, 15n
Cockayne, Sir William, lord mayor of London, 17–18, 126n, 141–42
Colclough, David, 43
Colebrooke, James, 11n
Coolahan, Marie-Louise, 4n, 5n, 27n, 31n, 32n
Cordivel, Mrs., 97
Corbett, Richard, bishop of Oxford and Norwich, 32–33, 120
Cowper [née Holled], Lady Sarah, 3, 7n
Crawford, Patricia, 2n, 14n, 23n

Cromwell, Battina, 39n
Cromwell, Elizabeth, 39n
Cromwell, Henry (1628–74), 39n
Cromwell, Oliver, 39n
Cropley, Sir Edward, 7, 121
Cropley [née Wilson], Martha, 6–8, 121n
Cruse, Mr., 95n, 152

Dale, T. C., 7n
Daniel, Samuel, 32, 171
David, 4, 16–17, 20, 26, 28–31, 37, 62, 66, 68, 81, 84, 97–98, 99, 101, 125, 127, 132, 136, 138–39, 160–61, 167
Davidson, Peter, 39n, 89n, 158n
Deborah, 20, 136
Delaval, Lady Elizabeth, 35
Donne, John, 3, 17–18, 21, 23, 27, 31, 33, 52, 53, 54, 56, 59, 62n, 63–64, 114n, 126n, 141–42
Dowd, Michelle M., 5n, 6n
Drapers' Company, 6
Dreams, 2, 16, 20, 21–26, 29, 32, 35, 37, 42–43, 52, 55–61, 64, 67, 70–71, 76–78, 82, 96, 106–7, 110–13, 119, 122, 124–25, 138, 148–49, 150n, 156n
Drury, Sir Robert, 59n
Duffield, Francis, 27, 52, 96, 97
Duffield, Mrs. (aunt of KA's husband, Thomas), 95, 96n
Duncan-Jones, Katherine, 30n
Durhams, 12–13, 15, 95, 167

East India Company, 7, 14
Eckerle, Julie A., 5n, 6n
Elijah, 62, 64
Elisha, 64
Erickson, Amy Louise, 8n
Essex, 6, 7, 13, 18, 22n, 35, 146, 148, 152, 164
Esther, 20, 136
Ezell, Margaret J. M., 5, 6n, 35, 39

Fairfax, Sir Thomas, third Lord Fairfax of Cameron, 56n
Fassler, Margot E., 124n

General Index

Featley, Daniel, 3, 21, 23, 52, 54, 64n, 65–66
Feeld (Field?), Uncle, 95
Fell, John, bishop of Oxford, 21, 23–25, 56
Fisken, Beth Wynne, 31n
Foster, Joseph, 9n, 19n
Foulke, Sara, 97
Fox, George, 24
Frith, Valerie, 1n
Fuller, Thomas, 21, 25, 27, 61, 77, 79, 123n

Galtres (or Gaultres), 9–10, 100n
Gauden, John, bishop of Worcester, 3, 21, 23, 62–64, 92n
George, Margaret, 14, 38n
Gibson, Jonathan, 2n, 43n, 158n
Gideon, 55, 64
Goliath, 160
Goodwin, Philip, 25n
Gowing, Laura, 2n
Graham, Elspeth, 4n, 5n, 28n, 37n, 38
Greenwich, 22, 57
Grundy, Isobel, 15n

Hagar, 55
Hague, The, 57
Hales, Judge, 59
Halkett [née Murray], Anne, Lady, 3, 4, 15, 29
Hall, Joseph, bishop of Norwich, 3, 24, 27–28, 30, 61
Halliwell-Phillipps, James Orchard, 71n
Hamlin, Hannibal, 31n
Hammond, Henry, 21, 23–24, 42, 52, 56–57
Hammons, Pamela, 2n, 8n, 14n, 15n, 33–34, 158n
Hannay, Margaret P., 4n, 29, 31n
Hardy, Deane, 152
Harley, Robert, first earl of Oxford, 22
Helicon, Mount, 159
Henry II, Holy Roman Emperor, 60
Herbert, Edward, first Baron Herbert of Cherbury, 77
Herbert, George, 32
Herbert [née Sidney], Mary, Countess of Pembroke, 31n, 32

Hezekiah, 16, 37, 67, 68n, 108, 113, 124–25
Highbury (or Newington Barrow), 1–2, 9–10, 11, 13, 15, 25, 33–34, 52–53, 59n, 90, 100n, 105, 107–8, 111–12, 115–16, 119, 121–22, 126, 129n, 130, 132n, 135, 140, 142, 151, 153, 156, 158–59, 162, 164–65, 167–68
Highlord, John, 7, 8, 13, 15, 53, 129, 143
Highlord, Katherine. *See* Wilson, Katherine
Hill, Thomas, 24
Hill, W. Speed, 43n
Hildegard of Bingen, 79
Hinds, Hilary, 4n, 5n
Hobbs, Mary, 33n
Hobby, Elaine, 4n, 5n
Hobson, Doctor, 79, 111n
Hoby, Margaret, Lady Hoby, 3n, 4, 29
Hodgkin, Katharine, 2n, 24n, 60n
Holland, Countess of, 61
Holland, Lady Diana, 61
Holland, Isabel, 61
Holland, Peter, 24n
Holland, Susan, 61
Houlbrooke, Ralph, 2n, 14
Howard, Joseph Jackson, 6n
Hunter, Michael, 44
Huntley, F. L., 27n
Hutchinson [née Apsley], Lucy, 9

Isaac, 20, 124–25, 136
Isaiah, 67n, 125
Islington, 1, 8n, 9, 10n, 13

Jackson, Charles, 37n, 38n
Jacob, 70
James, Bruno Scott, 84n
Job, 16–17, 28, 37, 100n, 124, 126n, 131, 155
Johnson, A. H., 6n
Jonson, Ben, 34n
Joseph, 70, 80
Joshua, 55
Josselin, Ralph, 22
Judith, 20, 136

King
    Charles I of England, 9, 9n, 11, 56n, 90
    Charles II of England, 122, 149, 152
    Edward VI of England, 81n
    Henry IV of England, 32, 76
    Henry VII of England, 21, 77
    Henry VIII of England, 84
    Philip IV of France, 78
King, Henry, bishop of Chichester, 32–33, 120
Kinnamon, Noel J., 31n
Kent, 60
Keynes, Geoffrey, 24n
Klene, Jean, 30n
Kugler, Anne, 3n, 7n

Lamb, Mary Ellen, 3n
Lancaster, Mr., 62
Lanyer, Aemilia, 34n
Laud, William, archbishop of Canterbury, 24, 61
Lesser, Zachary, 31n
Lewalski, Barbara, 31
Lincoln's Inn, 9, 18
Liu, Tai, 7n
London, 1, 6–8, 8n, 9, 10n, 12n, 17
    Blackfriars, 14
    Chancery Lane, 21, 59n
    Cheapside, 6
    Fleet Street (*see also* The Red Lion), 1, 12–13
    St Dunstan's in the West, 12, 131n
    St Leonard's Shoreditch, 9, 10n, 12, 15
    St Mary Colechurch, 6, 15
    St Olave's Hart Street, 7
    St Stephens Coleman Street, 8

Margaret, Aunt, 171
McDonald, James H., 30n
MacFarlane, Alan, 22n
McLuskie, Kathleen, 24n
Manchester, Lord, 87
Marcus, Leah S., 78n
Marotti, Arthur F., 33
Marshall, Peter, 23n
Medenham, 96
Melisande, Queen of Jerusalem, 84n

Mendelson, Sara Heller, 2n, 5n, 14n, 35
Middlesex, 1, 6, 8–9, 10n, 11n, 12, 13n, 14–15
Morecroft, Richard, 97
Moses, 63
Mueller, Janel, 78n

Nares, Robert, 71n
Nelson, John, 9n, 10n
Newington Barrow. *See* Highbury

O'Callaghan, Michelle, 2n, 60n
Ovid, 120n
Oxford, 9, 18, 52, 56n, 60n, 87, 88n, 133, 149, 152, 165, 168, 172
Oxfordshire, 7

Parliament, 10–11, 25, 47
Palmer, Sir Jeffery, 11, 168
Parnam, Cousin, 152
Parnassus, 159
Pearl, Valerie, 7n
Pelhams, Mrs., 101
Penelope (wife of Odysseus), 5, 148
Pepys, Samuel, 22
Pick, Daniel, 2n
Plague, 1, 18, 31, 36, 53, 129, 136–40, 141n, 146, 149, 151, 153, 155, 171
Plato, 78
Plot, Robert, 60n
Poole, Kirsten, 35n
Pope Clement V, 78
Pope Sylvester II, 76n
Pope Sylvester III, 76n
Popon/s, Colonel, 27, 89, 97
Popon/s, John, 27, 89–90, 97
Portents and prophecies, 2, 20, 21–26, 32, 43, 60–62, 64, 67, 71, 76–78, 82, 106–7, 110–13, 119, 124–25, 148–50, 156
Porter, Stanley, E., 4n
Price, Mary, 39n
Prier, Mr., 121
Prior, Mary, 1n, 5n,
Psalms, 3, 4, 26, 28–31, 37, 79, 97–99, 101, 103, 122, 124, 127, 131–32, 139–40, 161

General Index

Queen
   Elizabeth I of England, 60, 78, 81, 123
   Mary of England, 60n

Rathmell, J. C. A., 31n
Raworth, Mr., 88
Red Lion, The (*see also* Fleet Street), 1, 2, 10n, 12–13, 29–30, 112, 131–34, 162, 167, 169n
Rich, Mary, Countess of Warwick, 4, 29
Rich, Mr., 4, 83, 101
Roberts, Sasha, 3n
Robinson, Benedict S., 31n
Roper, Lyndal, 2n
Rose, Mary Beth, 78n
Ross, Sarah C. E., 2n, 3n, 34n, 158n
Rudd, Anne (KA's maternal grandmother), 6n, 51, 94, 97
Rudd, Uncle (KA's uncle), 97

Samuel, 55, 62
Satan, 124
Scot, Reginald, 24
Selden, John, 22
Sennacherib, 108
Sermons, 3, 17–18, 21, 23, 25, 43, 52, 54–56, 59n, 62–66, 70–76, 79, 81, 88, 114n, 126n, 141–42
Shakespeare, William, 32, 76
Sidney, Mary. *See* Herbert, Mary
Sidney, Sir Philip, 30, 32
Skinners' Company, 7
Socrates, 63, 78
Solomon, 62, 85, 105, 167
Small pox, 89–90, 96
Smith, Barbara, 2n
Smith, Mr, of Alderbury, 94
Smith, Nigel, 5n, 24n, 25n
Snook, Edith, 3n
Southwell [née Harris], Anne, Lady Southwell, 30
Southwell, Robert, S. J., 30
Spanish Armada, 78
St. Bernard of Clairvaux, 79, 84
St. John, 74
St. Paul, 20, 25, 55, 129, 136, 160
St. Peter, 20, 62, 136

Steen, Sara Jayne, 43
Stretton, Tim, 14n
Stevenson, Jane, 39n, 89n, 158n
Surrey, 59
Swan, The, 13, 129–30, 140, 152–53, 159, 164–65, 168
Symons, Mr., 101, 152

T. R., Cousin, 87
Taft, Robert F., 124n
Targoff, Ramie, 32n
Taylor, Jeremy, Church of Ireland bishop of Down and Connor, 3, 17, 21, 24, 27, 43, 44, 52, 62n, 63, 70–76, 78n, 80–82, 98
Thomas, Keith, 17–18, 24n, 108n
Thornton [née Wandesford], Alice, 4, 13, 14n, 28–29, 37–38
Thurland, Sir Edward, 21, 42, 59
Tilbury, 78
Tillingham, Essex, 148–49
Todd, Barbara, 1n, 14–15, 147n
Trill, Suzanne, 3n, 4n, 5n, 15n, 28n
Tudor, Edmund, first earl of Richmond, 78n
Twickenham, 79, 96n, 111
Twisden, Sir Thomas, 21, 42, 59

Van Dorsten, Jan, 30n
Varney, Cousin, 152
Venus and Adonis, 120
Visions, 2, 20–26, 55, 59, 62–63, 65, 82

Walker [née Sadler], Elizabeth, 28
Walsham, Alexandra, 17n, 22, 23n, 28n, 154n
Walteres, Roland, 121
Walton, Izaak, 21, 24n, 33, 59n, 60n
Warner, Lyndon, 2n
Weber, Max, 18n
Westminster, 10, 32, 61, 76, 121n, 168
Widowhood, 1, 2n, 5–7, 10–17, 32, 34n, 37–38, 69, 79, 84, 92–94, 100–1, 103, 105–6, 109, 112, 115–18, 120, 125n, 126, 128, 130, 133, 137, 141, 146–48, 151–52, 159, 161, 166
Wilcox, Helen, 4n, 5n

Wille, Doctor, 87
William, Cousin, 152, 164
Williams, Anna Cromwell, 39n
Wilson, Anne (KA's sister), 6
Wilson, Aunt, 121
Wilson, Johnny (KA's nephew), 172
Wilson [née Rudd, also Highlord], Katherine (KA's mother), 6, 6n, 7–8, 13, 14–15, 91n, 94, 106, 144, 159
Wilson, Martha (KA's sister). *See* Cropley, Martha
Wilson, Mary (KA's sister), 6, 8
Wilson, Parson, 87, 94
Wilson, Mrs. Richard, 97
Wilson, Richard (KA's brother), 6, 51, 97n
Wilson, Robert (KA's father), 6–8, 15, 21, 33, 59n, 129, 143
Wilson, Robert (KA's brother), 6

Wilson, Samuel, 121
Wilson, Thomas (KA's brother), 6
Wilson, Willy (KA's nephew), 36, 171–72
Winstanley, James, 12, 132–34
Wiseman, S. J., 2n, 60n
Wright, Thomas, 71n
Wood, Anthony, 22
Woods, Mr., 149
Wotton, Sir Edward (1489?–1551), 60n
Wotton, Sir Henry (1568–1639), 24, 59
Wotton, Sir Nicholas (*ca.* 1497–1567), dean of Canterbury and York, 24n, 60n
Wotton, Sir Robert (*ca.* 1463–1524), 60
Wotton, Thomas (*ca.* 1521–1587), 60
Wyatt, Sir Thomas [the younger] (*ca.* 1521–1554), 60, 81n

Young, Mrs. of Kingston, 97